COOP

THE MAKING OF A
SHOWTIME LAKERS LEGEND

Michael Cooper
with Jake Uitti

TRIUMPH
BOOKS

No part of this publication may be reproduced, stored in a retrieval system, or transmitted in any form by any means, electronic, mechanical, photocopying, or otherwise, without the prior written permission of the publisher, Triumph Books LLC, 814 North Franklin Street, Chicago, Illinois 60610.

Library of Congress Cataloging-in-Publication Data available upon request.

This book is available in quantity at special discounts for your group or organization. For further information, contact:

Triumph Books LLC
814 North Franklin Street
Chicago, Illinois 60610
(312) 337-0747
www.triumphbooks.com

Printed in U.S.A.
ISBN: 978-1-63727-760-7
Design by Patricia Frey

Photographs courtesy of the author unless otherwise noted.

For Mickey Cooper
—Coop

For Hendrix Michelle Uitti
—Jake

Contents

Foreword

MICHAEL COOPER WAS ESSENTIAL to the Los Angeles Lakers Showtime era. He was an all-world defender and an excellent spot-up shooter, and we couldn't have made history without him shutting down Larry Bird as our sixth man!

Today when I think of Coop, I think about his laugh—that robust sound emanating from the practice floor as we planned our great playoff runs or from the back of the team bus when we were hanging out talking about what we'd do after our playing careers ended. I often think back to those days, flying from city to city chalking up victories.

When I met Coop during my rookie year in 1980, I knew I'd found my NBA running mate. He would fly through the air for my alley-oops—aka Coop-a-Loops. We were locked in from that very first practice.

In Coop, I saw a winner. It was a pleasure to start our careers together in Los Angeles, because I recognized I had my guy in him. He pushed me in practice and made me a better point guard because of his defensive ability. In the games, he was a trustworthy purple-and-gold security blanket. Together we won five championship rings, and although we lost in the Finals in 1991 against the Bulls and a guy named Michael Jordan, I believe we could have taken that one too, had Coop still been on our roster.

To this day, he and I have remained close friends. Whenever we see each other, he puts a smile on my face. We had such a great time in Maui for our Showtime reunion in 2022 that our entire team wants to do it again. Remembering stories together—those epic battles against the Celtics and beating the 76ers or Pistons—is always a highlight for us.

In the end, Michael Cooper is my basketball brother. He's a wonderful person and had an NBA Hall of Fame basketball career. It's an honor to call him my trusted friend, and I'm so glad he was able to put this memoir together for Lakers fans everywhere. Here's to you, Coop!

—Earvin "Magic" Johnson

Foreword

WHEN I THINK OF COACH COOPER, I think of a person whom I love, who had a huge impact on my career and my success and my work ethic. I think about how I appreciate him taking the time during our Los Angeles Sparks off-season to meet me at 6:00 AM four days a week prior to the Lakers coming into the building to practice, just doing individual work with me. I also think about him being funny and laughing and dancing and even moody—sometimes throwing his clipboard and breaking it, and just being frustrated with the team. It'd seem he'd give up in one minute and then we might close the gap and then he's come back and coach us to victory. He's like a family member—you have a bunch of good times and a few tough times rolled up in there that help you to grow and love each other even more because you made it through tough times together.

One thing that stands out in my basketball career is that Coop gave me the nickname Smooth. And at times he'd say privately, "Smooth, don't let us lose." There would be times when he would tell me not to play so unselfishly and sometimes not to play the "right way," because we needed to win the game. And I appreciated him having that confidence in me. I also remember him being a protector, especially if I went out on the town. I would only go out if my coaches were going out, which I know is kind of weird, but I just didn't hang out a lot with my teammates, going out clubbing and things like that. I would only go if Coop were going, which was only a handful of times in my 11 years on the Sparks. I think about Coop dancing to his favorite song, "Magic Stick"!

There were fun times, such as grabbing luggage and loading it up—I just appreciated Coop being the man that he is, watching over us as women and making sure that we were safe. It was probably more than the role of a coach he was playing, you know; he was a father at times and a big brother at times to all of us. I knew that he was always watching over and being protective of us, probably beyond what the job really required.

Coop is a very compassionate man who is also a sensitive man. My son is also an Aries, so I understand my son because of Coop in some ways. He loves to win; he's a perfectionist. But Coop is also a very compassionate and caring person. He would help anybody. He would give his shirt and shoes to anybody. He would help anyone—old, young, Black, white. Coop loves people. And I see that also in my son.

We play a tough sport, and you have to be tough all the time. Coop played on the Showtime Lakers, and he was tough. He was the toughest defender that anybody's ever seen on the planet. Every opponent who played against Michael Cooper will tell you he's the best. And sometimes it would get overshadowed because Magic was the best and Kareem was the best. Everybody didn't necessarily highlight defense. But Michael Cooper is the best ever to play defense on anybody. Even in today's game, he would still be the top defender with his length and his quickness and his ability to jump and block shots. He always inspired me. I grew up watching the Showtime Lakers. I wouldn't be the player that I am without being in Inglewood and being able to watch the Lakers. Byron Scott graduated from my high school, and he's the person who allowed me to even come see the Lakers—like really see them up close and meet them, see their practice and see their games. I wouldn't have had that opportunity to meet Coach Cooper when I was 14 in ninth grade without Byron.

And obviously him and Michael Cooper, what they were to the Lakers and to Magic and James Worthy, was a highlight for me. So I'm that kid, that female, that's influenced by men's basketball and the Los Angeles Showtime Lakers. I'm a product of them as role models. That's why the pride of wearing Purple and Gold—that legacy and that culture—was created before the Showtime Lakers, but they carried it on and made it something that all of us from L.A. take pride in. Our knowledge, our basketball IQ as a city, is very high because of them. When Coach Cooper became the Sparks' assistant coach, we started to do this warm-up that the Lakers would do, which was called a three-minute run, with our hands up, running the baseline and sliding. And I think, knowing that he was from the Lakers, I personally knew he was going to instill in us whatever it took for that team to win. He had that in his DNA, so of course he dropped that into all of us.

Personally I showed up in a way that he was very proud of. He was proud that I worked as hard as I did, that I was a very good leader and a very good listener. There was never a time when he couldn't tell me something or teach me something. I think the reason why we got along so well was because I always respected him as the authority over my teammates and me. Just listening and following and learning. But his work ethic in the way that he coached us—we practiced as hard as we played, and probably even harder. That was something Coach Cooper instilled in us: our ability to run and be in shape. We would run for the first 20 minutes of our practice. It was all three-man weave, Olympic shooting drills. So we rarely really had to get on the line and run. We were in shape because of how we started our practices every single day, which is something he took from the Lakers and instilled in us too.

I remember this one practice—we were in training camp before the season, and there were people trying to make the team. Coop always showed up as a jerk at first because he's got to weed out all of these women who simply can't cut it. And you've got to think when you're trying out for a team, you're really trying out for the 10th, 11th, 12th, or 13th spot. So you have to be in great shape. But he would run those women to death. One day, we ran—and I was counting—a total of 83 17s, which is when we run side to side on the court. We would run for every missed layup. And I was just like in my head, *Coop, you'll never break me! It doesn't matter what you come up with!*

He would laugh on the side because he would look at me, and I'd roll my eyes at him, and he would know that I was pissed. But he would only cancel practice or give us a day off if I said we needed one. I didn't like days off because I felt like if you take a day off, it's actually worse. When we came back, Coop was going to run us like we were out of shape. So it was better to come in, get our practice over, and let him make it a shorter practice than take a full day off because he'd kill us! My teammates used to get mad, but I understood Coop and his mentality. One thing he wasn't going to do was put a team on the court that was not in better shape than the other team, and I always appreciated that. So I'll always remember those 83 17s that day because I was so mad at him! But I also understood the process as a veteran. Every time he said, "Get on the line!" my teammates would say, "Coop! No!" But I didn't say one word. I'd just get on the line and run. Get on the line, run. Don't say anything. Like today was just like a track day. So I always remember that—I wanted to punch him in the face, but I didn't!

Coop always had this weird high-five that he did where he'd act like he was about to hit my hand hard and then he'd just do it softly. That's what he did after I became the first woman to dunk in the WNBA. He appreciated me, and he'd give me a hug too. But I think me being, you know, one of his best players, I think the balance was that he never really tried to show favoritism. I think he did a good job with that, though I'm sure there are others who might say something different. But Coop didn't treat me differently than anyone else in my view. He was just proud of me; that's what I know. He didn't give me a whole lot of praise to my face, but he'd do it in the media or to other people.

The one thing Coop always said, though, was that I might be the only female that he thought could play in the NBA. But because of the physicality, the grind, and being hit by the guys—that would be the only reason I wouldn't be able to last. But because of my IQ and my ability to score, he would always say I could. That is the greatest compliment he's ever given me.

—Lisa "Smooth" Leslie

Coauthor's Note

MICHAEL COOPER IS A RABBLE-ROUSER. He's a man with a hearty, laughing spirit. But most of all, he cares about family, loyalty, and competition. These are the traits that define him, which made it easy and exceptionally fun to write a memoir with the all-time great. Through many interviews, the 1987 NBA Defensive Player of the Year and 2024 Hall of Fame inductee and I dove into his achievements to write this basketball record. Coop is, after all, one of only three Lakers—along with Kareem Abdul-Jabbar and Magic Johnson—to win five rings in the Showtime era. But Coop's career didn't end there.

You'll read how he helped identify a 17-year-old Kobe Bryant as a must-get for the Lakers before the 1996 NBA draft. And later, how he leveraged his experience with the Lakers for back-to-back rings as coach of the WNBA's L.A. Sparks in the early 2000s (while also helping to guide the careers of budding all-time greats Lisa Leslie and Candace Parker). Today he is still coaching, whether it's his son Nils, a standout at UC Davis, or at the Division II school Cal State L.A., where he's employed as an assistant.

Coop is an L.A. lifer, and because of this, he is an endless source of stories and history. Pose him a question, and he might unveil 2 or 10 minutes that will leave your jaw agape. From stories about covering

Larry Bird like a winter coat to running sprints on Riley's whistle to celebrating a win with Magic and beyond, these pages are proof.

—Jake Uitti

Introduction

THE LOS ANGELES LAKERS ERA KNOWN AS SHOWTIME began officially in the concluding seconds of our first regular-season game during the 1979–80 season, thanks to a one-point victory on the road against the San Diego Clippers. It was then when our captain, Kareem Abdul-Jabbar, hit one of his famous swooping skyhooks at the buzzer. Everyone on the team went crazy, leaping off the bench to hug our center. You should have seen us. We were like kids again.

From there, a decade and a dynasty unfurled. With Finals wins in 1980, 1982, 1985, and back-to-back in 1987 and '88 (the first team to repeat since the 1960s Boston Celtics), we changed the game, from how it was played to how it was perceived. Our home gym had its own nightclub, for goodness sake! And our owner, Dr. Jerry Buss, made as many headlines on the court as he made friends off it. Our stars burned at the brightest wattage, beginning with Earvin "Magic" Johnson.

For my part, I honed my game to help my teammates. We had scorers; we had focal points. So I became the league's best defender and won the award for it in 1987, the same year Magic won his first MVP and the Lakers won the first of our back-to-back titles. In pop culture, the mark of success is often summed up by one name: Madonna, Prince, Beyoncé, Cher, Adele. Showtime.

While it couldn't last forever, the memory assuredly will. In these pages, I wanted to add my part to the history books. Sure, I've told the press various stories ever since I became a member of the Lakers, but now that I've gone through nearly seven decades of life, I wanted to bring all my recollections together in one place. What follows is my point of view—how I experienced Showtime and, later, how I became a champion head coach in the WNBA and D-League.

ran the length of my leg to stabilize it. I had to wear that thing for 18 months, which felt like a lifetime.

After that, I had to wear a metal brace. For those who've seen *Forrest Gump*, it was a lot like that. In that movie, as Forrest runs from some bullies, his braces break off. Suddenly, he's *free*. But I wasn't free to run with mine! While I had the brace on one leg, my grandmother wouldn't let me leave the house. The farthest I could go was our front porch. But if she saw me there, she'd tell me to come back in and she'd set me in front of that big window. My brother and cousins would come inside and say how tired they were from their fun. It hurt my stomach to hear that, and I told myself that if I were ever able to get back outside, I'd never come back in.

That was the faith I held on to day after day. Hard as it was, I never gave in or admitted to myself that I wouldn't be back outside playing. I bided my time, patient even when it seemed like the most impossible thing. It helped knowing my grandmother prayed for me. I could feel her energy when she put her warm hands on my knee (like that Bill Withers song "Grandma's Hands") and asked God for help. I kept my faith and believed it would be okay. Then, finally, after I healed and was able to walk and jump on my left leg (despite the doctor's prediction), I made sure never to be inside before sundown. It took months, but I'd waited out the pain.

BUT I ENDURED more pain. Also when I was five, my father left our family, and I did not see him again until I was an L.A. Laker. Later, when I was about nine, my mother decided to marry a man named Phil, who was a full-blooded Cherokee from the Oklahoma tribe. His father was a chief, but unfortunately Phil was an alcoholic. I mean, he drank all the time, and as a result, he and my mother used to fight. She was very protective of me and my brother Mickey, who was three years younger. Our mother did everything she could to raise us without our father. She was one of 10 kids, and she knew what it took to maintain a family.

But soon things got really bad with Phil. We lived in Pasadena then, and my mother was working as a nurse in Los Angeles, trying to make a

Prologue
Hawaii 2022

HOW DO YOU KNOW WHEN YOU'RE PART OF A TEAM? Is it the uniforms? The structure, the coach, the players, the staff? Is it a *feeling*, a sense of camaraderie? Well, for the Showtime Los Angeles Lakers, it was all of those things wrapped up in an unforgettable decade. But if we'd ever had any doubt about our connection or place in history—any thoughts that a single moment was not quite what we'd remembered—then all of that was fixed in September 2022 with a trip to Hawaii exactly 34 years after our last Showtime championship. Our handful of days in paradise was unlike anything ever in the history of pro sports, something only we could have pulled off.

Traveling to Hawaii, the location of many Lakers training camps prior to our championship seasons in the 1980s, a few dozen of some of the most historic hoopers in history gathered to be around Coach Pat Riley. We ran drills (albeit gingerly), stretched in a big group, and shared memories from our glory days. It was part fantasy camp and part reunion, and guys such as Kareem Abdul-Jabbar, Magic Johnson, Jim Chones, Kurt Rambis, Mychal Thompson, James Worthy, Byron Scott, A.C. Green, Bob McAdoo, and many more dropped everything to take the time to reunite as Showtime once more. And it made waves, so to speak, with headlines and social media posts spreading far and wide.

There were MVPs, scoring and assist champs, and, most importantly, winners among our ranks. We joked about needing to shoot more three-pointers. Riley yelled (in good fun) things such as, "You guys got to wake up!" and "Cut!" Magic put up hook shots. Many of us were in our 60s and 70s, and it was the first time we'd all been together since 1989. We wore specially designed T-shirts with the Larry O'Brien Trophy emblazoned on the front surrounded by our championship years. It was a laugh to see so many of us old guys in shorts! In our playing days, we redefined basketball, so it was only right to go back and relive those days for one more week.

In the evenings, after practice, we hung out in the glorious warm weather, wearing Hawaiian leis and big ol' grins. All the players brought their lovely wives or girlfriends. One of the best moments came when we were gathered in a film room only to bust out singing in unison. Donning purple collared shirts and all-white leis, we sang karaoke to "Joy and Pain" by Maze, led by Magic (known as EJ the DJ). We did all the hand movements, mimicking rays of sunshine and droplets of rain coming down from the sky. A bunch of grown men singing in a big hotel room with our spouses—I never could have imagined it until it actually occurred.

Magic had the idea for the reunion first and had been thinking about it for several years. Over time he got it rolling with Pat Riley, Jeanie Buss, and Linda Rambis, calling everyone personally. When the 2020 pandemic hit, the concept was put on hold, but when the world opened up, we all decided we'd better get our butts to Maui for at least one last time. The experience brought back a lot of blessed memories, and receiving passes from Magic, running off screens from A.C., and seeing Kareem shoot was like a portal into the past. But more than anything, the trip showed how much we loved one another. While many of us were in first gear compared to our race car former selves, I wouldn't have changed a thing.

Some golfed, and others played cards or dominoes. At one point between meals, my wife and I went snorkeling with Kareem and Gary

Vitti, our old trainer and the man who kept us healthy through many playoff runs over the years. We spent two hours on a boat (though Kareem and I never got in the water!). We talked about our lives, our kids, anything at all. It was amazing watching people share these moments together. To see the familiar looks in their eyes that I'd come to rely on in the trenches as a player—the way a pupil flickers or a corner tightens—felt like we were young again, like we were 23 or 24 for just a few more terrific hours.

Our wives and girlfriends felt the love too. We saw them shed several tears of joy for what the occasion meant to us as people and to the history of the game that has done so much for all of us. In the mornings, we woke up early, grinning, ready to start the day and tell stories over breakfast in the Hawaiian sunshine. Throughout the afternoons, we reenacted several of the famed Showtime pictures from over the years. It was a blast to relive those moments, to remember what it meant to be part of Showtime.

In the late 1970s and into the early '80s, we held our training camps in Southern California. But as we started to win, which was something we did all throughout the decade, the Lakers' iconic owner, Dr. Jerry Buss, wanted to enjoy the finer things. So he started to send us to Honolulu for camp after we'd won our second consecutive championship in 1988. But that didn't mean we relaxed there. Not at all. Indeed, it wasn't about sun and girls; it was about work, sacrifice in paradise. That's what builds camaraderie—teamwork. We worked our butts off, wanting to get back to the promised land the next season. Maybe we had a night off in a week to enjoy the scenery—but just one. That's something people should know about the Showtime Lakers: we were workaholics.

Led by Magic, who demanded not only our best but our *most*, we worked ourselves so hard that the wheels essentially fell off at the end of the decade. Only Kareem, with his yoga regimen, was able to play into his 40s. The rest of us gave the world everything we had. When Showtime ended, a new era of Lakers basketball unfolded in the 1990s. Fast-forward more than three decades, and there we were again, marking one of the greatest decades in sports.

Sadly, not everyone could make it. Jerry West, Norm Nixon, Mike McGee, Mitch Kupchak, and Jamaal Wilkes had prior commitments. But aside from them, essentially everyone who helped win a ring for us back then was able to attend, other than those who had already passed on. And all who weren't in attendance were certainly missed. In the end, it was like a dream. A fantasy built on top of a decade of effort—*joy and pain*. We got the winning done when other teams couldn't. We respected each other and, because of that, pushed each other further than we thought we could ever go. We made each other better. You couldn't ask for anything more than that.

Chapter 1

The Doctor Said
I'd Never Run Again

I WAS BORN IN LOS ANGELES ON APRIL 15, 1956. Growing up in Los Angeles, my first favorite basketball team was, ironically, the Boston Celtics. Now, that's no joke; I promise you. Located 3,000 miles away, Boston was the franchise I followed as a boy, thanks to Tom, my uncle (his full name was Tom Butler, and we were prohibited from calling him Uncle Tom for obvious reasons). Because of him, I was 10 years old when I started to learn about the game. My eyes opened up to the NBA in the mid-1960s when Tom sat me down for the weekly televised games on his little black-and-white TV. My uncle loved the Celtics' center Bill Russell and small forward Satch Sanders. He would tell me, "Look at these guys! This is how you play the game."

We'd watch Bob Cousy running around—the "Houdini of the hardwood." We'd watch Russell blocking shots, keeping them in bounds so the Celtics could start their fast break. But the player I fell in love with most was John "Hondo" Havlicek. Drafted with the No. 9 pick in 1962, Havlicek became a 13-time NBA All-Star, 8-time All-Defensive player, 8-time NBA champion, top-75 player, and Hall of Famer. From the 1965–66 season until he retired, the 6'5" Hondo played on the All-Star team every year because he was the type of guy who'd do anything needed

1

to win, including coming off the bench. Hondo practically invented the concept of the sixth man.

And it's a role I would later duplicate in the 1980s. Havlicek could shoot, score, get the biggest steal—everything. Later, I was able to do all that too. At least partly because of how I'd built my game around his. People always used to say Havlicek had a third lung because he never got tired. Well, I wanted to be like that too: To play at the highest level on both ends of the floor. To occupy and guard virtually any position. To do the little things. Isn't it funny how as kids the things we spend time on end up becoming the building blocks of our adulthood? I didn't know it then, but seeing Hondo, a Celtic, so closely helped me become a champion Laker years later.

Still, despite this inspiration, even before I hit my teenage years, I remember when I almost quit basketball altogether. It was way before my career got going in earnest. At the time, I was playing in a league in the local YMCA. Rather, I *wasn't* playing. That was the problem. My coach was a white guy named Mr. Kelly. While I was no real star then, I still knew I was a pretty good player, and that I deserved at least to get in the games. For some reason, though, Mr. Kelly never put me in. Not even in what's known as garbage time, when a game is out of reach for either side.

It got so bad that I wanted to throw in the towel, to quit and move on to anything else. That, however, was when Tom pulled me aside and said something that changed my life. With my father gone and my mother, Dezzie Jean Cooper, living in San Francisco then, I was raised by my grandmother Ardessie Butler, along with aunts and uncles, including Tom, who was a former Negro Leagues baseball player. Naturally, I was thirsty for guidance, and Tom was there for me with plenty of it. He came to watch me play at the YMCA—well, *not* play, as was the case.

After seeing a few games, watching me sit through them all, Tom pulled me aside and asked, "Mike, how come you're not playing?" I told him, "I don't know!" This continued through the season until our team's second-to-last game. Mr. Kelly didn't put me in that one either. So I blurted out to Tom that I was going to quit playing basketball altogether. I was really mad at the whole thing. I felt I should have been part of the team all season. So forget all this, right? I thought, if basketball doesn't want me, I don't want it! So after the second-to-last matchup of the year, my uncle drove me home, and I said to him, "I'm going to quit. I'm going to go try football."

My family was known for playing sports. We played football, baseball, basketball—everything. Spring, summer, fall, winter. But my uncle just looked at me and said plainly, "Michael, do you love playing basketball?" I replied, "Yes, I love it." He asked, "Do you enjoy it?" I said, "I do!" That's when he told me the thing that changed my life: "Then don't ever let anybody take your joy. You started this, so I want you to finish it. Because you will play—sometime. This is a learning lesson for you." Right then, I knew he was completely right. So I resolved not to quit the team after all.

Instead, I went back to the YMCA the next week for our final game of the season, ready to sit it out. But this is where it gets a little eerie. I don't know if it was the basketball gods or what—though I do know for sure that my uncle never said anything directly to Mr. Kelly—but in that final game of the season, incredibly, Mr. Kelly put me in. And you know what? I played great. Scoring points, defending, rebounding. And we won the game. Afterward, Mr. Kelly pulled me aside and said, "Michael, I'm sorry. I should have been playing you all season." I was overjoyed. A rush of happiness raced through me from my head to my toenails.

But I just looked my coach in the eyes and said, "Mr. Kelly, that's okay." And I walked off the court, toward home, knowing that I'd been correct all along. For me, that was an important and early defining moment. That's when I knew I could play the game well, that I had talent and I just had to stick with it. But more than that, I knew, thanks to Tom, that I would never let anybody else control my happiness. I, Michael Jerome Cooper, was in charge of that, and I would be for the rest of my life. Throughout my career, I continued to think about that YMCA basketball experience. The overarching lesson? Follow your passion no matter what.

EVEN BEFORE MY issues with Mr. Kelly, as a young boy, I had to learn other important lessons when it came to patience. It began when I was five, in 1961, when I thought I might lose my left leg and never walk again. I still shudder thinking about it. Uncle George, who loved animals, brought home a German shepherd named Lady. Not long after, Lady had babies, so little puppies were always running around in the yard. On our back porch, my family also kept an old coffee can. Whenever someone made fried chicken or bacon, they'd pour the grease from the pan in there to use later or throw away at the appropriate time.

But one time the coffee can outside hadn't been opened correctly; my grandmother, bless her heart, hadn't gotten the top all the way off. And one day, one of the puppies must have knocked that can over on its side, with the jagged top edge pointing straight up. And on that day, just like on many others, I came running out of the house. But in a flash, I slipped, and before I knew it, my knee landed directly on the can. That gnarled edge went deep into my knee. The metal cut through my skin and muscle and went down to my bone, nicking a bit of that too.

The pain was so excruciating that all I saw were red lights. I screamed, and tears shot down my cheeks. After my family rushed me to the hospital, the doctor used 102 stitches to sew my left knee back together. It took him all night. My grandmother prayed powerfully for me the entire time, until dawn. When I wept, she comforted me, saying, "Michael, you're a blessed child. It's going to be all right. Don't worry." I stayed in the hospital for a few more days, and when I came home that week, I had to stay indoors. My grandmother, fearful I might get hurt again, wouldn't let me go outside.

Instead, I sat at a big picture window in our home and watched all the kids playing. The doctor who had sewed up my leg had said I would most likely never be able to run again. Imagine being a kid and hearing that. He said that I would *probably* be able to walk one day without a limp. But running or anything like that was out of the question. My grandmother kept praying, saying, "Michael, you're a blessed child. Don't worry, don't worry." Finally, after my stitches healed, the doctor put a cast on me that way for us. Growing up, you don't really compare your life to other kids' lives. No matter who or where you were, that's all there was, and it was just fine. If there was food, a roof, and time to play with your friends, that was enough. So I didn't see my life as any better or any worse than those of all the other kids I knew. But looking back on it, we had some tough times. The toughest came one night when my mother and Phil got into a big argument. During it, Phil threw an ashtray at my mother, and it sliced her arm open.

She came bursting into Mickey's and my bedroom around 3:00 in the morning. We weren't asleep, though. We had heard them fighting through the walls. But my mother had always told us that if we heard her and Phil arguing (or worse), not to leave the room. "Mommy can handle herself," she would say. She didn't want us getting involved, which itself hurt sometimes.

But that night, she'd had enough of Phil, so she came into our room and yanked us out of bed. "Get up," she said. "Come on!" The three of us got into her car, and I could see where she'd been cut by the ashtray; I could see her arm sparkling with dark red blood in the car's overhead light. My brother and I didn't know what had happened; we could just see the coagulating blood on her smooth brown skin. She turned the car's ignition and drove away from our home. My maternal grandmother lived just three blocks away, so my mother drove us there. When we arrived, she told us to get out of the car. Our grandmother had come outside and was standing on the front porch, and my brother and I ran to her. My mother, still in the car, drove away. That was the last time I saw her for years.

So I was about nine years old when my grandmother started taking care of Mickey and me. She raised us, along with our extended family of aunts and uncles. We had a bunch of cousins around at any given time too. We had a big family.

During the days, I was occupied with school and friends, but at night, I got sad and missed my mother. I thought of her most in the evenings. I missed her face, her voice. My grandmother told us, "Your mother loves you. She just can't be here right now." She needed to get away from Phil, and she needed us to be separated from him too. A few times, we saw his Corvette drive slowly past my grandmother's home to see if my mom was there. My grandma kept us inside whenever he did that. My mother's four brothers kept watch, standing outside by the door, scowling at Phil, who never stopped, thank God. My only connection with my mother for the next several years was the envelope she sent Mickey and me every Friday that contained a crisp $20 bill.

Our grandmother would hand us the envelope and say, "Boys, this is from your mother." I could still smell the perfume Mom wore on the money, as if when she put it in the envelope it stayed there from her wrist just for me. The sweet, fragrant smell was like flowers. I didn't even want to spend the money, didn't want to lose the scent memory.

I later learned the whole story of what happened after my mom drove away the night she dropped us off. She drove back to the house, and because Phil was a drunk, he'd already passed out when she arrived. My mother quickly and quietly got her things, and then she drove away. She drove first to Monrovia, where she stayed overnight with a friend. The next day, though, Phil found out where she was, and he went over there to find her. He took a gun with him and broke the front door down to get to her. He fired the gun, trying to kill her, but he missed.

My mother's friend Joe was standing behind the door when Phil broke in and started shooting. Joe was protecting my mom, and he came from behind the door, grabbing Phil's hand, trying to stop him. As this happened, my mother ran into the bedroom and jumped out the first-floor window to escape. When she told me this part of the story, she said that the last thing she'd heard as she leapt out was another gunshot. When she hit the lawn, she ran to another friend's house to hide, and she eventually made her way north to San Francisco. But the gunshot she'd heard was Phil shooting and killing Joe. After that, Phil went on the run from the police for as long as he could. But they eventually caught his ass. Before they caught him, we would see Phil drive by my grandmother's house in his Corvette, and my grandmother would say, "There he goes again. Why can't the police catch him? *There* he is!"

There was a murder trial after they caught him, and Phil was found guilty and sentenced to 25 years in prison. I remember it was a big deal, both in our house and in the city of Los Angeles. In the end, Phil served all 25 years in prison, but if you ask me, he should have stayed there to rot.

MY MOTHER'S PARENTS had moved to Los Angeles from New Hebron, Mississippi, a town in Lawrence County that had a very small population. They were looking for a better life, and they'd heard California could provide it. Coming out to L.A. was tough, but it was better than staying in the racist hotbed of Mississippi. One of my grandmother's sisters had come to L.A. in the 1940s, and my mother's parents had followed her. My grandmother knew her children needed a better place to live. She was a strong woman, as were all the women in my family. They had to be—life wasn't easy, especially for Black women.

With my mother living full-time in San Francisco after all that went down with Phil, it was my grandmother who raised Mickey and me for a significant portion of our young lives. She did all a grandmother could do for her grandsons. Because of her and my aunts and uncles, I had clothes on my back, food in my stomach, and a roof over my head. Yes, we had *enough*. I was raised with my other cousins. There were seven of us when I was young, but some 14 or 15 people were in and out of the house at any given time looking for a meal or a place to rest their heads. There was never a lot of food on the table, but it was never bare either.

My grandfather died when I was five years old. And what I remember most about that time was that my family took me to see him at Huntington Hospital in Pasadena. Only we had to stand outside his window to look in at him; we couldn't go into his room. It was three days before he died, and all I could do was wave at my grandfather through the glass. He saw us out there, but I never knew what he was thinking. From what I remember, he passed away from cancer, but I was too young to know any of the details. I just remember seeing him there, old and hurting, through the hospital window, seeing us wave.

When I was young, all of my grandmother's children were around—except for my mother, of course. At any time, we affectionately called my grandmother's place the Big House, and most of the family knew it as home. There were uncles, such as Tom, John, and George, and cousins, including Aaron, Avery, Braud (pronounced like *Brad*), Tammy, and more. The uncles had been good athletes, but they'd had to put sports away for the most part to earn a living and keep a roof over the family's head and clothes on our backs. Everyone had to sacrifice for the good of the family; that was the ethic of the Big House.

All the adults in the family worked or had money coming in. Three of my uncles had jobs at Vons grocery, for example. My grandmother got her Social Security too. So the kids were never without, and never dressed raggedy. We never had the best of the best, but who cared about that? My classmates never teased me, and we never knew how hard life really was, because our family shielded us from that. Looking back, I can't believe how much our family sacrificed for us. And I'll be forever grateful.

MY FATHER'S NAME was Marshall Cooper, and his entire family was from Paris, Texas. His family is still located there, and many have never left. His mother passed away several years ago at the age of 92, and my dad's father passed away when he was about 90. And when my dad died in 2014, he was 86. So at least he gave me good genes, if nothing else. My parents divorced when I was five. Before that, they would have terrible arguments. My father would beat on my mom, and so she eventually decided to leave him. I didn't see my father again until I was 20 years old, by which point I was a pro basketball player.

WHEN I WAS 13, my mother decided she wanted Mickey and me to move up to San Francisco and live with her full-time, so she sent for us. As a kid growing up without her there, I missed her, but I'd tried not to think about it much. I'd tried to just fill my life with friends, establish who I was, play sports, and get good grades in school. I also read a lot for a sense of escape.

My grandmother, who was very religious, had suggested naming me after the Archangel Michael, who fought Satan in the Bible and cast him out of heaven. So there were times I felt a sense of obligation to protect my family and to protect myself from all the things I could. My grandmother would say, "Michael, your mother loves you. She just has to be away from you now." In a way, Mom was always with me, though. Her absence was *there* in my stomach when I thought about it. I tried to keep it out of my mind until I couldn't anymore.

So when she sent for Mickey and me, I didn't know what to think. I was excited about the idea of seeing her more, but it also meant we would be moving 400 miles north, away from all that we knew (which would also take me away from my self-designated role of protector).

This wasn't the first contact we'd had with my mother, though. A couple of years earlier, when I was 11, my brother and I had gone to San Francisco on a few weekends to see her there. We'd take a Greyhound bus up on Friday, and then we'd take it back on Sunday because we had school the next morning. In San Francisco, my mother had found a new man, and she had a fine apartment. She worked as a nurse, giving private care to clients. We got to see her whole new established life on those weekend visits. She was doing well for herself, which I was proud to see.

So when she sent for us when I was 13, my brother and I went to stay with her for an entire year. It might be easy to think that we'd be overjoyed to be reunited with her. In all honesty, though, we didn't like it very much. Our grandmother missed us, and she'd tell my mother, "Send them kids back down here where they belong." Mickey and I ended up being latchkey kids in San Fran because my mom worked all the time. By 7:00 in the morning, she would wake with us to make us breakfast and ensure we got to school. But then she would go to work, only to come back around 1:00 AM. So Mickey and I rarely saw her.

But because I was 13 going on 14, I was old enough to look after him. We'd walk home together after school, and I remember we'd stop to get burgers at this little spot and take them home and chow down together. But after a year being away from L.A. and hardly ever seeing our mom, we moved back down to Southern California. From then on, I lived with my grandmother until the day I went off to college. That's where I felt most at home, with the people I knew best. You have to trust your gut when it comes to stuff like that. Like Tom told me, you can't let anyone else control your joy.

Chapter 2

Stealing Cigarettes

IF YOU DROVE AROUND LOS ANGELES in the 1960s and 1970s, you would likely have seen a lot of basketball hoops in the driveways. Rich kids had those big ol' backboards up on their two-car garages, and they'd pretend to be Jerry West or Elgin Baylor hitting game winners from the sidewalk. But while we weren't destitute by any means, my family didn't have the money for a professional-looking hoop for our own driveway.

So what I did was go to a lumberyard nearby and buy a big two-by-four. My cousin and I carried it home, and then we dug a hole in the backyard near a fence and jammed the two-by-four in there to build a hoop. After that, we got a big square piece of wood and nailed that to the top of the two-by-four, and that was our backboard. Before, I used to practice shooting into metal trashcans because I had no hoop. But then Tom, my uncle, brought me a real rim—nothing else but the rim. Back then, chain nets were the big thing, but those were dangerous if you wanted to dunk. They could rip your fingers off if you caught them the wrong way, and after my knee surgery, I didn't want to deal with any unnecessary injuries. Thankfully, Tom later bought me a 10-cent white nylon net from Johnny's Sport Shop, which is still standing today in L.A. I laced the net on the rim, and I got some white chalk and drew a square on the backboard to complete the setup.

I'd play basketball from sunup to sundown on my homemade setup. All I wanted to do was dunk on the hoop, and because the two-by-four we used was only about eight feet tall, there was plenty of opportunity for me to do just that. I'd pretend to be the high-flying Connie Hawkins or would shoot around like my idols John Havlicek, Jerry West, and skinny Charlie Scott. I'd watch games with Tom on his black-and-white TV, and then I'd go outside and jam on the hoop. I'd emulate the greats, not knowing that I was developing the skills that would one day make me a champion.

People wonder how I was so creative midair, how I could finish with such lighting quickness and style from a Magic Johnson pass—well, it was because of all the time I put in on that hoop I made out of wood. Back then, the only other place I could shoot hoops was the schoolyard, but the janitors at the school usually closed that down by 5:00. Every now and then, we'd get the gumption to jump the fence at the school and play anyway, but like clockwork, someone would come out and yell at us: "Get out of here!" So I most often stayed where I wouldn't be shooed away. I played with my cousins, and we were competitive and played hard.

When the hoop had taken too much abuse—if it broke or split at the bottom from dampness caused by the rain, fell down, or just got too old—we'd make another. We'd dig the old board out, get another two-by-four, and start all over. I also once made a wooden defender to shoot over and dribble around. Thanks to our ingenuity, I was able to experiment with moves and do it away from anyone else's influence. Sure Mickey and my cousins were around, but they were family. I could goof or I could get serious, but I never had to do it in front of anyone I didn't want to. It wasn't an intentional strategy, but it was one that let me develop on my own.

AS I MENTIONED, my grandmother's house was known as the Big House, but that did didn't mean that it didn't change locations. Throughout my youth, from elementary to middle school, we must have moved five or six times, which can be a pain for some, but I enjoyed it, always wanting to see what my new room or the new place would look like. Incredibly, my grandmother always found a four- or five-bedroom place with a big yard in front or out back. To this day, I'm not sure how she did it.

We lived in three different homes in Pasadena and two in Altadena, which was about a 10-minute drive north and closer to the mountains. The Altadena properties were even bigger than those in Pasadena, some combination between the L.A. suburbs and small farms. When we moved to Altadena, we had animals, including chickens, which my grandmother raised. One house we lived in during my childhood was near the intersection of Los Robles and Madison. That place had a whopping 12 bedrooms—you could spend a day touring the place and not get bored.

That was the first house where I had my own bedroom. I'd always grown up sleeping with other family members in the bed, from cousins such as Aaron and Braud to Mickey or my Uncle Ricky, who was just one year older than me and more like a brother than an uncle. If there were four of us in a bed, two would face one way and two would face the other, careful not to get a mouthful of feet. I got used to a lot sharing a room and a bed with family members. In one sense, it was not an ideal setup, but in another, getting used to things like that makes for strong character and a closeness among your family. That's very important, especially as you get older in this world.

LIFE ALWAYS HAS curve balls, such as the first time I experienced racism in 1973. I was about 17 years old and a junior at Pasadena High School. I have always had very dark skin, and there is no hiding my race (not that I would ever want to). But if bullies, like the police, were looking for a target, I easily stood out. On this particular occasion, my cousins and I were driving up to meet these three white girls from our school—Laurie, Sarah, and Abby—in Sierra Madre, a town east of Pasadena (I was dating Abby). Our high school was located between Altadena Drive and Sierra Madre Boulevard, and it pulled students from both towns. But when you headed into Sierra Madre, that was considered a "white area" of the city.

It was the evening, a little after 6:00 PM, when a cop pulled us over. We were driving up one of the main streets, Orange Grove Boulevard, and headed to Sierra Madre when the officer turned on his flashing red and blue lights. We pulled our car over, and he came up to the window and told us to get out of the vehicle. We complied. "What are you boys doing up here?" he asked. We told him we were going to see our friends, girls we were taking out.

Then the racist-ass cop told us, "You niggers aren't going to see anybody. What you need to do is turn this car around before I take you all to jail." That was the first time I'd ever been called the N-word. "You turn this car around," the police officer told us. "But," we implored, "we want to see our friends; we all go to school together." We were only a block and a half from Pasadena High School. "If you want to see your girlfriends," the police officer said, "you'll wait to see them at school." It was that night when I realized I was *Black* and that there was a major difference between that and being white. It showed there were thick racial lines.

Of course, I wasn't stupid growing up. Generally I knew there were differences between Black and white folks. But that cop was the first real exposure I had to that kind of aggressive, *hateful* racism. I'd never experienced it like that before, like I did that evening from that piece of shit cop. "Turn your car around and go back to your side of town," he said bitterly. I'd heard about racism from my family—it's what brought my mother's parents to California in many ways. But now I knew it wasn't just stories. It was right here, a block and a half from my high school. That was the first time it hit me, and it was shocking.

The fact that people thought that way was bad enough, but the fact that *law enforcement* thought that way—these people who are *sworn* to serve and protect the people—man, that was bad. The police are supposed to protect every law-abiding citizen, right? Of course we know they don't, and historically they never have. We saw it recently when a police officer murdered George Floyd for the world to witness (not to mention countless others, such as Eric Garner and Breonna Taylor). But that night in Sierra Madre was eye-opening. And you know what? We never went up there again. That shitty cop got his wish. Abby and I broke up a few weeks later.

A FEW YEARS before that, I'd had another life-changing experience, which I've never forgotten. I was 13 years old and living in Pasadena when, on a dare, I did something stupid. Ricky, Braud, and I were budding teenagers, and we were experimenting with smoking, as young people do. We wanted to grow up, and we were trying to act like we were men—we were coughing with nearly every puff, of course. Well, Ricky and Braud dared me to go to Ralph's grocery store with them to steal some more cigarettes. *Gulp.* I agreed.

To get to the supermarket, all we had to do was cross the street and hop an eight-foot brick wall that stood like a fence. We climbed the wall a lot, and we'd already set up a crate that we'd use that for a boost and get over pretty easily. So we did just that and went into Ralph's to snoop around. Inside, I could tell one of the bag guys—this young white guy— was looking right at us. He probably thought we were up to no good, and—well—on this day, he was right. I wandered near one of the cash registers, where the cigarettes were located, and quick as a flash, I reached out and grabbed a carton of Kools. Braud grabbed another for himself too. Then we took off.

We ran out of the market and darted out back where trucks made deliveries. We didn't think anyone was chasing us. I remember running as fast as I could. And when I turned a corner, I went for the crate by the brick wall. I jumped on top of it and lifted myself up. I threw my right leg over the wall, and just as I got to throwing my left leg over, the bagger from Ralph's grabbed me by my ankle and pulled me back down. I was stunned. And I never forgot what he told me. "You know what you are?" he shouted, breathing heavily. "You're a *thief*! That's what you are! And you'll never be anything *but* a thief!" The guy had me by the back of my shirt.

He pulled me back to the store, berating me at the same time. "A *thief*!" he said. The guy took me all the way into the back room at Ralph's and sat me down. "I'm going to call your parents," he said. "Where are *they*?" For some reason, I gave him our house number, and he called my uncle. Tom said he would come down to get me, and the whole time as we waited for him, the bagger called me a thief. "Thieves don't get anywhere in life," he said. "All you'll ever do is go to *jail*!" With each word, I got more and more scared. I was horrified by what he said. He broke my spirit. I felt so low, and I felt like a thief, which I guess I was.

I'd never considered myself a thief until then. It wasn't something I actually identified with. But if I thought about it, I was one now—at least a petty one. I'd stolen small things before, such as candy, and I'd never been caught. This was the first time I'd ever been nabbed by anyone. It felt awful. But then it got worse. When Tom came down, he talked with the people at the store. They told him I was never allowed in there again. My uncle agreed. Then he took me by the arm and took me home. "You all right?" he asked. "The guy didn't hurt you or anything, did he?" I told Tom that the guy kept calling me *worthless*, saying that I'd always be a *thief.*

Tom listened and nodded. "That's just him saying that," he replied. "Don't worry about what he thinks." Tom was calm when we got back to my grandmother's house. Almost sweetly, he said, "Listen, go upstairs and take all your clothes off." I told him, "Okay," even though, of course, I thought that was strange. But I went upstairs—and as I did, my grandmother threw her shoe at my head—and I got undressed. Then Tom came into my room and said, "Michael, you don't ever have to steal anything. If you want something, just ask, and we will provide it. If we can't, we'll work hard to get it for you." Then he took off his belt and proceeded to whip my ass.

Tom had this thick, black leather belt, and he used it to beat me good. People today would call it child abuse. But it taught me a lesson—one I needed to learn. He'd told me to take my clothes off so that I wouldn't have anything to block the belt or soften its strikes. He got all of me with that thing. But that was a big turning point for me. From then on, I never, ever, ever stole anything. I've had opportunities—there were times when friends or cousins would dare me. But I just shook it off. *You don't know what Tom will do to me if I steal that and get caught*, I thought. That event was the start of my moral education.

From then on, if I wanted something, I found a legitimate way to get it—no cutting corners. Tom beat that lesson into me with his belt that day. I remember it all like it was yesterday, even though it was more than 50 years ago. I've had a lot of hard times since then—weeks without money, living without my parents—but every time I considered the possibility of stealing, I thought about Tom's unforgiving leather belt. Since then, it's a lesson I've tried to teach my kids too (though without the belt): "You don't ever have to steal. We'll work for what you need. Besides, it's more gratifying that way. You won't have to look over your shoulder."

AS FAR AS basketball, my freshman year at Pasadena High School didn't get off to a flying start. I was cut from the varsity team as a freshman *and* a sophomore (I played JV). A late bloomer, I was skinny growing up. So skinny, in fact, that my grandmother started to call me Sticks as a nickname, because I looked like a pile of them. But though I was skinny, I was already blessed with athleticism. Sometimes that talent hurt me, though; I didn't always work as hard as I could have during my high school years.

That was true for basketball but even more so for my grades. PHS in the 1970s was about 90 percent white. But I'd never really seen any racial barriers until I was hanging around off campus and that cop pulled us over. Back at school, despite the racial disparity in my classes, you didn't see many issues between Blacks and whites. I'm sure there were underlying feelings harbored against my family and me—some teachers probably didn't think very highly of us—but no one ever voiced anything out loud.

I had a lot of white teammates on the basketball team (once I made it) too. And there was no blatant hatred for Blacks there, thank goodness. That included from the varsity coach at PHS, who was an Armenian guy named George Terzian. He was the guy who later introduced me to the Fellowship of Christian Athletes, an important group in my life. While I am a religious person, it's not something I flaunt. But it is something important to me, deep down in my soul. I grew up Baptist, and I still carry the faith with me. From the day I was born until the time I left for college in New Mexico, I went to church five days a week. Sunday mass was even held at our home in the Big House when I was a kid. When I went away to school, it was up to me to find a place of worship. Church has always been a big part of my life.

The Bible, I believe, remains important. The great basketball player George Gervin once asked me, "If the devil were running the world, what would it look like?" That stopped me in my tracks. It might look something like it does now. I'm not saying every person must be a saint, but we can all use some spirituality, faith, and religion in our lives. There is a lot to learn from the Bible—many solid tenets for life. Yes, plenty of bad things have been done in the name of religion, but many good things have been too. That's important for me to remember.

With the basketball team, Coach Terzian thankfully saw people as one kind. We were all his players, and I'll always be grateful for that mindset. There may have been racism in the streets outside of Pasadena High School but not within its walls—not that I ever experienced firsthand, anyway. It was only *after* you left campus that things about the outside world became a bit clearer—thanks in part to the police. But that's why so many of us prided ourselves on our faith and our family. We're close with each other so that we can support one another when the world works unfairly against us.

As an African American man in the United States, you grow up quickly due to the things you're exposed to. And I was growing up fast, beginning with my freshman year in high school. You learn to deal with things and then move on. You have to—there is no other real choice: adjust to the world, dodge, deflect, and adapt. Yet while much of my time and energy went into sports, I could have and should have studied more. But sports were always where my mind was—thanks, at least initially, to those times with Tom watching the Boston Celtics, seeing them beat my hometown Lakers. But while I'd quickly fallen in love with hoops, I also spent time playing football.

My favorite NFL team at the time was the Cleveland Browns. My favorite player on the team was Paul Warfield, who played for the squad for eight years, from 1964 through 1969 and again from 1976 through 1977. Warfield led the NFL in receiving touchdowns twice and landed in the Hall of Fame for his efforts. Because I was skinny and relatively tall for my age, I wanted to be a wide receiver just like him. My friends and I would go around to different blocks, challenging neighborhood kids to games. And when I was out on the playground playing, I'd jump in the air, trying to make these acrobatic catches like the great Paul Warfield.

But after one particular catlike attempt, the guy defending me, Herman Bluefur, hit me out of the air and knocked me unconscious. "You okay?" the other kids asked as I woke, trying to catch my breath. I was okay, thank God, but that play ended my football career (along with those other times I'd run into telephone poles in the street trying for a catch). It was all basketball after that. I watched guys such as John Havlicek, Jerry West, Bill Russell, Satch Sanders, and Elgin Baylor even closer. I got the bug. Another of my favorites was Connie Hawkins, who played for the Phoenix Suns. The Hawk was the first guy I saw palm the ball midair.

That was the fun part about growing up then. It was the era of hoops innovation. Players were finding out what they could do in the game to make themselves stand out. Players such as Connie were the first to do the things that guys now do routinely. That inspired me to no end. So when I got to high school, I was *determined* to make my mark—from trashcans to wooden hoops to the asphalt courts at the park and then, finally, to the indoor gyms of my school. But it was an uphill climb. In high school, I had a lot of nicknames, from Tarbaby (due to my dark skin) to Rope (because I was as thin as one). I needed to grow and fill out. I needed to mature.

Once I got good at the game, though, people just started calling me Coop, and that's the nickname I've always liked best. It would one day become a big part of my Lakers career, with my signature Coop-a-Loops, but I'll talk more about that later. When I was a Laker, I stood 6'7". But unlike some guys who grow super tall when they're in sixth or seventh grade, I was slower to sprout; my big growth spurt didn't come until late in high school. As a freshman at PHS, I was around six feet tall, and I didn't start growing until 11th or 12th grade, and then more when I got to college, when I shot up to 6'7".

In middle school, it was all outdoor playing. Either in the yard or trying to sneak into Madison middle school on the weekends before the janitors kicked us out. Great games took place at Victory Park. That was where I got my first taste of big-time competition. But the smell of an indoor gym always curled my toes. Growing up on asphalt, with skinned knees and having to play in all weather conditions, I got tough. I also learned to appreciate a gym. Playing in gyms was a sign you were advancing in your career. My first gym experiences came in the church, when the pastors would open the courts up after service. But in high school it all meant so much more.

Being in a family of 15, there were lots of hand-me-downs, and when it came to shoes, it was no different. My generation grew up with Chuck Taylor All-Stars, those canvas and rubber shoes from Converse. They're fashion statements today, but back then, they were performance-enhancing tools. Growing up, because I was on the taller side (though not a giant), my feet were the same size as Tom's. So Tom was always the source of my hand-me-down Chuck Taylors. But when you play ball—especially on asphalt—those sneakers can get torn up pretty quickly. Mine certainly did.

While I know some NBA players such as Dwyane Wade get a new pair of sneakers every game, when I was a kid, if you got a hole in your Chucks, you would have to cut out a piece of cardboard from a box and put that in the shoe to make it hang on and last another four or five days until the hole got so bad that you couldn't plug it with anymore.

That's when I'd get a new pair of shoes either from Tom or the store. I probably got a *new* pair of shoes twice a year, on my birthday in April and for Christmas. I would always try to keep my sneakers clean, though inevitably they would get dirty from playing outside.

You had to look good when you played. Look good, feel good, play better. Sometimes as I got older and played in the Los Angeles parks on the weekends, some of the best guys in the *world* would show up. That motivated me more. There was the bearded and burly Raymond Lewis from Watts, one of the best scorers California has ever seen, pro or otherwise. Today there is a documentary out about him, titled *Raymond Lewis: L.A. Legend*. Drafted by the Philadelphia 76ers in 1973, Ray unfortunately never played in the NBA, walking away from it after a contract dispute. There was also the incredible Marques Johnson, who went to high school in Crenshaw.

Dennis Johnson, who I'd later battle against in the NBA Finals when he played for the hated Celtics, was also an L.A. playground legend. We'd all run into each other at different parks. The summer leagues were big then, especially the one run by Joe Weakley in Crenshaw. Players from all over the city would hoop there in the sweltering months. Whether I was watching or playing, the leagues showed me guys from all over Southern California. But before I could shine, I had to work my way up the ranks at Pasadena High School, the four-year institution known for its program. It may not have been the *premier* school in California, but it was well up the list.

AS A 9TH, 10th, and 11th grader, I was thin, and I wasn't skyscraper-tall, either. I was about 6'2", maybe 6'3", as a junior in high school while I was on the junior varsity team. Of course, I hoped and prayed to join varsity as a senior. You had to be a good player to even *make* the varsity team, let alone get any playing time. But as a senior, finally it was my turn. I'd earned the big time, and then I got a lucky break. There was a player on the team who was set to start ahead of me, which would mean that I still wouldn't play much. Except suddenly he transferred, and just like that I got his spot in the starting five. And I kept it throughout the season. How? Well, I did whatever Coach Terzian told me to do. Coach was a great role model, and he said for me to stay in the game; I had to play defense and rebound. Done.

At PHS, the guys in my class were all in the shadow of a guy named Michael Gray, who'd made the varsity as a freshman. Standing 6'4" then, he was an awesome player. But by the time we were all seniors, Gray hadn't grown much. He was one of those guys who had fully matured by eighth grade. By our senior year, Gray was just an average player on the team, and I started to outshine even him.

We had a good team my senior season. We didn't win the state championship or anything like that, but we had a productive year. Historically, PHS was known for winning their city league and playing in the California Interscholastic Federation (CIF) state tournament. But we didn't go that far my senior year in 1974. Nevertheless, we were a strong squad. Wearing No. 42, I played forward and did a lot of things well, from scoring to rebounding and defending. I could shoot and I was light on my feet. Though I wasn't a highly recruited prospect, I'd come a long way since not playing at all on Mr. Kelly's YMCA team. I prided myself on my athleticism and speed, both of which helped my defensive prowess.

Coach Terzian was my first coach to prioritize defense. He set the tone for me, something that future coaches would refine. If it weren't for Coach Terzian and, later, my coaches in college, I wouldn't have had the experience to be a great defender when I got to the Lakers. Then in the hands of Pat Riley, one of the most detail-oriented coaches in history, I became one of the NBA's best defensive players (and *the* best in 1987). I was someone Larry Bird feared. His French Lick butt never wanted to see me! But without Coach Terzian and his teaching, which included wearing blinders to keep your eyes on the ball instead of looking at the entire gym, I wouldn't have gotten there.

Coach Terzian created various drills for me. First, he told me not to reach for the ball but to move my feet. Coach taught me the importance of sliding my feet. If he saw me reach, I'd have to run laps. He also attached a ball to the end of a long stick and used it to teach me how to block shots with two hands. The focus was not on slamming the ball out of bounds but on getting it to a teammate. Terzian showed me how to take charges. It was thanks to his help that I simply fell in love with defense; it became my calling card. The Hawk had scoring, Dr. J had his dunks, and I had maddening defense.

Everybody needs help, and Coach Terzian was mine. Thanks to my coach and love of basketball, I got an education. And that was my ultimate goal: to use the game to better my life. But it wasn't easy. Growing up, there were gang members in L.A. who wanted guys like me to join them and sell drugs, spend time in the streets, out at all hours. But I never wanted that, and neither did my grandmother. She told me, "Boy, don't you join no gang!" If she ever swore, she would have done so right there. But it was a hassle just getting to school sometimes, passing guys every day trying to recruit you. I had to fight my way through. Compared to that, basketball was easy.

HOWEVER, EVEN WHEN you're good, there's always someone who can frustrate you. For me, as a senior, it was a guy named Mark Wulfemeyer. He was a 6'1" guard from Troy High in L.A. Though Mark never made it as a pro, he was a star in high school who scored more than 2,600 points in those four years. He was the first white kid I'd seen who played like a brother (but not the last, Mr. Bird). He could dribble between his legs and play tough. He was handsome and could get the crowd going crazy. Mark could shoot from far out, and while we didn't have the three-point line then, if we had, he would have scored even more points and broken more records.

For the longest time, Wulfemeyer was also the kid who I couldn't stop on defense. He could drop 35 in an instant. I remember feeling scared to death when we had to play Troy my senior year. Once the game started, Mark hit his first three shots. But on his fourth attempt, I partially blocked his jumper. That's when my jitters melted away. I told myself,

Hey, you can play this game too! I'd blocked one of the best players in the city, so I realized I could play with the stars. Senior year was big for me after that—big for my self-esteem.

With each day, my confidence grew. That was an amazing thing. I'd seen players including Connie Hawkins and Wilt dunk. And when I did it, I felt somehow like one of their peers. Not that I was anywhere near as good as them, of course, but dunking became something we shared. I was part of the fraternity of slam dunkers. Because I was so light on my feet (and skinny), when I jumped, I could get up in the air pretty well. I was also fast. I'd started running track in high school, competing at the long and high jumps. At the time, the school record was around four feet for the high jump. And that was before the Fosbury flop, during which the jumper goes over the bar backward.

Before that, the technique we used was the Western Roll, where you get over the bar with your stomach parallel to it. Anyway, I was getting up in the air pretty high, even approaching the high school record as a tenth grader. As a long jumper, I was getting around 16 or 17 feet. I was good at both, but it was basketball that truly called to me. Coach Terzian eventually made me choose, saying he didn't keep two-sport players on his team, so I couldn't do both. But because he *wanted* me, I chose hoops. That's when I started to play more and how I got on varsity as a senior. And that's around when I first dunked—a tennis ball initially.

The first time I dunked anything on a 10-foot rim, I knew I was on to something special. It was the summer between my junior and senior years at PHS. I got hold of this tennis ball in our home gym; I'll never forget it. Everybody was trying to jump up and grab the rim, and one of the guys on the team, McKinley Taylor, who was a legit 6'5" and had big hands, went up and slammed it. Then it was my turn, and I followed him up. I wasn't nearly as big as he was, but I was able to put a tennis ball over the rim and then through. *Wait, did I just dunk? I just dunked!* I was ecstatic.

Not long after my tennis ball triumph, I was able to dunk a volleyball. Doing that felt even better. There was an eruption in my heart. More, more—I wanted *more*. It was exhilarating, the ultimate high. I felt like

Connie Hawkins and I shared something special: we both knew what a thrill it was to dunk. By the time I graduated from PHS, I was a little over 6'3", tall enough finally to dunk a basketball. I'd officially graduated in more ways than one. I could start to see the vague outline of a career unfold ahead of me too. The only question was, where would I play in college?

A lot of the guys on the team were getting scholarship offers, but I only received one, largely because my grades weren't great (I had a low C average), and in the end, the offer was extended to me as something of a favor to Coach Terzian. The head coach from Seattle Pacific University knew Terzian, and I think that was the reason why he made me an offer to play there there. PHS player Jim Marsh was at SPU, and so it would have been a fine fit, except that I had no idea where Seattle was. The concept of leaving L.A. was so foreign to me that though I only had the one scholarship offer, I decided to decline it. Instead, I enrolled at the junior college Pasadena City College. *Here we go!*

Chapter 3

Learning My Lessons

WHEN YOUNG PEOPLE ASK ME what I think about junior college, I tell them there's nothing wrong with it at all. Quite the opposite, actually. I went to Pasadena City College happily and look how I turned out! The history of basketball in America owes a great deal to junior colleges. In past decades, they were often the only options for Black players who were dissuaded from enrolling in historically white schools. Later, they became important for people like me who didn't have their academic priorities set at first, guys who needed a place to learn about the world, get an education and learn the game of basketball before going to the next level.

Friends like NBA champions Bob McAdoo, Spencer Haywood, and the late Earl Cureton did the same thing. Thank God PCC was there when I needed it. If it wasn't, I wouldn't be here today, with the accolades and accomplishments I've been able to accrue over time. It's thanks to PCC that I began to develop a certain personal philosophy that has helped me and others since. Like a cement worker, I began to lay the foundation. As it happened, my first season at PCC, my freshman year, we had a pretty good team, with a roster that included a few older guys who'd come back from the military and still had playing eligibility.

The school was also a former home to none other than the great Jackie Robinson. He is in the PCC (then Pasadena Junior College) Hall of

Fame, inducted in 1961. He played football and baseball and ran track for the school. He was the QB *and* the safety for the football team and the shortstop for the baseball team, and he broke track-and-field records. Jackie dove into his religious faith while at the school and later found himself embroiled in several run-ins with racist cops. While I would never compare myself to the man who broke baseball's color barrier, I do feel a kinship with him since we both attended PCC and both encountered racism on and off the field.

The team that Coach Joe Barnes assembled at PCC in 1975–76 was very good. My freshman year, I averaged about 15 points. And that's when I found out I had some explosiveness, that I could really jump out the gym. My goal my first year in college was to get at least one dunk per game. To do that, I knew I had to enhance my defense. How do you get lots of dunks? You get disruptive on defense and get steals. So I was always looking to take the ball away and get on the fast break. I learned how to anticipate passes and get into lanes, and I learned I was very good at that. But soon I absorbed some more significant lessons about discipline.

As I entered this next phase of my life, I considered myself an athlete-student, not the other way around. Class was merely a necessary evil. Even though I wasn't a highly touted recruit, I felt that basketball was my only real responsibility. It was the thing I prided myself on and the one thing I truly loved. But that's no excuse for sloughing off other aspects of my life. However, sometimes when you trip yourself up, you do so for a reason: that old "cry for help." Maybe that's what I was going through subconsciously at the time. As a student at PCC, you had to maintain a certain number of credits to stay eligible to play. Stupidly, I didn't maintain them.

Indeed, one late morning during my freshman year, as I was headed for school, I walked past Pasadena's Washington Park—the same park where my brother would be shot and killed five decades later—when a few guys I knew asked if I wanted to play. I should have declined and been on my way. But I didn't, thinking I deserved a nice break. "Ah, Coop, you don't need class," some of the guys said to me. "Come on!

Play a few games!" The siren song of the ambitionless. I weakly tried to tell them that I couldn't: "I have to go to class; I can't." But I soon gave in. "Coop, your coach will take care of you!" they said. In a way, they were right.

So I stayed in Washington Park and forgot about school. I got a run in, got a sweat going, and when the games were done, I went to PCC around 1:30 in the afternoon. We had our own game that night, and I was ready to dominate. But it was about 2:00 when I found myself in the locker room, and Coach Joe Barnes came over to me. "Coop," he said, "did you go to Professor Calvert's English class today?" Let that be a lesson to you: your coach always knows. "Yeah, I went," I lied. "Well, Coop," Coach Barnes said, "no you didn't, because if you had, you would've taken the test the professor gave out." Oh, right.

It got worse. Because I hadn't taken the test, my professor failed me, which meant I fell below the 12 credits I needed, which officially made me academically ineligible. I asked Barnes if he could fix it, and he said no. Professor Calvert wanted to make an example out of me. Just like that, my freshman season was over. "No need to dress," Coach said. "You're ineligible." I was crushed. But the silver lining was that this was the beginning of the philosophy I stick to every day, what I call Coop's Five D's (which, coincidentally, is what my report card used to look like!). Those stand for *Determination, Desire, Dedication, Discipline,* and *Decision-Making.* But with my season over, I had to figure out what was next.

JUST LIKE I had to learn the fundamentals of the game in college, I needed to learn academic and life skills too. But after I'd skipped class, lied about it, missed a test, lost credits, and was academically ineligible, I had forfeited what I loved most. It can be tempting to blame others in a situation like this. The reality, however, was that it was all my own doing. And while I hadn't lost my ability to play basketball—I could still play at the park and be a local "star" to the guys (until that eventually fizzled out with age)—I'd jeopardized my future and my standing as a collegiate athlete. It was about the dumbest thing I could have done to myself and to my team.

God had given me talent to be a player, and now I'd stunted myself—I could no longer play in school games. Thankfully, I took it as an opportunity to improve, not sulk. It was at this moment I changed things around for myself. I flipped the script and decided to become a student-athlete, not an athlete-student. I decided to go to all my classes and sit in the front row. I made sure to prioritize studying and getting passing grades.

Yes, I was determined to be in better standing with Pasadena City College. While I'd hurt my family and teammates (boy, were they mad at me), the only place I could go from there was up. In my absence, PCC had fallen from first to third in the division, and despite being one of the team's best players, there was nothing I could do. So I vowed to make it right the following season, and the first step in doing so was to pay attention in class. I also made sure not to fall in with the bad crowd, to stay away from drugs and the street. Instead, I studied and practiced. "Your skills can take you further than your family can afford," Coach Barnes had told me.

My teammates laughed at me when they found out I'd flunked. "Dummy," they said (that was not a *D* word I wanted to hear). "Why can't you be more successful?" they asked me. I told myself I'd prove them all wrong. As I had bettered myself on the court that second half of the year in practices, I did the same in the classroom. I made sure never, ever to forget that sick, embarrassed feeling. And you know what? I did well in school, and I was able to rejoin the team on a full-time level my sophomore year. In the end, it was a blessing that Professor Calvert and Coach Barnes, who was a chemistry professor and former football player, held me responsible and didn't let me slide.

Thanks to them, I'd learned a new sense of personal determination. I learned that I was in control of my own future. I'd also stoked the flames of my desire, realizing that was the fuel of my future. Things wouldn't just happen for me if I didn't push myself. I renewed my dedication to the game, to reading, and to my own well-being. But more than anything else, I strengthened my sense of discipline. On the court, if you're sloppy, if you're out of control, there is no way to score baskets consistently. The same is true in life. Once I was on the right path, I became an overall better decision-maker. And ultimately that is the key.

I carried these lessons with me through ups and downs in the NBA, through big wins and losses, through injuries, through tumultuous times in my personal life, and through moments when I didn't think I could go forward. No matter how successful you are, no matter whom you surround yourself with, there are dark times in everyone's lives. In mine, I've suffered plenty. But when you keep a credo—a personal philosophy— intact, that's a way to give yourself a chance at extricating yourself from any darkness, from any sorrows. Strangely, you can't learn these lessons without hard times along the way.

In fact, Coach Barnes had pulled me aside one day and made sure to drill the lesson into me. "You know what, Michael?" he said. "This is the best thing for you. There is a reason this happened to you. Somebody is telling you something." He encouraged me, gave me confidence. He didn't deride me or make things worse by twisting the knife. Instead, he made me see my failure as a type of opportunity. I will always love Coach Barnes for that. And while he passed away recently, his memory lives on today. "Get in here and do your work, Coop," he told me. "And you'll be the player you want to be." Between the lines and between my ears.

MY SOPHOMORE SEASON went much better, I'm grateful to report. I kept my focus on all of my responsibilities. While I wasn't a straight-A student, I knew that I wasn't unintelligent by any stretch of the imagination. So I applied myself in the classroom just like I did on the basketball court. Just as folks in high school had thought I was too skinny to play for a college team, I proved those at PCC wrong who thought I couldn't handle an academic load. Had I not gone through that ordeal, I may never have found the heights that I did with the Los Angeles Lakers in the 1980s. It's funny how life works. Sometimes you need to take a step back to bound forward.

During my second year at PCC, 1975, the sophomores who'd been there ahead of me—those former military guys such as 6'7" left-handed player Greg Minniefield—were gone and I was a starter for Coach Barnes. He told me then that I already had pro potential and that on defense I was like a tiger out of a cage. We had a strong year, and I averaged 24 points and was named All-Metro Conference first team and a Junior College All-American (I finished school with 1,070 points and a 20.2 point average). I got the recruitment letters I'd always wanted—from Michigan State (amazingly, I could have played with Magic Johnson), USC, UNLV, and New Mexico.

Importantly, I'd grown significantly since a few years before in high school, and I could feel it. Some mornings I woke up with burning soreness in my legs and knees; my whole body hurt. You're supposed to get growth spurts as a kid, and it's easier on you then if you do. But I was entering my twenties and getting these splitting pains. But it was that good kind of pain—growing is crucial for someone who wants to play basketball in the pros. I wasn't going to be a 5'3" Muggsy Bogues; I needed to be tall! But because I'd gotten my growth spurt late, I still had my guard skills from when I was shorter, which helped immensely.

At the end of the day, I decided to attend the University of New Mexico, and I was ready for it. I'd chosen against Michigan State because of the cold weather and against UNLV because they were stacked with great guys such as Reggie Theus. I picked New Mexico because I liked the head coach, Norm Ellenberger, who wasn't like other program leaders at the time, who were—for the most part—drill sergeants who seemed to relish in embarrassing you, like Indiana's Bob Knight.

Like many schools, the University of New Mexico had gone through plenty of ups and downs when I got there. For instance, in 1970, as students protested the Vietnam War and the shootings at Kent State University, the National Guard was called in to quell the dissent. Some students and journalists were even struck with bayonets and injured. In 1972 a peaceful sit-in protest led to tear gas, dozens of arrests, and the school declaring a state of emergency. But as far as its basketball program, the school had enjoyed many positive experiences, including the university's first major player, Mel Daniels, who was drafted in 1967 and went on to be a two-time MVP of the ABA.

In 1972 Coach Ellenberger moved up the ranks from assistant to head coach, replacing his mentor Bob King, who would go on to Indiana State, famously recruiting Larry Bird to the school in 1976. *Small world!* Once Ellenberger took over, he built the program quickly and feverishly. He was known around town as Stormin' Norman and was a local celebrity. His team won the Western Athletic Conference championship in 1974, but it dipped some the following year after losing a slew of players. So Coach Ellenberger looked to a new recruiting strategy. Starting with that class ahead of me, he had the idea of recruiting JUCO All-Americans, and he brought in big-time JUCO guys to fill his roster, which eventually included me.

Notably, however, many of the Black players in that 1975–76 class that came in a year before I did, quit on Norm and the team during the season in a boycott, citing racial reasons and making accusations against Norm. So when I came in the next year, along with players such as Marvin "Automatic" Johnson (a big-time scorer, who once got 50 points in a game for us), Jimmy Allen, Will Smiley, Willie Howard, and future pro Billy Reid, we had the relative run of the place, even though we were a bit cautious of Norm and the school. We were the new names in town. I didn't know exactly what had happened with the class prior, but I kept my guard up.

In the end, I decided to trust Norm, and I'm glad I did. Like I said, I'd had options, including one of UNM's rivals, UNLV, with their famous towel-biting head coach Jerry Tarkanian. The Runnin' Rebels were stacked with talent, though, and I knew I would have had to sit behind some of them, including Theus. Norm, however, said he would play guys not based on reputation and recruitment but on how we earned it in practice. He told me, "I'm going to throw the ball up, and the best five will start." That was a draw for me, and why I picked UNM. And by the grace of God, I had two great years with the Lobos.

The University of New Mexico is located in Albuquerque, some 800 miles from Los Angeles along Interstate 40. New Mexico is an arid place, dry and relatively barren, especially outside the city. Compared to L.A., it's a world away. But that just meant I could focus on my game and classes. In my family, only my mom and one aunt were lucky enough to go to college before me. And I was my grandmother's first grandchild to get a degree, which I did by receiving an associate's from PCC. That was another reason she looked at me as a special child. Now I had to prove how special I was on the court.

Coach Ellenberger preached tenacity on defense. When I came to the Lobos, he would tell me, "Coop! You gotta get up there! You got to beat him to the spot! Get in his *jersey!*" When he yelled, Ellenberger had spit shooting out of his mouth. "*Coop!* You've got to become *one* with that guy!" I would have run through a wall for him during practice if I'd had to. But while he yelled, it was encouragement. He *believed* I could stop anyone. By now, I was 6'7", and I had long arms and big hands. I was still skinny, but I was very quick. Every step of the way, one of my coaches was priming me for who I would become in the NBA: a rabid defender.

It had begun with Coach Terzian and then continued with Barnes, and now Ellenberger. Good habits start early, and these were men who believed in the fundamentals—from good footwork to proper hand positioning—in building up a player right, each step of the way. Norm added that sense of tenacity. He was a great coach. "Coop! Get in their *face!* Become *one!*" He was maniacal about defense. He set the template for the fiery, wiry Michael Cooper. He made me look my opponents up and down and let them know, "You ain't scoring on me tonight." Later, Coach Riley refined it on the Lakers with his detail-oriented schemes and incessant prep work.

All my coaches taught me a lot. In the end, I could annihilate anyone on defense. That was my superpower, and I knew it. I used that skill as a junior with the Lobos, jump-starting my career with hopes of more beyond. While we started the year lukewarm, going 6–4, we played some big teams tight, including No. 9 UNLV and No. 10 Arizona. We finished the season at 19–11 (who said the collegiate game was only good on the East Coast?), good for third place in the conference. I was first-team all-Western Athletic Conference, and my New Mexico team voted me MVP and our best defender.

But it was my senior year when we all came to play in a major way. That was when Ellenberger instituted a new offense dependent on pace and passing, which helped me flourish. We were talented and versatile, and we took advantage of it all, especially so with our full-court press that endlessly disrupted opponents. I was even earning praise from pro coaches such as Larry Brown, who said of me, "He's an *athlete*." I was beginning to show I could stand out not only in college but at the next level in the pros. Just like the giant Southwest horizon, the sky was the limit going into my senior year.

FOR MY SENIOR season at UNM, I was named co-captain. We started 7–2 but then won 14 in a row. We beat UNLV *twice*, which helped us earn a top 10 ranking in the country. As a team, we led the nation in scoring with 97.5 points. Our games at home in the Pit were legendary, packed with 17,000-plus students. The gym itself was built in a 37-foot hole in 1966 (hence the name). Then in 1975, the school did a $2.2 million renovation because games were so popular with students. They just flocked to the place. Inside the gym, it was, and is, intimating. There is a long half-mile tunnel from the locker rooms to the court. Some of the older coaches have to take a cart.

Along with being the highest-scoring team, we drew the second-most fans in the country. Over the last 50 years, the school has averaged some 15,000-plus fans per game, and we even outdid that. Oftentimes it was standing room only. That year, we won the WAC again and finished ranked No. 5 in the country. But then came a blow: we lost in the first round of the NCAA tournament to Cal State Fullerton. That was a tough game to swallow. For my part, I notched 12 points and 4 rebounds in the game, but we couldn't fulfill the hope we'd built up. Success is based on expectations, and we just didn't meet our own lofty goals then, sadly.

Though we were 24–4 for the season, with Ellenberger finishing second in the Coach of the Year vote from the basketball writers, we were disappointed. However, I already had new fish to fry. Since we'd been so good and fun to watch, scouts were coming to see us play. And while every NBA scout in the country was coming to watch Marvin (aka Automatic), and not me, I told myself, "You know what? Let me prove a little something too!" Off the court, I kept my head on straight and did my classwork, but on the court, I knew I had to help myself toward the next step in my career. So I worked to raise eyebrows.

One of Ellenberger's assistants, Gary Colson, who took over as head coach a season after Norm left in the late 1970s (more on that later), was friends with the Lakers' former star, coach, and now GM, Jerry West (who sadly just passed away in 2024). Colson, who was also an advocate for the college three-point line, got the Logo (West's nickname, as he was known for being the silhouette of the NBA emblem) to come see the Lobos. Life is often about timing, and the chance to impress Jerry during one of our high-pressure, high-scoring games was what I lived for. And I did just that, scoring 18 points and grabbing 15 big rebounds against Wyoming, earning Jerry's deep respect.

West also liked to play golf with Ellenberger. Part of that, I think, was Jerry's way of keeping tabs on New Mexico's roster, from Marvin to me. And I know Jerry also came to see us again when we played the University of Utah, which had players such as the future All-Star Tom Chambers and future pros (and cousins) Jeff Judkins and Danny Vranes. Against the Utes, I had a big game with 18 points and 16 rebounds, and I played excellent defense on Vranes, locking him down. But my biggest break was when Jerry saw me lock up future All-Star and Celtics rival Danny Ainge when UNM played BYU. To this day, Ainge will barely talk to me in public!

I loved my time at the University of New Mexico; the games we played were tight. And our success was important for the state—it even helped ease racial tensions. Many around the university never thought the team could achieve the heights that it had in the past, but we brought the school back and breathed new life into the program with each win. I was very proud to be a part of the healing of the larger community too.

Sports is a big unifier—in stadiums across the world, people forget their differences and cheer for the same team. That's big. Watching games, people have a tendency to forget about race, color, and anything else that might divide. We're all rooting for the same uniforms. Going 24–4 that season played a big part of that in the state, on the campus, and in UNM's Black Student Union. Winning brought us together, and I loved being at the center of that. After our team did so well, the school was able to land other significant recruits, including the Australian center Luc Longley, who won three rings with Michael Jordan and the 1990s Bulls. Other big names include All-Star Danny Granger from the Pacers and veteran Kenny Thomas. And the program is still going strong!

MY OWN AMBITIONS when it came to basketball were never about individual accolades. It's a team game, and the proof is in the pudding of winning. There is only one real question that matters, and that's "Did you win?" It's nice to have awards, but I play team-first basketball and always have. Throughout my career I've learned that *team* is the most important word in sports. Anyone who talks to me for a few minutes will hear me say, "Together Everyone Achieves More." If you follow that credo, good things will come to you. The ultimate goal is a championship ring, which is won by a *team*, not a person.

Still, I did take home my fair share of hardware. For my career at the University of New Mexico, I averaged 15.6 points, 5.3 rebounds, and 3.8 assists, and I was named to the First-Team All-WAC twice. I was also bestowed a great honor during my senior year, named as a First-Team All-American by the U.S. Basketball Writers Association. I also achieved First-Team All-WAC in 1977 and 1978. Not bad for a skinny, no-name kid from L.A. who no one thought would be able to play in college, huh? A kid who sliced his knee, had to wait to play varsity as a senior, who nearly lost hope after becoming academically ineligible—I did pretty well.

But success in one area doesn't always determine success in another, unfortunately. While I would be drafted to my hometown Los Angeles Lakers after my senior season (the 60th player in the third round in 1978), I was not able to earn my four-year college degree from the University of New Mexico, falling just short in credits. For my final two years, I majored in Therapeutic Recreation, which I don't mind saying wasn't the most rigorous of subjects. Have you ever even heard of that class? Heck no, you haven't! Nevertheless, I'd earned the grades I needed to keep playing, and I'd done my classwork. Then I let go of the rope, so to speak.

Once I finished my senior season, I stopped thinking about school. I know it's stupid, but it was the reality at the moment. When I got drafted that summer, there was no going back to the books. I put myself behind the eight ball. Thankfully, I made it in the pros. Not everyone is so lucky. That's one thing I tell my teenage son Nils today. There is a life after basketball. Get your degree! You never know what it will mean for you when your career is all said and done. Thankfully, all my other kids have their degrees by now. That's always been important to me as a parent.

I knew I was a gifted athlete, so I didn't think I needed to apply myself academically. But today I wish I had. If I knew then what I know now, I would have been keen on getting my four-year degree. For one thing, to coach at many schools, you're required to have one. So without that paper, I limited myself. But that's one of the reasons why I love to coach—I get to help young people not make the same mistakes I did (and I wish I could have done so at New Mexico).

Now, though, it was time for my next chapter. Time to prepare myself during the summer after my senior year, to get the bad taste of the NCAA tournament loss out of my mouth, and to get in the best shape of my life. The NBA Draft was on the horizon. In the 1970s for people like me, it was about becoming an NBA ballplayer—that or bust. If I didn't make it, I knew I would be a blue-collar worker. *I had to make it or else.* Little did I know just how painful the next year of my life would be.

Chapter 4

Draft Day

ON JUNE 9, 1978, THE L.A. LAKERS SELECTED ME with the 60th pick in
the NBA Draft. That year, high flyer Mychal Thompson was picked first
by the Trail Blazers out of Minnesota. He was college teammates with
future Celtic Kevin McHale, and after leaving the Northwest, Thompson
would become a teammate of mine in L.A. (Later, he would father future
NBA superstar Klay Thompson, one-half of the Splash Brothers with
another NBA son, Stephen Curry.) Phil Ford was selected No. 2, Rick
Robey went third to the Pacers, Michael Ray Richardson went fourth to
the Knicks, and Larry Bird went sixth to the Celtics (though he'd return
to college for his senior season).

It's impossible to imagine what it's like to be drafted into the NBA.
And I thank my higher power for putting me in the position to be able to
enter the league with my hometown team. I did a lot to make it happen,
sure, but I couldn't have done any of it without help. Despite that, back
in 1978, while it was special to be picked, the draft wasn't nearly what
it is now. Future four-time All-Star Michael Ray said he was shooting
hoops when he found out he was drafted. And that's only because Willis
Reed called to tell him. A year later, two-time NBA champ Earl Cureton
found out he was picked while he was stripping floors.

For me, getting picked by the Los Angeles Lakers was a life-changing moment, the culmination of a lot of work and faith. There were many times in high school and even in college when I could have thrown in the towel and lowered my expectations. Thank goodness I never succumbed to that. Faith was a major player in my decision to stay strong. In high school, Coach Terzian was the first person to show me that someone could maintain faith and still play basketball. I'd always thought it had to be one or the other, like they were mutually exclusive.

But Coach Terzian turned me on to the Fellowship of Christian Athletes. The international nonprofit, which was founded in 1954 and is based in Kansas City, Missouri, connects players with the Bible and God, the source of all our talent. It's important to remember where our success comes from, and the Fellowship of Christian Athletes helps me do this in my life. It was also something to lean on in times of doubt, like when everyone on my high school team was getting scholarship offers and I wasn't, or when my playing was in doubt at Pasadena City College. Faith has always been helpful to me in that way.

One of the ways I connected the two was by prizing team over individuality, which is something spirituality also teaches us. Coach Barnes drilled that idea into me. "Michael, listen," he said. "I don't want you to be bigger than the team. I want you to *be* the team." In other words, he wanted me to embody the idea of it, not to try and transcend it. It's a subtle but clear distinction.

WHEN THE LOS ANGELES LAKERS selected me in 1978, I signed for $30,000, which was a lot to me. Of course, history is a funny thing. The legendary Kobe Bryant was *born* in 1978 (the son of former NBA player Jellybean Bryant), and 18 years later, he signed a $3.5 million contract with L.A. Also in 1978, the league had *10* draft rounds, with 202 players selected. After the fourth, GMs would throw darts at a board, and they'd pick whomever they hit. Not exactly a scientific process. The benefit was that if you were selected, you would at least get an invitation to training camp. But then once you arrived, you'd have to compete against dozens more.

First it was the rookie camps; then, if you made it past those, there would be the veteran camps with the rest of the team. In today's era, I wouldn't even have been drafted, since there are only two rounds. When I found out about the news, though, I couldn't believe it. In college, all the scouts were watching Marvin "Automatic" Johnson, UNM's big-time scorer. I was just trying to make my mark any way I could—especially on defense. The day the draft took place, I was at the park, shooting. After the Lakers selected me, though, Tom sent my cousin Braud down to the court to get me. "Michael, you're wanted at the house," my cousin said.

All I could think of was that something bad had happened. "For what?" Then my cousin said, "Michael, you got drafted!" I still couldn't believe it. "By who?" All my cousin said was, "I don't know." When I got home, my uncle told me it was the hometown Lakers. My head began to spin—I couldn't believe it. "They're going to be calling you," Tom told me. I began to think back to my time meeting Jerry West. While he had scouted New Mexico when I was there, I had met him years before that when I was young, attending his Camp Clutch at Occidental College, a half hour outside L.A. But I doubted he remembered that.

It's wild to think that I knew Jerry for 50 years, may his soul rest in peace. In order for me to get one of the six scholarships to that camp, I had to shoot free throws at the local Boys & Girls Club, and whoever made the most would go to the camp. In the end, I was one of the people chosen. Then, at the camp, the Logo picked me out of the crowd of about 300 kids and told me to get up and shoot free throws in front of everybody. When I did, he told me, "Young man, you've got great form." This was before college, when I was still a skinny, no-name 13-year-old. Thankfully, I made all my free throws; I didn't buckle under the immense pressure.

Today, I love thinking about that memory. Maybe Jerry actually *did* remember that when he saw me in college or when he drafted me. But either way, there I was—part of the Lakers organization, thanks to him. And over the years, Jerry would play a major part in my life, from putting me on the team to teaching me how to be an even better shooter. He used to tell me his secret: right before he was about to shoot, he'd dribble the ball especially hard so that it would bounce back up to his hands and he'd be ready to take a jumper in the same motion. That's why he had such a quick release and was such a prolific scorer.

Prior to the Lakers selecting me, my impression of the league was that every player from California got picked by some team *outside* of the state. Reggie Theus was taken in the same draft as me (in the first round) by the Chicago Bulls. Two years earlier, Dennis Johnson had been picked by the Seattle SuperSonics in the second round. Even Marvin was drafted outside of L.A. in 1978 (also by Chicago). It just seemed like few players, if any, were taken by their local teams. But now I had been, and I was over the moon. The only question was whether or not I would actually make the roster. I figured there was a slim chance, and in reality, I was just happy my name was uttered.

Ahead of the draft, I'd bought a huge coat. Thinking that East Coast winters or Pacific Northwest rains were in my future, I got the biggest one I could find. I figured maybe New York, New Jersey, or Cleveland would take me. But after I was selected by L.A., I immediately sold that sucker. It wasn't hard for me to get rid of it. And I was honored to be staying in town. The Lakers had won the championship in 1972 with Wilt Chamberlain, Gail Goodrich, and Jerry West. But they'd struggled since; after going 69–13 in their victorious season, they followed it up with 60 wins, then 47, 30, 40, 53, and 45 respectively over the subsequent six seasons. Not awful but not especially glitzy, either.

While I may not be the most famous person to be taken by his hometown team—that has to go to Akron's LeBron James, who was selected by his Cleveland Cavaliers in 2003—I am one of the few. That's one thing I'm proud of. Unlike LeBron, I played for one team my entire career. To me, it's all about loyalty. I didn't want to go anywhere else. Why would I? That summer, after L.A. selected me, I played basketball all day, every day. I got ready for training camp. And while I didn't quite know what to expect, I wanted to be as prepared as possible to show out and, with hope, make the squad.

My agent, Harold Daniels, walked me through the process. He said he would deal with things off the court so I could deal with everything on it. So I went and got in the best shape of my life. Even though the Lakers weren't *the Lakers* yet (Dr. Jerry Buss hadn't yet bought the team), it was still a huge deal. I still remember that first day walking into the gym at Loyola Marymount University for Lakers training camp. Norm Nixon and Jamaal Wilkes were practicing. I saw Kareem Abdul-Jabbar at the other end of the court shooting his signature skyhooks, and I almost peed my pants! I'd just walked in, and there was a legend. Kareem was already an NBA champion and MVP, and I remembered seeing him at UCLA, dominating for Coach John Wooden, the beacon of excellence on and off the court.

You can't overstate how important Kareem is to the Lakers, the NBA, and the world. He was so good that they outlawed the dunk because of him years before! Seeing him in training camp was an honor. But when I went up to say hello, he told me, "Man, what the fuck are you looking at? The fucking locker room is over there. Go get your shit ready!" Okay, then! I followed orders. Once I got dressed, I had to go and suit up to compete with the other rookies.

Part of that early work happened at the NBA's summer league, which was held at Cal State in L.A. (the school where coincidentally I am coaching today). During one of the games, against Phoenix, something horrible happened. I was running back on defense on one play when Suns guard Andre Wakefield came down the court and got tangled with another guy.

Andre tripped, and suddenly bodies flew, twisted up. The next thing I knew, Wakefield was barreling into my right knee (not the one that had 102 stitches) and I felt a deep, surging pain run down my leg. His left knee hit my right one, and in that moment, I tore my right medial collateral ligament (MCL). I was on the floor, writhing in pain. During my young career, I'd hurt ankles and fingers, as all basketball players do, but this was the first time since slicing my left leg as a kid that any major damage had been done to any other part of my body. It was the first time something tore. Just like that, my dreams of the NBA were in peril. I couldn't even walk. That night, I cried myself to sleep.

WHAT HAPPENED NEXT was totally out of my control but miraculous. Sometimes you just have to let go and let the world work its magic. In this case, I couldn't have been more fortunate, despite the freak injury. Strangely, getting hurt was likely the best thing for me. It set my career right on track. Going into training camp, I wasn't sure if I was going to make the Lakers roster. I was a third-round pick, and there were plenty of guys ahead of me who could've landed a permanent spot. Guys including eight-time All-Star Ron Boone, six-time All-Stars Lou Hudson, Adrian Dantley (a future scoring champ), and All-Star Jim Price. Those were some big names.

The Lakers had also drafted shooting guard Ron Carter in the second round in 1978. In other words, there was some real competition at my position. It was going to be hard for me to make the team, even if my knees were made of gold. But after I was injured, the Lakers couldn't cut me. That was a rule in the NBA at the time—you couldn't get cut from a roster due to injury (which was not the case in sports such as the NFL). I was put on injured reserve. As I sat on my butt, unable to play, Jerry West said, "Coop, young man, your job right now is to keep your head up and get as healthy as you can. Sometimes good things come when least expected."

The thing was, I hadn't signed my contract with the team when I got hurt, so they could have cut me. But West and the iconic radio broadcaster Chick Hearn, who was also the team's assistant GM, had faith in me. They convinced owner Jack Kent Cooke to keep me on, and for that I'll forever be in their debt. While no one, not even me, knew what my career would be down the line, God smiled on me in that moment. The Lakers signed me to that $30,000 rookie minimum for the season, and that was fine by me. As I healed, I read every book I could about the MCL. And when I could, I started my rehab, running in pools and up countless flights of stairs.

Jerry trusted me, and I didn't want to let him down, so that's all I did after my surgery—work to get healthy. When I wasn't playing, he would come over to me to lift me up and make sure my spirits were in the right place. "Hey, Coop. How are you doing? Everything okay?" That meant the world to me. Here was this legend in the game thinking about *me*, taking the time for little old Coop, the once-skinny guy who made his own makeshift basketball hoops in his yard. But Jerry was always a real person like that, the salt of the earth. A former West Virginia star, he knew what the world of basketball was all about: teamwork and humility.

But you can't find the fruits of those without self-belief. Again, my Five D's served me here. As my leg healed after the catastrophic injury, I leaned into the tools that had helped me thus far in my life. In these dark, difficult moments, it can be easy to fall off the path. Some turn to drugs, others look to vices such as sex and spending money. But I dug down and remained determined to stay on the team. I let Jerry West's words continue to add fuel to the fire of my hopes and desire. I remained dedicated and disciplined. I didn't sway from my internal sense of good decision-making. It's all interconnected. In other words, I stayed the course. Thank God I did.

Eventually, the Lakers had to cut some guys, but I wasn't one of them. In an unpredictable way, getting hurt was a blessing in disguise. And when I was finally healthy, I worked my tail off to prove I was worth the wait and that I could bring value to the team. But I was able to play in only three games that first season, testing out my knee in the middle of the year. In total, I suited up against the Washington Bullets on December 22, the Portland Trail Blazers on December 29, and the New York Knicks on January 9. I got in for a total of seven minutes, scoring a meager total of six points. But it was enough to keep me in Purple and Gold.

What I remember most was the game in New York, in Madison Square Garden, the mecca of Basketball. As a young player, I'd watched the Knicks win rings in 1970 and 1973 with the likes of Willis Reed, the captain who limped out in Game 7 of the 1970 Finals to will his team to victory. I'd seen them battle Boston with stars such as Walt "Clyde"

Frazier and Dave DeBusschere. So being there in MSG and getting to score even a single basket, even in "garbage time," gave me goose bumps. The other bonus from those three games was we won them all—a signal of much more to come. Somehow I knew I'd be a major factor in Los Angeles soon.

But for now the good thing about those games was that I was even there. It's embarrassing to say, but there was one time during the season when I missed a flight. I was a rookie, so I guess I'll chalk it up to that. Still, I shake my head now. This was when you could walk on to the planes from the street; there wasn't all the extra security of today. So I guess I felt I had time to make the plane leaving for a road trip. But I was late. And let me tell you, that was the last time I was ever late to a flight, and certainly the last time I ever missed one. I can still see my teammates' faces watching me from the airplane windows, wondering what the heck I was still doing there.

For the 1978–79 season, the Lakers finished 47–35. It also marked Jerry West's last as head coach for the franchise. The new decade would bring in great changes, including a big-time, smiling No. 1 draft pick by the name of Magic Johnson—someone I'd soon share a lot of Denny's breakfasts with. What that would mean for the team, city, and league as a whole would soon be determined. For my part, however, I was glad to still be on the roster, to have people looking out for me. Even if I had missed a flight, embarrassing myself. But I knew I had potential. I knew it, and Jerry West knew it. Now, it was just a matter of proving it to everyone else.

Chapter 5

Championship Trophy No. 1

MY SECOND YEAR IN THE LEAGUE WAS A HISTORIC ONE. Coming to the Lakers, I wasn't thought of as any sort of great offensive player. So I knew I had to stay defensive-minded. In the league, there were many great offensive challenges, from George Gervin to David Thompson to Dennis Johnson (my old L.A. foe) to Danny Ainge. There seemed to be a world-class guy every night. When I got in, I knew I had to match my skills against theirs, and I had to come out on top more often than they did. Have a plan, be resilient, be relentless—these were all lessons I learned along the way to the NBA. Now, they were about to pay off.

Mostly a bench player, I watched the starters set the tone, and I paid close attention to who was doing what. What were my matchup's tendencies? Did he like to go right or left? Was he a jump-shooter or a driver? Quick or plodding? Could he rebound or was he someone who liked to push the pace. If we were up in a game, I had to help keep the lead. And if we were down, I knew I had to play good enough defense to help us come back, maybe even score a few too. That's the role of a bench guy: pay close attention and fill in where you're needed. I learned that while injured, and I perfected it in my first season.

When I'd been hurt my rookie year, I thought back to the days when my knee was sliced up by the coffee can. The patience I had to maintain to get back from that was like a boot camp for whatever else I faced. That was key. Prayer and faith combined with my grandmother's attention helped me learn how to overcome whatever peril or hurdle was in front of me. Back then, she kept telling me, "Michael, you're a blessed child." Other factors were also important, including Jerry West, who gave me time to heal. Thankfully, I also had a great surgeon, Dr. Stephen Lombardo, who did an incredible job on my MCL.

It also helped that I wasn't a particularly heavy person. During my years with the Lakers, I weighed about 176 pounds, and being thin aided my recovery. I didn't get too down, especially since the people around the Lakers organization, from the staff to my teammates, said I'd make a complete comeback soon enough. And I believed what they told me. I had no concept of giving up or throwing in the towel. For some, being injured can cause a great deal of stress and anxiety. They wonder about their pay and their playing time. But I was extremely lucky that wasn't my case. My desire never wavered.

IF I HAD been drafted by Philly or Seattle or New Jersey, who knows what would have happened to me after my injury? But the truth of the matter was that I was able to recover in my home city and around family. That also meant I was able to be around my wife, Wanda (more on her in a moment). I was lucky I'd had the experience as a young person, with all those stitches, with my leg hanging by a thread. That helped me learn to heal. I've also always tried to take care of my body, to eat well and stay in shape. Of the 15 people in my family, I've always been one of the thinnest. Many of them have grown to weigh more than 300 pounds, and I never wanted that for myself.

THANKFULLY, GOD IS good, and I've continued to walk with Him in His glory and with my faith. Part of that meant taking part in the sacrament of marriage. I met Wanda Juzang at the University of New Mexico, and we were married after college, just before my rookie season with the Lakers. Ever since, she's been influential in my life. We met one day in school. I was sitting in the quad with my teammates early during my senior year, shooting the breeze, when I happened to see this young woman walk across the campus and into the cafeteria. I told my friends, "That's the woman I'm going to marry."

Of course, they laughed me off. I'd seen her before here and there, but I'd never *noticed* her in that way. That day, I went to class after lunch and I sat down in the second row. That's when I noticed someone drop a pencil. When I went to pick it up, I couldn't believe it. The girl who it belonged to looked me in the eyes, and it was *her*, sitting in front of me. I said, "Hey, how are you doing?" And we started talking. I asked her for help on a term paper, and we went to her place for her to help me. It was a week before we came up for air! Later, we got our own place together.

We married eight months after that, taking our excited selves down to an L.A. courthouse, where we were wed by Judge Brown. Wanda and I would stay together for some 20 years, throughout my entire Lakers tenure. Together, we have three children. But the life of an NBA player can be hard on a marriage. Wanda faced a lot of difficult situations, several of which I put her through. But for now, let's highlight the good parts. Together, we became parents to Michael Cooper II; Simone Cooper, who's named after Wanda's favorite singer, Nina Simone; and Miles Cooper, who we adopted at just nine months and who is named after my favorite artist, trumpeter Miles Davis.

We were fortunate to have Miles come into our lives. It happened during the 1985–86 season. Wanda and I knew we wanted another child, and back then, there was a push from adoption agencies to bring kids into loving homes. In fact, Wanda's mother worked at an adoption home in Albuquerque, where Wanda is from. So during the NBA off-season, we went back to her home in New Mexico and visited with her mother, who would tell us about the children she knew at the facility. That triggered us, and we made the move. We were able to adopt Miles thanks to Magic's help. Magic wrote us a glowing letter of recommendation that really helped. (He and his wife, Cookie, would later adopt a daughter, Elisa.)

Prior, the agencies had told us it would take a year or two to find a baby, but we weren't comfortable with that. Wanda and I prayed about it, and the next thing we knew, a young couple from Hobbs, New Mexico, said they had a child they wanted to put up for adoption. The white mother was a volleyball player and the Black dad played football. They faced racial prejudice—the mother's parents didn't want them to have the Black child, to raise it with their family. The mother was young, a teenager. So all of a sudden, things happened quickly.

One day we heard about the possibility, and the next day we were brought in for an interview. Magic wrote his letter, and in just about a week, we were able to meet little Miles, a smiling, wide-eyed little boy. He was a beautiful baby. We call Miles our Child from God because it was a miracle we were able to bring him into our home, and so quickly. Today he is married and he has a master's degree from USC. He works at UTEP with student crisis management. Michael II is doing well too. He's married and is a former assistant coach at USC and a D-League assistant GM; he's since started a company called Two One Sports. He also runs 5D United, which is based my Five D's. It bridges the common language of sports with community and education. As for my daughter, Simone, she's a social worker and psychologist. She received her degree from USC and is married. Her husband just retired from the military. Simone also works in the prison system, undertaking psychological evaluations of incarcerated inmates.

And now I have a fourth child, Nils, with my beautiful wife Yvonne, who I met in 2000 (more on her later). Born on February 18, 2005, Nils is a standout basketball player who went from Pepperdine as a freshman to UC Davis as a sophomore. A 6'7" guard, Nils is tall and quick—a triple threat with a bright hoops future ahead of him. I'm even getting some calls from pro scouts about him. They call me up and ask, "Hey, Coop, is that your son? I'm going to keep my eyes on him!" Nils is an excellent defender—he may even be better than me one day. I've never pushed him or any of my kids to follow in my footsteps, but he is the one who has really taken to hoops. And I'm all for it! Growing up, Nils was actually a better soccer player than he was a basketball player, but basketball is his first love, and at 19 years old, standing 6'7", with long arms and a great head on his shoulders, he can go far.

BACK TO BASKETBALL. When I got to the Lakers, I knew the team didn't need another scorer. The squad had the best bucket-getter ever in Kareem Abdul-Jabbar. Norm Nixon was an All-Star point guard, and All-Star Jamaal Wilkes could score with the best, even with his slingshot shooting motion (which his college coach John Wooden used to hate). He was in the middle of a five-year stretch in which he averaged more than 20 points and 5 boards. So if I wanted to stick, I knew I had to fill another role— one a little less glamorous but still crucial: to be the guy who *sparked* our offense by playing world-class defense. I could do that and then some.

I thought, *Bring it on—I'll guard anyone!* Heck, I'd come back after people said I'd maybe never walk again. Now, they talked about me on TV newscasts saying that I could *fly*. My legs healed and I could leap with the best. Soon, Magic and I would develop our famous Coop-a-Loop play, where I'd slam so many basketballs through the rim off his passes that other teams didn't know what to do. But before that, we had to master playing together, which I knew would be a piece of cake. While I'd technically been in the NBA for a year, I considered the 1979–80 term as my rookie season. And it was also Magic's. Just a couple of guys making their way together.

The year prior, Magic had won the 1979 NCAA title with Michigan State over Larry Bird's Indiana State team. That game was the most watched college basketball game ever at the time, and remains so to this day. The folks in L.A. were excited to have the smiling 6'9" Magic wearing Purple and Gold, and the Lakers picked him No. 1 overall. Not only that, but Dr. Jerry Buss had just purchased the team from Jack Kent Cooke in one of the wildest transactions in league history, involving the swapping of assets including New York's Chrysler building. But those affairs were far out of my purview. I was just a young guy with high ambitions trying to find my place on a talented roster.

The Celtics drafted Bird the year prior thanks to a loophole in NBA rules, and while he stayed in school for his senior year, that allowed both Magic and Bird to enter the NBA at the same time. Not only that, but they came in playing for the most storied teams in the league. Their rivalry—which would go on to bolster, if not save, the league—began in college. Those two took the NBA to heights never before seen. Their passing ignited the league. And I was happy to be along for the historic ride.

That year also marked the first cable television deal between the NBA and the upstart USA Network, and it was the first season that the league adopted the three-point line, taking it from the ABA, which had borrowed it from the now-defunct ABL. It was the birth of the modern league. And during the 1979–80 season, Bird would help his Boston team to the biggest regular-season turnaround in history, from 29–53 without him to 61–21 with (despite a loss to us on December 28, 1979). But while Bird and his team won the regular-season ring, Magic began to focus on much bigger team goals.

THE SUMMER BEFORE the 1979–80 season was all business for me and the Lakers. I'd healed my knee and studied what I could do to contribute. I stayed in touch with the entire coaching staff, peppering them with questions. Our new head coach was Jack McKinney, who had come to L.A. from the Trail Blazers. McKinney, an acolyte of Dr. Jack Ramsay, who had won the title with Bill Walton (who sadly just passed away in May 2024) and Maurice Lucas in Portland in 1976–77 with a pass-first offense built around pace and teamwork, was grandfatherly and soft-spoken. His assistant was Paul Westhead, who boasted a good basketball mind, and one for poetry and literature too.

McKinney, who was hired by Buss and West to try and re-create his Portland system in Southern California, told me what I needed to do for us to win and for me to stay on the team. He cared about defense, and his plan was well thought-out on both sides of the court. McKinney said, "Coop, I need a defensive player." I told him, "Jack, I'm your guy." I went out to prove it in practice every day, spending a ton of time in the gym. I had to find a way to be noticed on a roster full of veteran egos. It was friendly competition with guys such as Ron Carter, but we were also fighting for our livelihoods. Showing McKinney that I cared about defense saved me.

But so did my friendship with Magic. We were friends, and Earvin wanted me on the roster. He liked to throw me alley-oops, and he liked how I could help him on D too. We'd play together in the summers at Fox Hills Park in Culver City, a 10-acre spot with hoops, picnic tables, and BBQ grills. We would run through situations and dream about what was ahead of us, this giant backcourt that prized team play over everything else. We'd meet up at Fox Hills or we'd get together at local gyms in L.A., melding our minds. The off months were never *off*; they were always about basketball. All the while, I was getting stronger, this wiry kid from Pasadena.

Had I not been prepared to take on that role by each and every coach before, I don't know what I would have done or if I would have been able to stay on the Lakers roster. Destiny is wild, I tell you. On the team, I went from almost being cut to playing in all 82 regular-season games in 1979–80 and averaging 24.1 minutes to go along with 2.7 assists, 2.8 rebounds, a steal, and 8.8 points. How did I manage? Well, I just didn't back down. I observed and did whatever I could to help the team win. By doing that, I told myself, I would stick. It helped being on the same team with Magic, a great player, who many of us dubbed the Enhancer.

My second year, the Michigan-born Magic and I bonded. In one preseason game at Cal State L.A., we played the Detroit Pistons. It was a huge game that officials had to open to hundreds of people since there was such interest in Magic (normally summer league games drew about 50 people). Magic's old college teammate Greg Kelser was on Detroit too. Well, we won that one, and in the locker room after the game, Magic yelled, "Yeah! Yeah! The Lakers! That's who we are!" It was also the game when Magic and I first started talking about what would become the

Coop-a-Loop play. He turned to me and said, "Coop, we gotta get you a play." And boy, did we.

Magic's infectious talents made everyone want to run with him. He was a great rebounder and passer, and he knew how to make people better. The team already had the trio of Norm, Wilkes, and Kareem, who we called Cap, for Captain, and now they had added Magic and me. It was the foundation for greatness. We just knew it. Our world changed real quick with him at the helm. Magic was a terrific team defender, which also made our jobs easier on the other end. Quickly, I began to fit in. I could finish Coop-a-Loop plays with my high-flying dunks, I could shoot from the outside, and I never let up defending. I even set a career high with 13 boards that season. What more could you want from a young player?

OFF THE COURT during my rookie season(s) while recuperating from surgery, I had to carry the stinky gym bags for guys such as Adrian Dantley. In my rookie year at training camp in Palm Desert, I did the dirty work for Dantley (who was later traded to Utah for Spencer Haywood ahead of the 1979–80 year), Ron Boone, and Lou Hudson. My job was to get their laundry after practice and make sure it was cleaned. Rookie Ron Carter was subjected to the same. The Lakers had eight or nine veterans on the team and few rookies. So we youngsters had our share of jobs. During the breaks in practice, I also had to get all the veterans full cups of Gatorade.

I couldn't spill a single drop—that was the rule. When Ron was cut from the team (I beat him out!), I became Kareem's rookie. He was one of the hardest to work for due to his morning requests. Cap wanted a copy of the *Wall Street Journal* at his doorstep by 5:00 AM each morning. So I had to go out and find one. Luckily, there was an IHOP near where we stayed for camp. So I'd run there at dawn, put my quarter (my money, not Kareem's) in, and get the paper. He liked it folded, and so I did all that and placed it by his door before the sun rose. If I didn't have it done, he'd take it to me in practice.

The thing was, I had to do all this *both* my rookie year and the following year! Because I hadn't played in 1978–79 due to my injury, I wasn't allowed to skip my duties in 1979–80. Along with me in 1979–80, Magic wasn't spared either. Not even the No. 1 pick—well, *especially* not the No. 1 pick—got out of it. Magic, who the vets called Buck, became Kareem's rookie during his rookie year too. He also did things for Kenny Carr, such as like washing his laundry after practices at the College of the Desert. That went on for the entire two weeks of camp—*both* years for me. While it was nothing severe, in the end the vets did test your spirit, playfully degrading you.

I had never done anything like that before, especially for a man. My mother and grandmother had always done *my* laundry! (God bless them.) Despite these tasks, I was still becoming more and more of a valuable part of the Lakers roster. Jerry West liked me for my aggression, long arms, and competitive nature. He also saw I complemented my teammates, not trying to take over in spots where they were more equipped. As for Jerry Buss, he was a great new owner just starting to build his sports empire, which included the revamped Forum Club, celebrities, and beautiful lady friends galore. But Buss was a genius in how he listened.

He let you talk, and he'd ask you questions. For him, Earvin was that missing ingredient to Lakers success, the proverbial straw that stirred our drink. Magic provided leadership, scoring, and easy buckets on the hardwood. He was no-nonsense. We could have fun, but Magic made it clear we better always be ready to play—if you weren't, he might get your ass traded. And Buss provided stability, business acumen, and guidance—a match made in heaven. I was just glad to be along for the ride, filling in wherever I could. After we started winning rings, Buss flew us out to the University of Hawaii in Honolulu for training camp. But for now, in 1979–80 and 1980–81, we stayed closer to home. Later, he started to spring for finer things. Buss always wanted the best in life, no matter what.

He was also very active with our team. Today, I consider him the greatest owner in sports history. While I can only judge by my experience, and I technically didn't play for any others, it's clear how smart he was. He was a man of both his word and vision. He always told us that our job was to "entertain the entertainers." That's what Showtime was all about. Just as we might go home after a tough day and watch a movie, it was our job to put on a big-time show when people such as Jack Nicholson came to the Forum. That's how the Laker Girls came about around 1979 and 1980—that and Buss seeing the Dallas Cowboys cheerleaders.

Buss loved what Jerry Jones did with the NFL. Dr. Buss would always come in before every game, and he'd walk around the Forum. He'd have 13 or 14 girls with him at a time, a femme entourage, and they'd walk the arena, as if blessing it with their sexy energy. Then he'd walk up to his seat high above in the rafters, by the jerseys with the iconic Lakers retired numbers, and the girls would keep walking the Forum's hallways, maintaining that sexy energy. I bit my lip—they were some beautiful young ladies. While I don't want to say there was a *carnival* atmosphere on game day, it was something like that.

Buss made the Forum the place to be. He wanted it to be the spot where you might meet a new friend or girlfriend. He wanted that kind of vibe. It was enticing to fans. He wanted the people to come back to the games over and over. He was very savvy about things like that. And along the way, he taught his favorite players a little bit about it—I like to think I was one of them. Furthermore, whenever it was time for me to negotiate a new contract, it was always with Dr. Buss, one-on-one. I only dealt with him. We'd sit down, hash it out, and finish with a handshake. He'd always ask, "Coop, are you okay with this?" And I'd reply, "Yes, Dr. Buss." And when you walked out, it was final. The lawyers on each side would then finalize the deal.

Buss made the game about more than basketball, taking the sport to the next level. And he was beloved for it; even the discerning Jerry West called him a "fantastic man." What's more, with Magic on the team, we had substance behind the glitz. He was perfect for the fans that Buss cultivated at the Fabulous Forum. The place became a hub for celebrities and American culture itself. We had to make a lot of shots with flashbulbs going off in our faces.

ANYONE WHO'S EVER seen me on a basketball court has likely noticed my unusual attire. Every game as a pro, I wore my socks up high, my short shorts' drawstrings out, and sweatbands on each arm. That trend started for me way back in high school. A varsity player my senior season back then, I was getting pretty good. Reporters were writing about me in the paper, and as I got better, I garnered more attention. I even began to score more. Around this time, L.A. hoops officials brought back the local high school game of the week.

It was 1974, and my grandmother was still alive then (though, sadly, not for much longer). She had glaucoma and wasn't doing well health-wise. Pasadena High School was invited to play in the game of the week. We were matched up against El Rancho High School from Pico River, and it was the first game of the week since 1968. It was also the first time I'd be on TV. When I told my grandmother the good news, she said, "Michael, you have to do something to separate yourself from the other kids!" She didn't necessarily mean in terms of my overall performance on the court. She just meant so that she could tell me apart from the others on her little black-and-white TV.

My idea was to play the game with my high white socks (to hide my skinny legs), sweatbands, and strings pulled out of my red uniform shorts—*really* different. And it worked! She could tell who I was on her TV. Ever since, that's been how I stood out to fans in L.A. It was how I built my identity and how I'm remembered even now. It's how the legend of Coop began! Oh, and in that game, I scored 25 points and grabbed 15 rebounds along with a handful of blocked shots and big dunks. After that, I quietly began to think about playing in the NBA. Little did I know what would be in store for me—the journey it would take to get there.

IN 1980, BACK in the Southwest at the University of New Mexico, they experienced another low for the school. While it was after my time and I had nothing to do with it, it still hurt to see. The issue is known today as Lobogate, and it was horrible for the school. It involved forged transcripts and illegal payments and academic credentials. The FBI even got involved, indicting Ellenberger on seven counts of fraud and forgery. He was fired because of it (later, he coached in the pros). But while all the counts were dismissed, it was still sad. The program was put on probation, banned from March Madness for three years, and six players were dismissed. Ugly stuff, unfortunately.

AS FOR MY 1979–80 season, the Lakers were off to a great start, thanks to McKinney's diligent planning. We won 14 of our opening 19 games, which included a 103–102 win over the San Diego Clippers in our first game. That was the beginning of Showtime. While I only played one minute in the game, it was Magic and Kareem who stole the show. It was their first game together (though they'd actually met 10 years earlier when a young Earvin sought an autograph from an aloof Kareem in the Pistons' locker room when Detroit played Milwaukee). There were only a few ticks of the clock left in the San Diego game, and we were down by a single point.

The Clippers' World B. Free had torched us for 46 points, and we were still in the game. Kobe's dad, Joe "Jellybean" Bryant, was on the court too. It was tense but as with all great players, when the rubber meets the road, they don't let you lose. The game had been back and forth, but then it came down to the final moments. Kareem got the ball at the elbow, made a move, and swished an 18-foot skyhook at the buzzer. We all went berserk. Somehow we knew that win was the beginning of something special. Magic leapt into Kareem's arms and hugged him, smiling like the Cheshire cat. The rest of us were all jumping around with joy.

Then Cap, who'd go on to win the MVP that year, turned to Magic and said, "Hey, rookie, calm down. It's just 1 of 82." But there was no sense in tamping it down. You should have seen us. We were all so happy to get that first victory as a team. We'd won the opening game! Wilkes had 19 points and Norm added another 12. It felt like a blissful dream.

In previous seasons, the Lakers had been mediocre. But now with Magic, me, and the other guys, we were looking to rejuvenate the team's winning spirit. It was only a matter of time—*Showtime*. History was about to unfold in front of us.

As a team, we had all the pieces, including the greatest rookie ever to play the game (acquired by L.A. after trading Gail Goodrich to New Orleans for what turned out to be the No. 1 pick). The Lakers had thought to select Sidney Moncrief in the draft ahead of Magic until Dr. Jerry Buss, the team's brand-new owner, vetoed that and said he wanted the smiling new collegiate champion. And winning that first game showed us what we were all about, what we were going to do in the not-too-distant future. That's what Magic did for us. Before Magic and Larry Bird, the NBA was ho-hum, too cool for school. Now it was about to become an amusement park.

IN THE EARLY stretches of the season, we all just played to have fun. Magic built camaraderie, an infectious and enthusiastic atmosphere. It was work, but we still had fun. He'd tell us to keep our hands up, or else our heads would get taken off by one of his passes! McKinney brought the Portland system to L.A. with Kareem as Bill Walton, Magic as a bigger Lionel Hollins, and me as Bob Gross. Going through our work, we didn't talk about winning a ring. It was just about winning tonight's game and going on to the next. But for the year, we finished 60–22, good for first in the Pacific Division. However, the problem came when we lost Coach McKinney.

Just 14 games into the year, he suffered a horrific accident. A health nut, he was out for a bike ride when he hit something in the road and, without a helmet, flipped over his handlebars. He was hospitalized for months fighting for his life. In his place, Paul Westhead took over, and we finished the season 50–18. There'd been talk of Jerry West taking over again, but since he'd retired from the job the year before, there was no going back.

The ordeal put a cloud over the team. Jack had established the system, and now we had to adjust, shell-shocked. There was a bad feeling in the air. Here was our leader—showing us how to get it all done, how to win—and now he was gone. While Magic knew how to win on a collegiate level, this was a new thing entirely. Kareem had won a ring with the Bucks about a decade before, but everyone else was new to it. The good news was Westhead didn't change much—he just wanted to move *faster*. He told Magic to get the ball after makes or misses and *push*. He wanted us to get downcourt and play. In that sense, the season was so much fun. In truth, it felt almost like a college team. Practices on off days were shorter, maybe an hour and a half compared to the 150-minute ones many other coaches preferred. But they were jam-packed with running and strategy.

After he'd taken over, Westhead chose a little-known person for his assistant—a mop-topped Patrick James Riley. The son of a minor league baseball lifer, Pat played college basketball at the University of Kentucky. From there, he was drafted No. 7 by the San Diego Rockets. After three seasons, he became a Laker in the 1970–71 season, winning a ring the next with Wilt, West, and Elgin Baylor. He played for the Lakers for five-plus years, his best coming in the 1974–75 season, when he averaged 11 points (though he only played in 46 games). In 1977 the 32-year-old signed on as a color broadcaster for Lakers radio with the golden-voiced Chick Hearn.

Pat, who had a haircut like Paul McCartney, had come in from the beach one day to pick up some mail at the Forum, and just then, Chick's broadcasting partner, Keith Erickson, a former great for UCLA, was moving on to other things. So when Chick saw Pat coming in to get his mail, he asked him if he wanted to fill in for Keith. "You want to try out?" Chick asked. Pat said, "Sure." Simple as that. All of a sudden, he was sitting next to Chick Hearn, the guy who'd invented the term "slam dunk," on the broadcast. But after McKinney went down and people were looking at what to do, Pat was there once again at the right place and time. So Paul tapped him to help.

You can't make this stuff up, even in Hollywood! Now, with every victory on the court, our Lakers squad began to cement our crucial team-first mentality. Each game, something pulled us closer. But perhaps the most important thing came at the All-Star break. We'd just beaten Chicago 107–97 to go 38–17 on the year. I played 25 minutes in that game, scoring four points with three assists and three rebounds. Kareem had 27, Magic had 11 assists, and Wilkes added 28. But it was what Magic said after that made all the difference. While both he and Kareem were All-Star starters in the February game in Maryland, he didn't want the rest of us resting.

Magic told us that while players normally get four days off for the break, that wouldn't be our fate. He organized our own practices around the All-Star Game. I think that was a big turning point for our whole season. We didn't splinter and go our separate directions like most teams. No, we stayed together, kept working, gelled. So when we came back after the break, we were a fine-tuned team for the stretch run. We won 9 out of our next 10 games and finished the year winning 22 out of 27. Two of those wins were against the vaunted Seattle SuperSonics, the team that had won the 1979 championship the year prior.

We played them twice ahead of the season's end, once on February 26 and then again on March 22. Both victories helped us edge them out for the top spot in the division. Seattle was locked and loaded at the time, with players such as Dennis Johnson (a former Finals MVP), Gus Williams, Jack Sikma, and Fred Brown. And we were the new kids on the block. In the February win against them, Kareem had 31 points and 11 rebounds, Magic had 18 points and 13 assists, and I scored 10 with 2 blocks. Dennis Johnson, who was always tough on Magic, torched us for 30, but it wasn't enough and we blew them out 131–108 in Los Angeles. That felt good.

In the second game, our victory was narrower, and we won 97–92. Norm Nixon was the star in that one, scoring 23 with 10 assists. I had 6 points with a steal in 22 minutes. For Seattle, Sikma had 25 and Gus had 22, but we outlasted them. Why this is important is because in the playoffs that year, we matched up against Seattle in the Western

Conference Finals. We'd shot past Phoenix 4–1 in the semifinals and then we got to Seattle, trouncing them 4–1 in the conference finals. Iron sharpens iron, and getting past Seattle really helped us learn how to win big. They got us ready to play in the Finals that year against the Philadelphia 76ers and Julius "Dr. J" Erving.

The crazy thing was, Seattle had beaten us in the first playoff game of the series—in L.A., no less. Just as we'd won by a point in our first regular-season game that year, we lost by one in that first playoff game against Seattle. But then we came back with four in a row, including two wins in the Emerald City. Strangely, though, we didn't play them at the Kingdome in Seattle, their home gym. We played them at the Hec Edmundson Pavilion on the University of Washington campus. We may have lost to them had we matched up in the Kingdome, but there was something about the Hec that made it feel like a college game.

And that's where Magic shined. The Mariners were playing at home, so the Kingdome was out of use. So we got the break of playing at the Hec. It's that kind of luck that makes me believe in the Basketball Gods. In the Kingdome, the crowd was far away and you felt like you were on an island. But at the Hec, the fans were on top of you. Magic was in his element, and so we blew them out. Dr. Buss had traveled there to see us, and when we knew we had the games in hand, I looked up to him in the rafters and saw he was raising a fist with pride. Even Kareem got into the collegiate camaraderie, pumping his fists, and so did everyone else. It was all smiles.

ONCE WE'D WON and were set for the Finals, we hoped it would be Boston and Larry Bird, who'd won Rookie of the Year that season over Magic. But his Celtics couldn't get past Philly—*boo-hoo*. Yet the 76ers were no slouch. They had a talented team with Dr. J, Henry Bibby, Maurice Cheeks, Darryl Dawkins (who I helped Kareem defend, flying over his shoulder to double-team), Bobby Jones, Lionel Hollins, and Caldwell Jones. In 1977 the 76ers had lost to Jack Ramsay and Portland in the

Finals. An Eastern Conference team, they played physical ball; they wanted to bruise and break you. But we showed them how to *run*.

Dr. J was a formidable foe. Yet we were the team of destiny (he got his in 1983). I remember the first time I played against Dr. J that year in the regular season. Like so many, I'd watched him growing up, his big Afro flying backward as he dunked the ball with one hand. But the first time I saw him in a game, I lined up next to him while someone shot free throws. I caught myself, like, *Oh, fuck, I'm here with the one and only Dr. J, one of the greatest ever to do it!* But I didn't say anything, and neither did he. He just had his hands on his hips. And the next thing I knew, he was running up court, gone, while I stood gawking, mesmerized.

To do anything against him, I had to tell myself I wasn't guarding Julius Erving; instead he was just a 76ers player. Not the guy I emulated while dunking tennis balls in my backyard but just another dude. So when I matched up against him in the Finals in 1980, you can imagine the mindfuck it was. This was for a championship, and what would have been his first in the NBA. (Later, Dr. J would famously dunk on me with his Rock the Baby jam, but we can leave that story for another chapter.) In the 1980 series, we took the first game 109–102 at home. Then Philly fought back and beat us 107–104 in our gym.

We split the next two in Philly, winning game three 111–101 and then losing the next 105–102. But it was in Game 4 of the Finals that Dr. J shocked us, and the world. That's when he pulled off the greatest move maybe in NBA history—this balletic shot that started from the right elbow. He dribbled by Mark Landsberger, went past Cap, and jumped behind the backboard. Magic and I were sitting on the baseline, front-row view. And his arm went behind the backboard and he hung in the air like he had wings on his feet. Then he swooped his arm with his big hand holding the ball and did a reverse layup that our minds couldn't fully understand.

But that was Doc. He defied gravity and expectations. That put them up 91–84 in the game and helped them win Game 4. In Game 5, back in Los Angeles, we won again, 108–103, gathering momentum. And the climax for the series came in Game 6—sadly, with Kareem hurt. The big fella had won Game 5 for us in L.A. with a heroic Willis Reed–like performance, scoring 14 points in the fourth quarter on a bad ankle. (When he'd hurt it, the Forum crowd went silent. Only the 76ers were cheering.) Cap had to sit out Game 6 at home while we flew to Philly for it.

To start the year, we'd never imagined winning a ring, yet here it was on our doorstep. Except we were without Kareem. As we were sitting in the L.A. airport waiting for our flight to Philadelphia, everyone was quiet. We figured we'd already lost without our All-Star center, and we'd be coming back to L.A. Still, we had two games to try and win a ring, with a potential Game 7 set for Los Angeles back home. But that's when Magic gave us a new hope, like a Black Luke Skywalker.

As we waited to board the plane, Magic and his blaring boom box (probably Luther Vandross) came to the team's gate. The last to arrive, Earvin had that big million-dollar smile on his face. He said his enthusiastic hellos to us, and then he managed to be the first one of us to get on the plane. Normally, Kareem would have been sitting in the front first-class seat, the one with all the legroom, and Magic and I would have been sitting in the second row (one of us in the aisle, one of us at the window). But since Magic got on first, he took that front-row seat that Cap would have occupied. And once everyone sat down quietly and we were about 10 to 15 minutes from takeoff, Magic turned to all of us and said, "What's wrong with y'all?"

Nobody said a word. Then he said, "Have no fear! Magic fucking Johnson is here!" With that, we all busted up. He'd set the tone for the entire trip. Magic broke the tension, and we all laughed. Then he said, "[Number] 33 ain't here; 32 is!" And he sat back down in Kareem's spot. The long plane ride was completely different after that than it would have been. And so was our time in Philly. We could have been stewing in worry, preparing ourselves for a blowout against Dr. J, Darryl Dawkins, Maurice Cheeks, and the others, but Magic changed it all, as if flipping a vinyl record to the other side and playing a new batch of songs. That was EJ the DJ. He was a genius.

THE NIGHT BEFORE the game, after we got to the hotel from the cross-country flight, Magic pulled a bunch of us aside and said, "Hey, we're going to the movies!" We looked at him like he was crazy. Someone said, "No, we're not!" But he said, "No, no, no! Coop, Nixon, Jamaal, you guys, let's go. We're going to the movies!" Magic liked those shoot-'em-up films, and so that's what we went to see. Sitting in the dark theater, we completely forgot about basketball. When we got back afterward, it was close to midnight. And the next morning when we got on the bus, the vibe had totally changed. "You guys, we *got* this," Magic said. And he was right.

In Philly before the game, we had a great practice, and warm-ups were smooth. Magic hyped us up in the locker room going from guy to guy and giving him words of advice. Then just before tip-off, we were all in the huddle, and Coach Westhead said, "All right, Jim Chones, you're going to jump center." But Magic burst in, "No, no, no. Let me jump center, Coach." Everyone looked at him like he was nuts. But thinking about it now, I think Magic had that idea up his sleeve the whole plane ride. He was all about surprises that put uncertainty in the minds of his opponents. He wanted the other team to look at us and go, "What are they doing?"

When Magic got to midcourt to begin the game, Philly's nearly seven-foot center Caldwell Jones looked around big-eyed like he wasn't sure what day it was. Fans in the stands began to *Ooooo*. But it wasn't about winning the tip itself (he didn't); it was about taking up space in the other team's mind. The ball went up, and Magic ruled the day. In that game, he scored 42 points, grabbed 15 rebounds, and dished 7 assists. With the performance, Earvin became the first, and still only, rookie to get the NBA Finals MVP and only the third player to win a college championship and then the NBA championship the following season. (Back home, Bird must have fumed.)

In that final game, there was a big scare for me. I was guarding Dr. J at the top of the key, and when he made a pass down low, Jim "Crusher" Chones knocked the ball loose. It ended up in my hands, and suddenly we were racing down to the other end. I came down the lane, dribbled past Doc, and got into the air on the left side of the basket. But when I went up for the layup, out of nowhere, Dawkins jumped over Magic, clotheslined me, and knocked me to the ground as I shot. Then he fell on me as I lay on the floor. It took me several minutes to get up with the help of our trainer Jack Kern's smelling salts. We were up 95–89. Thankfully, we didn't look back.

We won Game 6 123–107, silencing 76ers fans. After, we celebrated (especially so for Jerry West, who'd lost many Finals as a player). It was the culmination of a year starting with that San Diego win. Showtime had arrived! But it wasn't a party for the *entire* summer. Just as he'd got us together at the All-Star break, Magic said we had two weeks off before we had to be back to train for the next season. He did that for us his whole career. And if we didn't win a ring, we worked even harder. Today, I'm proud to say that the Lakers went to the Finals eight times during my tenure, and we won five. We would have won more if it hadn't been for a few errors along the way.

AS MY CAREER progressed, I would take a few weeks off in summer to go back to Albuquerque and run coed camps and talk about the Five D's. Since I didn't have a father growing up, I knew what mentorship could do for a person, and I wanted to invest in that. After, though, I'd join the team, and we'd be back in the gym. For the Lakers, camp wasn't about *getting* in shape. Magic said our butts had better *be* in shape by then, ready to learn what we needed to do to whoop ass. With his showing in that Game 6, he'd ushered in a new idea of positionless basketball. He'd jumped center, but he played everywhere, including point. We were all versatile.

We flew around the court, caring more about playing hard defense than which individual was in front of us in the moment. Today, the concept of positionless basketball is all the rage. But it was something we kicked off in 1980, especially in that final game. I was in the starting lineup for that one too, playing 39 minutes, scoring 16 points, grabbing 4 boards, dishing 6 assists, and getting 2 steals. It was a career highlight. Coach Westhead hadn't said I was going to start until a few minutes before taking the court in Philadelphia. Like Magic keeping his idea to jump center close to his chest, Paul did the same thing with his roster moves that game.

Shortly before tip, Paul said, "Coop, you're going to start for us." My heart nearly skipped a beat when he told me. On defense, Jamaal Wilkes took Dr. J, Magic had Bobby Jones, Norm had Maurice Cheeks, and I started on Lionel Hollins. But because we were all so interchangeable, Magic and I would often switch assignments. If there were a down screen set on one of us, the other would jump out on the man shooting to the wing. In the 1980 Finals, I scored just under nine points a game to go along with four rebounds, four assists, more than a steal, and nearly a block per game. I was also a solid 13 of 16 from the free throw line.

Two years into the league, and I'd already won. It also marked Magic's first NBA championship. The victory gave Paul Westhead his first ring as a coach too. As for our captain, the big fella, Kareem Abdul-Jabbar, it gave him his first championship in Lakers Purple and Gold. Despite all his dominance in the NBA prior, he'd not won a ring in Los Angeles until then, despite joining the team ahead of the 1975–76 season. The win in 1980 also gave Dr. Jerry Buss his first Finals victory as an owner—in his first season, no less. It was amazing how all these legends started thanks to that win. We'd played free-flowing. We were happy teammates, and it worked.

Today I tell people that the win set the tone not only for the L.A. Lakers but for the player Magic would become. Yet it took all of us to pull it off. Stars don't win without good role players. For example, people forget, but Kareem had a career-high 37 points. And I did my thing too. Sometimes that gets overshadowed because of Magic's stats, and I understand that. But it was also my first chance to step into the limelight, my own coming-out party, showing my worth. I was counted on to stop the 76ers' wings, and I did it with flying colors. But it wouldn't be the last time we'd see Philly in the Finals or the last time I'd have to defend the best.

AFTERWARD, SOME TRIED to make a big deal of Magic winning the Finals MVP over Kareem, who'd had an outstanding series, averaging 33.4 points. (Cap did win the regular-season MVP, his sixth.) But I never saw any tension between them. Our team was a family. Sure, maybe an older brother got annoyed by a younger brother here and there, but it wasn't anything to fret about. Nothing bad. Kareem and Magic had a wonderful relationship (despite what that show *Winning Time* tried to peddle). I suppose I could be wrong or that I missed something—I was always sort of the happy-go-lucky guy on the roster. But that's certainly my point of view of it.

One tough moment for us did happen during the 1980 Finals, though, when our backup center, Spencer Haywood, was kicked off the team. He was a former ABA MVP who was brought in to help Kareem in the post—a guy who'd played 76 games for us during the year, averaging 10 points and 5 rebounds in 20 minutes. Back then, cocaine was everywhere, and Spencer, a former "indentured servant"—as he called it—from Mississippi, sadly wasn't immune. He'd gotten involved in drugs, and it ended up cutting his time with us short. Coach Westhead dismissed him *during* the Finals for falling asleep at team stretches. That was sad—though he did get a ring.

Just a note here on Spencer Haywood: He is one of the most important people in the history of professional basketball. Not only did he take the NBA to the Supreme Court while he was in Seattle, thus paving the way for underclassmen to enter the league, but he is also one of pro hoops' most accomplished players. A Hall of Famer, he was an outstanding scorer and rebounder, and after his retirement, he has helped to usher in new initiatives with the National Basketball Retired Players Association, including health care for older players. Spencer is a great friend and a legend, despite a few issues during his early life.

Winning is hard, so there will always be issues, but there was no fissure in the locker room or anything like that. As for my life then, things were great. It was a blessing to be in L.A., and that my family could see me play. It was hectic to get tickets for everyone, sometimes 30 a night! But my wife Wanda and I were making the best of it together at home. During the holidays, we'd host get-togethers, and the team would come over. She was a great cook; everyone loved her meals. With some teams, when the games are done, you stop seeing everyone, but that wasn't the case with us. We were different. We spent time together, ate, went to the movies, and trained as one.

Teammate Testimonial

Spencer Haywood

Right now I'm thinking about Michael Cooper because he just made the Hall of Fame! As for 1979–80, when I got to the Lakers, you're always looking for a young person to be around, to mentor a little bit. So Coop was my guy. Whenever there was a little something going on with the coach, I would always kind of be there to back up Coop, because I love him dearly.

That's my heart, man. Our connection—maybe it's because we both have real dark skin! It's sort of a joke but not a joke too. Black folks have jokes with each other. Everybody says, "You love him, Spencer, because he's darker than you!" But I don't know. Especially when you got Kareem there too! Oh, that's a bad joke!

But with Coop, I loved his competition. I love the way he competed. We lived near each other too, so we'd ride to practice at the same time—not together but in our own cars. We were all in Jerry Buss's compound! Jerry had these apartments in Fox Hills, or wherever it was. We all would go to practice from there.

Then when we got to practice, Coop would always try to guard me, but he was too little! Like, "Get the fuck out of here!" But jokes aside, you just knew right off that he had his eye on one prize, which was, *I'm going to stop somebody!*

One night we were wondering who was going to play legend David Thompson, and Coop reached out up front and said, "I want him!" I was like, "Rookie, get out of here! What are you talking about?" But that was his attitude.

Then you got to see him develop and develop. It was a beautiful thing to watch. That was my 10th year, so I'd been around players that you saw what they had, and I saw that Coop had it. He paid close attention to detail, both on offense and defense. He knew not to clog up the middle where the bigs were. He just kept his movement going, kept his continuity. Instead of going to the post where Kareem, Jamaal Wilkes, and I were, he said, "Let me run with Magic! I'm going to get a few layups out of this!" And if they laid off him, he'd pop his jumper on them.

Our team was like a jazz band. You had Kareem as your piano player, sitting in the middle there. Me as your bass over there on the left. You got Jamaal over on the other side as the drummer keeping the timing going. Then you got Coop playing all kinds of good trumpet. Then here comes Magic as John Coltrane blowing all kinds of shit. You better catch up; otherwise you'll be lost.

I always looked at that team like a jazz team. Me and Kareem—all we did was sit around and play jazz. There it is! But to end this, Coop and I had a really wonderful time during our Hawaii reunion. I had a wonderful time with all the guys, but it was really special for me and Coop. Maybe it was the sun! Two Black guys in the sun! Then James Worthy was in there too. Oh, boy!

Chapter 6

Brutal Defeat No. 1

As it turned out, despite our best efforts, the 1980–81 season didn't end quite like the 1979–80 one had. So let's not talk about it, okay? All right, fine—we can, but just a little. The story of the season begins with Larry Bird and the Boston Celtics—the team we measured ourselves against and the player with whom Magic would forever be intertwined. To this day, you can't mention one without the other. And while Bird and his green goblins weren't in the 1980 Finals, we knew we would have to reckon with them somehow this season, whether we liked it or not. During the regular season that year, we played Boston twice and lost both times. Just know I hate saying that.

The first game took place at the Boston Garden on January 18, 1981. We lost that one by a mere two points, 98–96. Both Kareem and Jamaal had great games, combining for 61 and 14 boards. For Boston, Tiny Archibald, the newly acquired Robert Parish, and the trash-talking Cedric Maxwell each scored 22. But Bird wasn't himself, scoring only 11, thanks in part to my defense. I started the game because Magic was injured. In the second tilt on February 11, Magic was still out, and I got to start again. Bird scored 36 with a whopping 21 boards. Kareem got 32, but we lost 105–91.

Those losses hurt, but what pained us even more was Magic's injury. Missing him for more than half the season (45 games) killed us, costing us a number of wins and a lot of team chemistry along the way. But his absence due to injury was just one of the many issues we faced over the next few months. Since we'd won it all in 1980 with Westhead, the Lakers brought the coach back for the following season, which meant Jack McKinney, who had started the Showtime era, had to go to another team. He landed with the Pacers, thanks to the help of Dr. Buss, who had close ties with the team from prior business dealings. Jerry was just a good man like that.

Dr. Buss treated his roster as family, not as athletes. That's why so many of us worked for him after we retired. For instance, Jim "Crusher" Chones told me a story once about how he and Dr. Buss went to the Playboy Mansion in L.A. to watch a prize fight. When Hugh Hefner, who had a macho rivalry with Dr. Buss, passed out a bag of numbers, Chones and Buss each grabbed a random one. If the fight ended on your digit, you won the prize. But the number Jim got was Buss's "lucky number," so they traded. Then Buss won (causing Hefner to storm out!). But he didn't keep all the cash; he fairly split the $60,000 with Jim.

But Magic and Paul, on the other hand, didn't have the right chemistry that season. All Magic—who'd liked Paul at first—thought about was Bird. But all Paul thought about was his "system." When we'd won it all in 1980, while it was one of the hardest things any of us had to do, we did it almost on instinct. We'd played with such natural joy and enthusiasm that we didn't realize what it took out of us until we'd earned the victory in that final Philly game. We didn't know how crazy what we'd done actually was. Now we were going to learn—the hard way. We were going to find out the meaning of the words *heartbreak* and *pain* when it came to the season.

WHEN IT CAME to Magic and Larry, there was always a sense of one-upmanship. Magic got his in college and then the next year in the pros. This had to irk Bird. Magic was driven by him, and vice versa. They needed each other to achieve heights no one had ever seen before in the NBA. Bill Russell won 11 rings, but the NBA wasn't nearly as big then in terms of number of teams or attention. Magic wouldn't let the competition die down between him and Bird. When we talked ahead of the 1980–81 season, he said, "Man, Coop, I want to see him again. I want to see Bird." He meant in the NBA Finals that year. He wanted to win and beat Bird every time.

That meant beating Boston too. When it comes to the Finals, you want the two best teams and the two best players facing off. Well, that's what we were planning for that season. But what's the saying? "Man plans, God laughs." Well, there must have been a big chortle up in heaven at our expense. Indeed, other teams had something to say about our big plans. We didn't see Boston in 1980 because they'd fallen to Philly. But in 1981 we'd be the absent party in the championship series. Truth be told, the entire year was a mess for us. From the beginning of camp through the final shot of the season and the very last buzzer. *Ugh.*

It would be easy to blame it all on Magic's knee injury, but that wouldn't be the full story, not by a long shot. In truth, the entire dynamic of the team changed. With Coach Westhead, whom I liked, now fully entrenched as the head coach, thanks to a contract extension, he wanted to make adjustments. Like I said, *ugh.* This is why I try to forget the 1980–81 season as much as I can. Really, I try to forget every season in which we didn't win it all—to blank them out intentionally. We had the potential to repeat as champions, but we just didn't play up to it. Losing our point guard and instigator for half the year was a huge reason why. Our mojo was gone.

Magic had torn cartilage in his left knee in a game against the Kansas City Kings (before they moved to Sacramento in 1985) early in the season on November 18, 1980. Prior to that, he'd been averaging 22.4 points, 8.8 assists, 8.5 rebounds, and 3.5 steals per game. He was out until February 27, 1981, and we limped along in his absence. We lost five out of our next eight games. Then we won five in a row before losing six out of our next nine. The entire year, even when Magic came back, wondering if he'd be the same, we couldn't find our footing well enough, though he averaged 21.8 points, 8.5 assists, and 9.2 rebounds upon his return.

Magic—whose locker was next to mine—said that during his time out, rehab was one of the lowest points of his career. He *needed* the competition, the fun. The problem was too that with Magic out, our 6'2" point guard Norm Nixon became the full-time ball handler. In his career, Norm would be a two-time NBA All-Star. In the 1980–81 season, he tallied 17.1 points, 8.8 assists, 2.9 rebounds, and 1.8 steals. But Norm wasn't a pass-first guy like Magic. He didn't live and die for assists. Yet they were both talented guards on a talented team. Naturally, a feud began to brew between them (even leading to blows during a heated practice). So Dr. Buss had to squash it personally.

It was tough for Norm, who helped me a ton as a rookie and who had been with the Lakers before Magic arrived. With him, Wilkes, and Kareem, the team was stacked pre-Showtime. But they hadn't won it all. Magic helped make them winners. Norm was one of the fastest players in the NBA with the ball, along with the Clippers' Randy Smith. Norm could stop on a dime and score with the best. He could hit the midrange jumper and, well, he felt the Lakers were his team. His nickname was Mr. Big! But then this young buck—Magic—arrives with his smile and boom box, and the world flips. So whose team was it? In the end, it had to be Magic's.

That Dr. Buss and most of the other guys backed Magic hurt Norm. Now, he was being asked to play second or third fiddle. That *divide*, as our assistant coach Pat Riley called it, hurt the squad. And as a supporting cast, we didn't know who to pass the ball to after the other team scored or when we were set to run a fast break. Magic even told Norm, "I want you to score 30 points." He wanted to help him get there. But Norm said he could do it without Magic passing him the ball. While we were able to make all this work in 1980, we weren't in 1981 after we'd gotten our rings. In the end, we were good with Norm, but we were *great* with Magic.

THAT SEASON, THE Lakers logo might as well have been a giant target. Everywhere we went, we were introduced as the world champions, and rightly so. But that only made other teams want to knock us off. We were the biggest game on everyone's schedule, and for a group of guys just getting used to winning, this didn't make our job any easier. By the regular season's end, we'd finished 54–28. And for our troubles, we faced the sub-.500 Houston Rockets in the first round, a team that had finished at 40–42. But the Rockets boasted one of the best players in the league in center Moses Malone, who'd won the MVP award in 1979 (he'd get two more in 1982 and 1983).

During the 1980–81 year, Moses averaged 27.8 points and a league-leading 14.8 rebounds. He was also a big, burly guy, which made it tough for the thinner Kareem down low. Moses was a bully on the court (off the court, he was one of the nicest guys). He was so good the 76ers traded for him in 1983, propelling them to a Finals win (more on that later). The 5'9" Calvin Murphy was another star for Houston. He'd averaged 25.6 points three years prior, 20.2 two years prior, and 20 the year before. In 1980–81 he averaged 16.7. He was also the NBA's best free throw shooter that season, sinking them 95.8 percent of the time.

But the Rockets didn't beat us in that series; we beat ourselves. There was too much pressure to go along with too much dysfunction. We all felt it. To start, we lost the first game to Houston at home 111–107. In that one, Moses scored 38 points and grabbed 23 rebounds. In the second game, we pulled it together and won 111–106 with all five starters, including me, scoring in double digits—Norm had 21, Kareem had 27, Jamaal got 22, I had 17, and Magic got 15 points to go with 18 rebounds and 8 assists. But in the third and final game back at home, we fell to Houston 89–86. That one came down to the final shot—one I'd also like to forget.

With just 15 seconds left, Wilkes inbounded the ball to Magic. The Rockets were up by one point, 87–86. With Kareem calling for it on the left block, Magic dribbled up the court with Houston's Tom Henderson guarding him. Magic put the ball behind his back and then jumped in the air to take a floater, a shot Chick Hearn called a "leaping leaner." But the ball didn't even hit the rim and Moses just leapt up and corralled the air ball. I could only scratch my head as I saw the whole thing transpire from the three-point line. Houston added two free throws, and it was over after a last-second heave by Wilkes. We lost by three measly points. Our season was done.

Should Magic have passed the ball to Cap? That's the lingering question from the series. But he had a good shot, and Henderson was about six inches shorter than him. So why not? He'd won it for us in 1980, and he could have done it again in 1981 had his shot floated just six inches farther. Also, at the time, Kareem was draped by Moses; it wouldn't have been simple for Kareem to score on him. Magic wasn't afraid of the big moment. You can't be if you want to become a superstar. He failed at that moment, yes. But he didn't fail our team. Not in my eyes. We wouldn't have even been that close without him. The whole team—*all* of us—laid an egg.

For the season, my averages were the best of my career. I scored 9.4 points per game to go along with 1 block, 1.6 steals, 4.1 assists, and 4.1 rebounds per game. I'd even gotten a few MVP votes, finishing No. 24. The following season, I'd come in even higher in that voting, finishing No. 17, the highest of my NBA career. I never thought about myself as an MVP candidate, but that was never up to me anyway. All I cared about was winning, and we hadn't come close during the 1981 playoffs. But maybe the 1981–82 season would be better—we could only hope.

Teammate Testimonial
Jim Chones

Cleveland traded me to the Lakers during the exhibition season in 1979, and Coop was a rookie with the team. He was very unassuming—until the games started. The drills, he was all right, not impressive. But when the game started, he started blocking shots, getting steals, getting in the passing lanes, and not backing off from anybody no matter who it was. That was his moniker. He was fearless. Coop wasn't a nice guy on the court—he was nasty! He and Bird used to go at it. Bird said Michael Cooper guarded him the best out of anyone. He gave him credit for that.

I was like a big brother to Coop. He was married at the time, so after practice he would go home to his beautiful wife and family and I'd go home to mine. I only had one child at the time. My second year with the Lakers, my second daughter came, the one who works for the Knicks. And now my oldest daughter is the senior vice president of the Bucks. But the thing I always liked about Coop was he was loyal. If there was any fighting or any antagonistic behavior, he was right in the middle of it, trying to defend his teammates.

He and Norm Nixon made a tremendous defensive tandem during those couple years. Nix could defend. He would turn his guy, and Coop would come from behind and make a steal. They'd do that two to three times a game. The thing I liked about Coop was that he kept getting better, especially on the offensive end. He could always dunk on you, do tip-ins, and get on the break and finish at the rim. But he developed a three-point shot, and he became one of the best in the league at it.

But most of my favorite memories of him have to do with what kind of person he is. Coop was basically from a single-parent household. He had a beautiful mother. He was a kid trying to make it. He didn't have a big name, even though he was great at New Mexico. He didn't have a great big name, but when the game started, his competitive nature took over. Whether it was an NBA game, a scrimmage, a three-on-three, or a one-on-one. He was unmatched on our team. Most of that comes from the way most of us were raised.

My father was never around either. So we were always trying to prove that we could. Just that phrase—always trying to prove that we could. We were never afraid, based on what we went through as kids in the hood. Basketball—there's no room for fear. If you go out there and you play courageously and play with your heart and play to win, you'll never have a bad game. And Coop personified that. Plus he's loving; he's just a good guy. When we went to Maui this summer, he was the toast of the group.

Coop brought everybody together. He hugged everybody, went to various tables, talked to people. He made it easier for us to reunite. I just love him like a little brother. But don't let him fool you! He speaks really well, but if you ever compete against him—look at some of the old film! Coop is special. He always will be. He's fearless. If you want to win, make sure Michael Cooper is on your side. They never talked about two-way players until Coop came along, but that's Michael Cooper.

Chapter 7

Riley Takes Over

AFTER THE 1980–81 REGULAR SEASON, Dr. Jerry Buss had made Magic a rich man beyond his wildest dreams. He signed Earvin to a 25-year, $25 million contract, which was the highest in sports history at the time. Today, that would be worth about $80 million, which is much closer to what stars make in a single year! *Yeesh.* For my part, though I made significantly less, I'd earned my first big-time NBA accolade. For the 1980–81 season, I'd been named to the NBA's All-Defensive Second Team. That was a high honor, to already be recognized as one of the league's best defenders. In one particular game, I'd set a career high with seven steals.

A relentless competitive edge got me the nod, and I wasn't going to back off on the way I approached the game in the new year. Yes, the 1981–82 season would be a fresh start for us as a team after the horrible playoff loss to Houston. We'd be the comeback kids. Sadly, the Boston Celtics team had won the championship without us showing up to the 1981 Finals. They beat Houston in six games, and Boston's Cedric Maxwell was named the Finals MVP. Now Magic and Larry each had one NBA championship. It was setting up to be a great heavyweight bout, and the only question was, who would land the next big punch?

OUR ROSTER WAS stacked during the 1981–82 season: Kareem, Magic, Jamaal, Norm, and me, along with newcomers Mitch Kupchak, Kurt "Clark Kent" Rambis, and former MVP and three-time scoring champ Bob McAdoo. Sometimes I wonder how one Showtime team would do against another from the decade, but the 1981–82 team might have been the best among the bunch. While I embraced my role coming off the bench, in my heart of hearts, it wasn't always easy. But because of the all-important idea of *team*, I sucked up any reservations and played my part. A lot of guys over the years had to sacrifice for us to win. It takes a special personality to do that.

Where we weren't at our best was with our guy on the sideline—Paul Westhead. It wasn't that he was a bad coach; it was just that he was a bad fit for our team at the time. Later, Westhead would be a successful college coach at Loyola Marymount with guys such as Hank Gathers (who died after collapsing in a game) and Bo Kimble. Paul would coach in the NBA again too, with Chicago, Denver, and Golden State. But in L.A., there was too often a sense of friction. Like gears grinding. There was no oil in our team's big machine. Don't get me wrong, I appreciated many things Coach Westhead gave us, but we needed a different voice.

Paul was a book-smart coach, and while many of us were educated, even more than intellectual motivation we needed someone to rev our engines, to kick some ass. But because he was so studied, Paul got along swimmingly with Kareem. In the end, his approach and motivation style was geared more toward the big fella than anyone else. Coach Westhead came at things with a philosophical point of view. He would quote Shakespeare. Kareem, now in his 12th season, loved it, and they bonded, talking about ideas and theories. But a lot of the stuff Coach told us went over our heads at the moment. Like I said, it wasn't the avenue the *team* needed.

We weren't students, despite how we were depicted in that November 9, 1981, *Sports Illustrated* photo with Kareem, Jamaal, Mitch, Norm, and me sitting at desks in a classroom with Coach (Magic stood, refusing to sit like a student). That stuff was better suited for real college kids.

Yet you can't take away Westhead's (and before him, Jack McKinney's) influence on our speed, on Showtime. But Westhead didn't do it the right way; it was backward. We needed to run *first*. And then if there wasn't anything, we could get the ball to our skilled center, Kareem. Westhead wanted us to walk it up too much of the time and go through Cap at the outset.

What was great about how we played was that Magic made you want to bust your ass, to run down the right or left side at any chance you had, after a make or a miss, and get on the break to get a no-look pass and an easy layup. It was about pace, freedom of movement, and passing. Not about waiting, finding your spot, and plodding to predetermined points. That's where Paul had it wrong and where Magic had it right. It always seemed that while Coach Westhead wanted us to run, he didn't have supreme confidence in it. And that's where he and the Lakers suffered in the 1980–81 season, and that's also how we started the 1981–82 campaign too.

Magic's gift was that he could pass from anywhere. Part of his genius was that he could be all the way at the other end of the floor or in the backcourt, and he could zip one to you right on point for a bucket. Paul's "system," though, could never account for that. Norm, Jamaal, I, and the other guys wanted to run, to practically break our necks to get out on the break, but Paul wanted us to be in those damn spots. But it was Magic, who Westhead at times played at power forward, who fueled what Dr. Buss wanted: to entertain the entertainers. After all, we were a basketball team, and Paul was quoting works from centuries before.

WE OPENED THE year undefeated in the preseason exhibition games. But despite that, it wasn't any fun. We were like racehorses, greyhounds trying to run in two feet of mud. While we didn't *mind* mud, it wasn't what we thrived on. Combined with our failure to win a ring the season before, the team was an unhappy mess. It all came to a head early in the year. To start the regular season, we lost to Houston, the team that had knocked us out in the playoffs, 113–112 in double overtime. Moses had 36 points and 10 rebounds. And though Kareem had 33 and 10, Jamaal had 27 and 10, and Magic had a triple-double, it wasn't enough.

We lost our next game too, in Portland, 102–100. We were too slow and predictable. We barely won our next one against Seattle 106–103, but then we lost again to Phoenix 101–99. We beat the lowly Dallas Mavericks 121–111 and then were blown out by the Spurs in San Antonio 128–102. They didn't even have George Gervin in the lineup, and they still killed us. Ron Brewer dropped 44, his career high, against us. After the game, we traveled to Houston to play the Rockets again, and while we beat them 95–93 to rise to 3–4 on the season, Magic was visibly distraught.

There was even a moment in Houston that crystallized the whole thing for us. With the team charter bus stopped near Hobby Airport, Magic left us and stood outside in a patch of grass on a median in the *middle of the road*. Not sure what he was thinking, I went out to him. "E, you okay, man?" He said, "Coop, I can't play like this. I'm just not having fun. This ain't us. We run; we don't walk." He felt like a pawn, a piece in the "system." When your star isn't having fun, changes must be made. In the NBA, guys don't get traded; coaches get fired. So that began Paul's demise. It may have been unfair, but it's what happened. Today, history books get it wrong by saying that Magic got Paul fired. But that came from West and Buss.

Tough times help make great teams, though. Either you rise to the challenge and adapt or fold. We were winning games to begin the season, but it was a slog. And for anyone who knows the effervescent Magic Johnson with the big smile and magnetic, generous personality, a slog is not what you want. When we won in 1980, it was electric joy. And it was positionless. Now it was the opposite. Everything should have been fluid, easy. Earvin was my best friend on the team, and I felt bad for him. But it was four games later on November 18, playing in Utah, when it all changed. We'd beaten the Jazz 113–110 when Magic, in the locker room, told reporters he wanted out.

After enough sniping back and forth with Paul, who'd given Earvin a postgame lecture after the Jazz game, Magic said he couldn't play "here anymore" and that the Lakers could trade him and he could go somewhere else to play if the team wanted to keep Paul's system. "I'm not happy," Earvin said, adding that he and Paul didn't see "eye to eye on a lot of things." That, of course, sent a shock wave through the organization, from the players in the locker room to upper management. Dr. Buss urged everyone not to "panic." But no one in L.A. wanted to lose Magic, so there was only one other choice.

In the end, Dr. Buss fired Coach Westhead after just 11 games of the season. He'd finished his season at just 7–4. Some saw it as not fair, but that's how it goes in the NBA. Even then, it was a players' league. The guys in the team jerseys play the game, and that's who the fans come to see. And they most definitely were coming to see Magic. He was the draw for Showtime. The only question now was, who would coach us? At the next day's press conference, Dr. Buss said he wanted Jerry West to coach (West had been the coach my rookie year). But West didn't want to coach anymore; he wanted to keep doing his work behind the scenes. Enter Pat Riley.

Pat was a former broadcaster with Chick Hearn. Paul Westhead had hired Pat to be an assistant, and now Pat was there to replace Westhead. It was an awkward situation but something that was also best for what we needed. Winning is hard; it can get ugly in the trenches. That's life. So West agreed to be an assistant for Pat early on—his "offensive coach." But really it was now all in the hands of Riley, the team's new interim head man. That didn't end the turmoil for Magic, though. Combined with our playoff loss the previous year (and his air ball), fans thought he got Westhead fired, and that pushed them to boo in arenas all over, even at the Forum.

Buss came out in support of Magic and said he'd been planning to let Paul go even before Magic talked to the reporters in Utah. It was Jerry West and the team's GM Bill Sharman who had slowed his hand. While Buss and Magic were like father and son, hanging out together often,

Buss wasn't going to do just *whatever* Magic told him. He was his own boss, despite what people said. So he pulled the trigger when the time was right. Still, though, fans booed the young Magic, thinking he had too much influence on the team. Boy, would they soon eat their words. In the meantime, Riley made the game fun for us again. He leaned in to what made us special.

Basketball is supposed to be entertaining (in that way, the old ABA had it right). We became the pinnacle of that again. *It was Showtime!* In our first game under Pat, we beat the Spurs—the same team that had blown us out a few games prior—136–116. Kareem had 30 and 8 boards, and Magic had 20 points, 16 assists, and 10 rebounds. We were back! When you have a guy like Magic, you don't want to waste seasons, and so it was good the Lakers acted. Now it was time for us to show our appreciation. Riley lit a fire under us. We won 16 of our next 19, including 8 blowouts of 10-plus points. He got us running. Sure, there was structure, but we felt free.

What was the major difference? Well, Pat was a former player. He knew what it was like to be in our shoes, and that was better for our team. Practices were in tune with what benefited the players. You can't just run people into the ground, and Pat was intuitive in those ways. He had his finger on the pulse of the team. If you've never played in the NBA, you might run your guys for hours, but Riley could tell when all we had was a good 15 minutes left in our legs. That's the kind of stuff that builds morale, not tears it down. We started to enjoy practicing again, even Kareem! Magic got his joy back too. Pat allowed us to be the best versions of ourselves.

Riley, a natural head coach, also instituted a half-court trap on defense. When your team is built on the fast break and a jazzlike transition game, it's good to force turnovers. So pressure was key in spurts. We pressed full court here and there, but we also used a 1-3-1 trap in the halfcourt to disrupt opponents. That's where I shined too, flying around, double-teaming guys, and using my long arms and quickness to get into passing lanes. Pat motivated us with many original maxims, which only grew in number over the years. One he *constantly* repeated was "No rebounds, no rings." Another was, "Defense is the disposition to dominate your opponent."

While it was a shock in some ways that Riley was now the Lakers' head coach—for a time, I thought things were going to smooth out with Paul—I could see the vision now with Riley. And it still offered some sense of consistency, since he had already been on the bench with us as an assistant. Pat was experienced; he'd learned his basketball regimen at the University of Kentucky and his greatness in Los Angeles with the Lakers. Amazingly, he was only three years older than Cap, and the two had played against each other in high school in the early 1960s. Riley became a master motivator, always knowing just what to say, the right phrase for the right time.

In that same way, Pat knew about player combinations too—just whom to put in the right positions. He defined our roles, which was something Coach McKinney and Coach Westhead never quite figured out. Pat vocalized who our leaders were: Cap, Magic, Jamaal, and Norm. Kurt Rambis was our blue-collar guy who started the break with rebounds. McAdoo was our bench scorer. And I was our defensive stopper. Pat told me, "Coop, you're good enough to start on many teams. But we need you to be our sixth man." He showed me just where I could be great for my Lakers, not merely a contributor.

That was music to my ears. I'd worked hard to earn my spot. In fact, that year, some of my teammates who usually just called me Coop were now calling me All Summer, because I kept talking about how *all summer* I'd put in so much work to become a well-rounded player. Even though part of me wanted to be a starter on the team, I knew I was playing behind two all-pro guards and with other legends, such as Kareem. So if it meant we would keep winning, I knew it was best for me and for the team to keep my ego in check and do what was best for the squad. Turns out that move would keep me around for years to come, and through many victories.

THEN THERE WAS Jerry West. He was like a father to so many of us. Jerry saw talent in you that you didn't know you had and gave you confidence along the way, which is what he did for me, taking me in the third round with the 60th pick and letting me heal for an entire year before we won the 1980 title. Later, he'd find diamonds in the rough such as A.C. Green and make trades for key Lakers players such as Mychal Thompson. West was always orchestrating something behind the scenes, and he'd continue to do so for the Lakers in the 21st century. I played for Jerry as a coach in 1978–79, my rookie season. And I've been around him seemingly my entire life.

As a coach, West suffered from something a lot of great ones deal with. They just can't get why everyone can't be great like they were on the court. It's the old saying: most great players don't make good coaches (with few exceptions, of course). I think Jerry took the coaching role early on to stay close to the game. He had great assistants, including Jack McCloskey and Stan Albeck. But in the end, the Logo was more suited for other opportunities in the league. And as far as the Lakers are concerned, thank God he listened to his inner voice. Yet even in the team's front office, he would still pull us aside in the middle of practice and give us little tips to think about.

West was always watching everything because he knew the secret to basketball—that it's about chemistry and personality as much as it is about overall talent. Jerry would meet with players and give it to us straight, no matter if it was good or bad news. He never tried to overshadow the coach on the sideline, either. Like Riley, he knew what it was like to be a player in the league—and a star, at that. So he knew what we needed in a head coach. A 14-time All-Star; a scoring, assist, and NBA champion; a five-time All-Defensive player; a Finals MVP (for a losing team!); and an All-Star MVP, Jerry West is a Hall of Famer if there ever was one.

But somehow, though, he was even better at working in the front office. The secret to his success was that he didn't always pick the consensus best player. Rather, he just wanted the best player for the *team*. Case in point: Ahead of the 1982–83 season, high-flyer Dominique Wilkins was available, and we had the No. 1 pick. But Jerry selected the nimble James Worthy, an excellent college recruit. More than his talent versus Wilkins's, it was about who would be better for us. And Jerry got that one right, to be sure. The deer-quick Worthy soon became Big Game James and an icon in Lakers lore, winning three rings.

Another great example is Mychal Thompson, who played with Kevin McHale in college at the University of Minnesota. When we needed help defending the gangly Boston Celtic, West knew that Mychal, of all people, knew how to guard him. So he went and got him from San Antonio in 1987 for our title run then. Jerry swapped Frank Brickowski and a pick for Mychal, and boom, it did what West was sure it would. The hardest trade he had to make, though, happened after the 1983 season (we'll talk more on that later). For now, we were rolling with Riley at the helm. As it concluded, we finished 57–25, including a 10–2 run down the stretch. *Playoff time!*

WHEN THE POSTSEASON began, we were off like a shot. And while we had big-name stars, I believe that our real advantage was our bench. Throughout the 1980s, we had the best one in the league, if I do say so myself. The 6'9" power forward Mitch Kupchak had come over from Washington, where he'd played with the strong Wes Unseld (a guy who used to knock my behind down on screens), and Mitch brought us some toughness. Unfortunately, he'd gotten hurt ahead of the playoffs, so fans never really saw what he could do in the postseason. Later, he'd be a GM for the Lake Show era after Jerry West left L.A.

But in the regular season, Kupchak had helped set the tone along with another University of North Carolina product, Bob "Offense Wins Championships" McAdoo. The Greensboro-born McAdoo, whom we all called 'Do, was instant offense. He'd earned all the individual accolades in Buffalo, including an MVP and scoring championships, and now he wanted to add a ring to his trophy case. In the playoffs in 1982, he averaged 16.7 points and 6.8 rebounds in 27.7 minutes per game. In February earlier in the year, I scored my career-high 31 points too, picking up where 'Do left off. And another bench star was second-year hustler Kurt Rambis.

Riley knew Kurt could rebound, play hard-nosed defense, and inbound the ball quick on makes. That got our fast break (which was sometimes better than sex!) rolling. Because our bench was so good, it made practices between games more intense. It was the kind of stuff that helped us win big that season in 1982. Practices often were harder than the games, in fact. Coach Riley designed them that way. Unlike today's star players, who regularly sit out practices, we always ran hard during ours; that included Kareem and Magic. Our practices were meant to be competitive. So much so that when we played a new team, we said, "Damn, it's time for fresh meat!"

Practicing made me better; it made us all better. McAdoo and Kareem battled, talking trash the whole time. Magic and I would go at it too, sometimes with hard fouls. Mike McGee and Jamaal would scrape and claw. Indeed, our second unit would give our first unit fits. But we always ran the scrimmages with the same sense of teamwork that led to rings. Through these efforts, our relationships grew. Magic and I became tight in those early years, and though I was a family man, staying home with Wanda and the kids while Earvin explored the world and celebrity, we stayed close while sharpening each other's skills.

Our closeness led to our on-court weapon, which we took advantage of often—what Chick Hearn dubbed the Coop-a-Loop. In college, Magic had great chemistry with his Michigan State teammate, the high-flying Greg Kelser, who was the recipient of many of Earvin's alley-oop passes. Well, in the pros, Magic needed another finisher like that, and he saw that my long leaping legs could help me fit the bill. He knew that if I were in the game, I had to be a threat to score, not just defend. So we devised a plan. In games—especially crucial playoff ones—our opponent's best offensive player would usually guard me, thinking he could rest. So we wanted to take advantage of that.

Magic and I would set up a pick-and-roll at the top of the three-point arc. So instead of defenders being able to slack off on me, we put them right in the action, and when they went to double-team Magic, I would slip and roll to the basket for a pass up top and a slam dunk. Magic and I got so good at it, we wouldn't even have to set a screen—or speak. Instead, I knew that if I got into a certain spot either on the break or in the halfcourt, he'd put the ball up there and I'd score. We could just sense what the other was thinking. Then when Chick gave the play its now-famous nickname, it became a household name.

BILL RUSSELL (PRO SPORTS' first Black coach) helped my basketball career even more. The great former Celtic, known for his 11 rings and all-world defense, saw something in me during the playoffs that year and into the Finals, and he praised me for it on TV. In the Western Conference Semifinals, we swept the Phoenix Suns 4–0, and then in the Conference Finals, we swept the Spurs 4–0. Ever since Riley had taken over the team, we were thinking championship, and now it was within our grasp. In the Finals, though, we faced the Philadelphia 76ers, the team we'd beaten two years prior for the title. And the team, still led by Dr. J, wanted revenge.

The 1982 NBA Finals were the first since 1978 not to be broadcast on tape delay. It was a sign the league was growing in importance and popularity, which had to do with both our and the Celtics' success. Though we wanted to see Bird in the Finals, it was Philly that had knocked them off, even as Boston fans chanted, "Beat L.A.!" *Oh well.* We won the first game in Philly 124–117. Norm, Jamaal, and Kareem each scored 20-plus, and Magic got 10 points, 9 assists, and 14 boards. Off the bench, I added 17, 5 assists, and 5 rebounds, and McAdoo had 14. Philly won Game 2 110–94, but it mattered little since we'd gotten the necessary split on the road.

Back in L.A., we won both games at home. The first was a blowout, 129–108, thanks to 29 from Norm. For Philly, star guard Andrew Toney torched us for 36 and Dr. J had 21, but it was too little too late. In the next game, we won 111–101. Toney, known as the Boston Strangler for how he killed the Celtics, again went off. He was one of the hardest players to guard. But we had five players in double digits, giving us plenty to win. The 76ers blew us out in Game 5, 135–102, and then the series headed back to L.A. for Game 6, which we won 114–104. Kareem hit skyhooks from all over the court, and Jamaal capped a great series with 27 smooth points.

Magic notched a triple-double in Game 6, and I added 16 off the bench, along with 5 assists. Throughout the series, Philly's coach, Billy Cunningham, made sure his team hit me with hard picks as often as they could. I heard him yelling, "We've got to get Cooper off our scorers!" I was suffocating the guys. Darryl Dawkins, Caldwell Jones, Earl Cureton—they all made sure to hit me with their big bodies whenever they were screening for their man. Cunningham was trying to free up Julius, Maurice Cheeks, and Toney so they could score. But it just wasn't enough. And it was Russell, a TV commentator during the Finals, who sang my praises for the entire six games.

Russ was one of my all-time biggest fans, in love with how I played defense. I think I reminded him of some of his best teammates back with the 1960s Celtics, such as K.C. Jones and Satch Sanders—guys who I followed and adored as a youth. Russell said things on the broadcast like, "Keep your eyes on the young Michael Cooper out there. He plays the game right!" Bill knew Jamaal, Magic, and Kareem were our stars, but he loved my style too, which means the world to me in hindsight. By the end of the series, we'd fulfilled our mission. Riley, who coached a masterful Finals, got his first ring as a head coach, and McAdoo got his first as a player.

WINNING A RING is all about buying into the system. McAdoo, who said he came from the "apartheid" American South, is a prime example of that. He didn't *want* to come off the bench, but it was the best thing for us. It was because of selfless acts like this that we knew we were going to win in 1982. While we wished it had been over Boston, a title is a title. The only thing about the series that bugged me was that Philly brought in the jazz artist Grover Washington Jr. to play the national anthem. I was a big fan of his, but seeing him in Philadelphia—suddenly I hated his music! But Dr. Buss got singer Jeffrey Osborne to sing for us in L.A., which helped.

More than any song, it was Riley who navigated the season. By the end of the 1981–82 season, we were champions once again. On top of that, I was named to the NBA's All-Defensive First Team for the first time. And I was helping to make the idea of the sixth man cool again in the league. You didn't have to start to be effective—look at me. I'd learned it all from John Havlicek.

PLAYING IN 76 games and starting in 14, I averaged 11.9 points, 1.6 steals, 3 assists, 3.5 boards, with nearly a block per game. As someone who had made just $30,000 per year in my first three seasons (I was a steal!), I earned a new contract in the summer of 1982 for about 10 times that. And while I would have played for free if I'd had to, I'd earned my bigger deal. By winning and garnering some celebrity thanks to Russell, I also booked commercials and endorsement deals that only grew over my career, including one for bubble gum and, later, one with Larry Bird advertising beef! As champions, we weren't lacking.

It was fun seeing our success pay off in real time—for individual players, for our team, and for the league. We knew we were part of something special. It was largely thanks to Magic and Bird—their love of the game and their passing skills—that the NBA boomed. Not to mention all the rings. It made other teams in the NBA want to do the same. Philly, Atlanta, Milwaukee, Houston, Utah, and Golden State— they all wanted to squash the idea that they were doormats. So they got smarter. While most fans wanted to see the Lakers and Celtics in the Finals, other teams now tried to spoil that. It was all they thought about while we held up the trophy.

Teammate Testimonial
Norm Nixon

Coop came to the Lakers in my second year. But he got hurt his rookie season. That same year, rookie Ron Carter was a friend of mine from back in Pittsburgh, where I played in college, and I know he and Coop were going after the same spot on the team. And Coop came in and took his job! But then he got hurt. So I didn't have the opportunity to play with him much that year.

But Coop came back the next season, and he and Magic were playing for us my third year. I was happy to see those guys, because I got tired of being spanked by the Seattle SuperSonics guys, including Gus Williams and Dennis Johnson. At the time, I had some veteran guards like Lou Hudson and Ron Boone, but they were at the tail end of their careers.

But with Coop and Magic, there were now some young guys on the team. Seattle had an offense that was guard-oriented, so they were working me! But with Magic and Coop, I was happy to have two young guys in the backcourt. Coop had the ability to change the course of a game with his defense.

He'd come in off the bench and change the whole complexion of the game. He's a great defensive player. He played hard defense in practice every day. I didn't want to play against him—"Like, dude, come on, it's practice!" But we were very good friends. We all went out together. That's the origin of the Three Amigos—Magic, Coop, and me.

We were some young guys, and we were trying to win championships. We played against a lot of great guards, and we took pride in being the young guys who came out and played against the veterans, the older and more established guys in the league. We felt the combination of us was arguably the best three in the league.

With us, you got everything: assists, defense, and scoring. So I thought the three of us could match up against any backcourt in the league and outplay them. Man, I just have so many memories of Coop. One I really remember is throwing Coop those alley-oops. We laugh about it now—in practice, he was always pointing up, like, "Norm, throw the ball up!"

But I would never do it. Finally, I just got tired of him asking, and one day I threw it in the air and he jumped up and dunked the thing. After that, I knew if a guy was running side by side with Coop, if I threw it up there, that guy was getting dunked on! From that moment on, we looked for it in the games. But it just happened in practice first because I got tired of him saying it.

At first, I couldn't see what he was seeing. But once he got to it, I was like, "Oh my goodness!" That made an indelible mark in my head. Then the year Magic got hurt, the year we got upset in the playoffs, Coop and I started in the backcourt extensively, and we played extremely well together. Unfortunately, we got upset that season in 1981.

Coop and I ended up being neighbors. He moved a few blocks from me, and we're still friends to this day. We have lots of stories I can't say! But we had a good time playing together. I think that's one of the elements that has to be part of a championship team—we spent lots of time on the road, going to movie theaters, and that's probably why we're still close to this day.

Chapter 8

Back-to-Back?

IN THE SUMMER AFTER OUR FINALS WIN, I went back to Albuquerque to run a camp. It was there where my Five D's idea started to really crystallize in a way that I could make it clear for others. As a star athlete—indeed, as a celebrity of any kind—you become part famous person and part professor. People look up to you, even if you're like Sir Charles Barkley, who didn't want to be a role model in his famous Nike ad. So I told my campers about the value of the Five D's concept. I told them stories from my life about when determination, desire, dedication, discipline, and decision-making pulled me through. They watched with wide eyes, at times nodding their little heads.

That's when I knew I was on to something. To be a hardworking player takes a well-rounded skill set and mindset. Like a tough playoff game, they must be tested. But the only way to come out on top is with the tools for success. At the camp, I invited guests to speak, from teammates such as Magic to experts including Cheryl Miller and world-class sprinter Jim Hines, who tutored the Lakers on how to run during games. He suggested starting low at first to decrease resistance. Then you should increase your strides as you speed up and straighten up. There's an art to it, and knowing that helped our fast breaks (and I would set a career high in assists in 1983 with 17).

As for Magic, he reminded the campers to "see the vision," or to watch a play unfold before it did. It was one of his gifts, which he tried to impart to them. At my camps, which I held from New Mexico to Pasadena, I stressed fundamentals, especially defensively. Knowing the game's building blocks helps you grow as a player. We did drills and underscored sportsmanship and mental toughness. I liked to help mold the future student-athletes of America. But the summer held more good news: L.A. had drafted James Worthy from UNC at No. 1. A former teammate of *Mike* Jordan, James was a great addition to our agile, quick team.

Worthy had won a national championship in college in 1982, just before getting drafted by us. Over the course of his three-year career in Chapel Hill, he averaged 14.5 points, 1.1 blocks, 1.4 steals, 2.5 assists, and 7.4 rebounds per game. Adding him with the No. 1 pick in the 1982 draft, the rich (us) just got richer. Today, James is still the only player picked first by an NBA defending champion. The Lakers had received the No. 1 selection from the Cleveland Cavaliers in a trade that created the Stepien Rule (named after Cavs owner Ted Stepien), which forbids franchises from trading their first-round draft pick in consecutive years, saving them from themselves.

Worthy came into a wild cast of characters on the team that year, which included Joe Cooper (another Cooper!), Mark Landsberger, Eddie Jordan, McAdoo, McGee, Steve Mix, Norm, Kurt, Jamaal, Magic, Kareem, and me. We were feeling good about ourselves, having just won a second title with a bright future ahead of us. As the kids today say, you couldn't tell us nothing! But that didn't mean we weren't ready to work hard. Magic continued to push us, and we followed his lead—"Coop," he'd say, "do your job!" And I got on him too. We'd already found the promised land twice in the past three years, and the future continued to look wide-open.

Thankfully, when James came to us that summer, he did a great job. While he averaged 13.4 points, 5.2 rebounds, and 1.7 assists that first season, you could see the potential for even more. Today, people know him as Big Game James, a nickname he earned after the 1988 Finals. At first, though, he was just Jay Dub to us. James played forward at UNC alongside Sam Perkins. But until he came to camp, we had no idea just how fast he was. He is also a likable, mild-mannered guy. James grew up with religious parents, and he brought those sensibilities to the Lakers, which was something he and I bonded over.

The thing about us at the time—if a rookie came into camp and didn't show he had a work ethic, we would make sure he learned. And if he still didn't respond, he was cut or traded. But James's work ethic was special. He wanted to be great, and he knew he had a chance to be that with us. He made sure to fit in with the team concept. Now, James is one of a few stars to play with the same franchise his whole career, along with the likes of Magic and me. Over the years, he got better and better, first on defense and then as a perimeter shooter. He worked on his midrange jumper and his low-post skills.

He had great touch around the rim, and we needed his inside presence to go along with Kareem. James could go left or right, and he earned his nickname, given to him by Chick Hearn. During the seasons, he ate many meals at my house, chowing down on Wanda's cooking. James has a particular affection for spicy food. Sometimes I'd have to get him a towel, he was perspiring so much from the heat—sweating like he was playing Boston! But we always had fun, engaging conversations, which often tended toward basketball or spirituality. He'd grown up in a small country town on a dirt road.

Though giant Virginia center Ralph Sampson (who decided not to come out in 1982) and Dominique Wilkins were hard to pass up, I was glad James declared for the draft and we got him. He fit right in. I can't imagine the Los Angeles Lakers without him now. He's that connected to the team's history. When you think of the Showtime Lakers today, he's one of the guys who first comes to mind. Big Game streaking down the sideline, getting a Magic Johnson pass for one of his signature Statue of Liberty dunks. His face with those round goggles on, perspiring after another big win.

THAT SAME YEAR, 1982, I actually got my own shoe. Well, kind of. In 1982 Nike put out its original Air Force 1 sneaker, and for the marketing campaign they hired six NBA players—Moses Malone, Jamaal Wilkes, Bobby Jones, Mychal Thompson, Calvin Natt, and me. (It was a far cry from Tom's old hand-me-downs.) We got our own poster too: the six of us standing at sunrise wearing space suits in front of a giant jet. Nike flew us to Seattle for that, and we had to be there at 4:00 in the morning to get the right shot of the sunrise. Nike also had to cut up Moses's flight suit so it would fit his big frame. If you look closely, you can see it's held together with pins. I liked the sneakers (their thick soles gave me another two inches of height), but they were a little hard to play in. Today they're maybe the most popular shoes with kids! Indeed, when you're an L.A. Laker, you get these kinds of perks.

We were getting so famous by then that we had to get out of Los Angeles to work and focus. It wasn't about local girls or spending time in bars. It was about our singular goal for the new year: winning another championship. We obsessed over it, especially Pat and Magic. There was no time for "fun in the sun." By then, we'd gotten a taste of winning it all (twice) and we remained thirsty. But we weren't the only ones wanting to get the taste of victory champagne again. Our fans were crazy for it too. And as always, so was Boston.

We sold out the 1982–83 season, welcoming in some 598,000 fans to the Fabulous Forum that season. Not only did they like to come see a winner, but Jerry Buss was a genius with outreach, which included giving big-name celebrities such as Jack Nicholson free tickets so that they would help draw more people to the Forum and to its oasis, the Forum Club. He even sent his limo to pick them up and bring them out. And it worked. The Lakers were the hottest ticket in town. It seemed like with each passing day, Buss was inventing some new way to titillate the area fans. He was early on the cable TV revolution too, constantly thinking outside the box.

And the apple doesn't fall too far from the tree. Over the years, Jerry Buss's daughter Jeanie came around more. She was 21 at the start of the

1982–83 season, and you could see her with her dad, soaking up the scenes while also learning the business like a rising star. She was a sponge. When we practiced during the year at the Forum, which sometimes included two practices and a film session, Jeanie would be up there in the stands with her dad. Sometimes she'd come down to talk to the players, but either way she always seemed to be present. And when Buss bought the famous Mary Pickford House in Beverly Hills, guess who else was onsite when we did the team photo. Jeanie!

She was clever, always operating under the radar. Jeanie never wanted to be the star of the show. But she never wanted to be absent, either. At the time, her two brothers, Johnny and Jim, were doing their own things. Later, all three kids would become more a part of Jerry's business, from the team to his real estate, with Buss delegating responsibility to each. At the outset, though, it was Jeanie. One of her first jobs was general manager of the Los Angeles Strings, a professional tennis team, which she started at just 19 years old. Today, at 63, she is the big boss when it comes to the Lakers, and you could see it all start way back when.

In the 1980s the Lakers could've printed money. With the team winning; the stars, including Magic and Kareem, on the roster; the Forum Club, which Wanda hated, bumping; and all the glitz and glamour of the local celebrity culture, there was nothing better. Truth be told, there are a lot of secrets that I still can't share about the goings-on with the team. The sheer star power and level of beauty that would be walking around, sipping drinks at the Forum Club was incredible. A married man, I didn't spend too much time there myself, but I heard plenty of stories from those who did.

Perhaps the biggest fan the Lakers had at the time, though, was Michael Jackson. The pop star of pop stars, the creator of *Thriller* and *Bad*, the former Jackson 5 member, he loved coming to games at the Forum. But because he was so famous, he would have to dress up like an old man with a hat just to be able to walk around among the thousands of fans. Magic always knew when he was there, though. He'd tell me, "Coop, you see that guy there in Row F, Seat 5? That's Michael Jackson!" And I'd see him sitting across from our bench and I'd laugh, knowing those around him had no idea who they were next to. *Entertain the entertainers*—Buss was so right.

OKAY, LET'S GET this out of the way finally: As it turned out, 1983 was not a good year for me. But it was a *great* year for Dr. J, at my expense. The first moment came on January 5, 1983, when we were playing the 76ers in Philly during the regular season. We came into the game 25–7, and the Sixers were 24–5. The spring before, we'd beaten them in the Finals, and they were out for blood. Turns out they got it! In the final minutes of that January game, Dr. J stole the ball from us, and suddenly I was chasing him down as he raced toward the basket. In a blink he was close enough to the hoop to begin his leap. As I flew by below, he slammed it home.

As he broke down the sideline in a sprint, I was thinking this was my chance to make a great play against a great player. But as I got close to him and he rose up, Erving did his now-famous rock the baby cradle move and I was toast (second-best after the one in the 1980 Finals). At that moment, I knew I wasn't going to be able to turn around fast enough midair. But if I had gotten up a split second ahead of him and gotten my right hand out, it would have been *my* highlight. Instead, it's become one of his most famous dunks. What could have been known as perhaps the greatest block was instead an offensive highlight for Julius! Oh well, that's how it goes.

A few weeks later, on February 13, 1983, L.A. hosted the NBA All-Star Game at the Fabulous Forum in Inglewood. And guess who was the MVP of the game? That's right: Julius Erving. After entering pro hoops with the ABA's Virginia Squires a dozen years prior in 1971 (and helping force the ABA-NBA merger in 1976), 1982–83 was turning out to be *his* year. The coaches of the All-Star Game were the same two who had matched up in the Finals the spring before and the same two who would match up in the Finals again this year, Pat Riley and Philly's Billy Cunningham. Not only that, but 1983 was the year Marvin Gaye sang the national anthem like an angel!

In the playoffs later, the 76ers were feeling themselves. Their MVP center, Moses Malone, predicted his team would go through sweeping every opponent, famously saying, "Fo' fo' fo'," as in they would win 4–0, 4–0, and 4–0. After finishing the season 58–24 (I made the All-Defensive Second Team again), we knew we'd have something to say about that, and we wanted to shut his big country mouth up. The Western Conference's top seed, we beat Mychal Thompson and Portland 4–1 in our opening series and then George Gervin's San Antonio 4–2 in the Conference Finals. And who was waiting for us in the Finals but Dr. J, Moses, and the 76ers—again.

Now, while it's true that Philly swept us in the series, something I loathe saying, what is also true is that we were injured almost beyond belief. This was the third time in four years that we matched up against Philly in the Finals, and they wanted to win at least one. But in the first game, they got lucky. Our guard Norm Nixon injured himself in a bad collision with Philly's Andrew Toney, and while he kept playing, Norm suffered a separated shoulder. On top of that, during the San Antonio series, McAdoo tore his hamstring, leaving him severely hobbled for the Finals. But the biggest blow came even before the playoffs that year.

On April 10 against the Phoenix Suns, James Worthy broke his leg when he landed badly after trying to tip in a missed shot. And he was out. Without James, Bob, and Norm, we were a shell of ourselves. Not to mention, in the first game of the series, as we tried to keep things close, Philly got some unexpected scoring from reserve Clint Richardson. The guy had the game of his life, going 7–12 from the field and scoring 15 points with 3 assists. With Toney out from his collision with Norm, Philly's coach, Billy Cunningham, put in Clint, and he won the game for them. Afterward Riley said, "If I have to devise a defense to stop Clint Richardson, we're in trouble."

We were in trouble, all right. We lost Game 1 113–107. In the second, another of Philly's bench players scored a big bucket for his team. With Moses Malone sitting out due to foul trouble in the third quarter of Game 2, Philly's backup, big Earl Cureton, came in and kept the ship afloat.

The 6'9" forward-center known as the Twirl hit a skyhook over Kareem to extend Philly's lead against us. Philly wound up winning Game 2 by 10 points, 103–93. It only got worse from there. We lost Game 3 in L.A., 111–94, and the sweep was complete in Game 4, with the 76ers winning 115–108. Moses, the greatest rebounder ever, got the Finals MVP.

I finished the season averaging 7.8 points, 3.8 assists, and 3.3 rebounds to go along with 1.4 steals and half a block per game. In the playoffs, I'd averaged 9.4 points, with 1.7 steals, 2.9 assists, and 3.9 rebounds. But a lot of the stuff I did on the court didn't show up in the box score. I knew that, and my teammates knew it too. That's why all I cared about was winning—something we'd failed to do. We had to watch Philly celebrate, only hoping we would be back to the promised land the next season, hopefully whooping either Philly's or Boston's butt in the process. Time would have to tell.

THANKS TO THE 1983 win for Philly, Julius Erving got his elusive first NBA title. He'd won two rings in the ABA before the league merged with the NBA, and now he had an NBA ring too. I was happy for him. But still, even today, more than any other year, thinking about the 1983 Finals makes me angry. While Philly was hungry, I believe we would have won that series had we been fully healthy. I hate losing, and I hated giving Moses—who kept head-butting Kareem in the post during the series—the satisfaction of predicting the sweep (the 76ers only lost one game during the playoffs that year, against Milwaukee in the Eastern Conference Finals).

But hard times build your character, and we knew we would be back soon. Though, the same couldn't be said for the aging Philly squad. That had been their last chance. Next season they were knocked out in the first round by Michael "Sugar" Ray Richardson's scrappy Nets team. And while it hurt to fall in 1983, that wouldn't be the end of the pain for us that summer. We were about to lose one of our best teammates, a fan favorite, and bring in an untested, brash rookie. It would prove to be the kind of move that made Jerry West an icon, but it was also one that felt like a second gut punch in just weeks.

Chapter 9

I Hate the Color Green

NORM NIXON WAS AN ICON IN LOS ANGELES. So when Jerry West shipped him to the San Diego Clippers, we were all stunned. Not only had we not gone back-to-back, losing to Philly, but now we were losing one of our best players. Logically, it made sense. Norm and Magic played the same position. But emotionally, it was really hard for me. I got along well with Norm; he was a friend, someone I'd known since my first days in the league. The NBA is a business, and I get it. But that didn't make it any easier. And who did Jerry West get in return? Well, it was rookie Byron Scott, who'd been taken by San Diego with the fourth pick in the draft.

Jerry got Byron and Swen Nater on October 10, 1983, for Norm, Eddie Jordan, and two second-round picks. Making the swap took courage and vision. Norm was one of *the* famous guys on the team. There were rumors Norm was partying too much and that Jerry had hired private investigators to follow him (and even follow me), believing he was using drugs. While that angered Norm—and rightly so—it was impossible to escape the fact that with the Lakers, girls and parties and nightlife often followed. It was America in the 1980s. Even our goofy forward Mark Landsberger loved to go out and hit the strip clubs (always looking for a woman to take home). From the Forum Club and beyond, our lives were packed with good times and temptations. In the end, it would seem, that was one of the reasons Jerry West pushed to trade Norm.

In fact, a few of those escapades got some of the players in trouble with their girlfriends and wives over the years. Our blockheaded forward Mark Landsberger ended up spilling the beans about some private stuff involving strip clubs to his wife one night, and she went and told the other players' significant others. That caused a big stir in our locker room, and, well, Mark didn't come back to the team for the 1983–84 season, waived by management. Good riddance! But I digress. With Norm out and Byron in, we had to figure out a new balance in the backcourt. The benefit was that Byron was a shooting guard, not a ball handler.

That meant he wasn't going to take the ball away from Magic. Instead, he'd work his butt off trying to get open and be the recipient of Magic's pinpoint passing. In this way, Byron was a better fit positionally. Byron had a pure jump shot, while Norm on the other hand needed the ball all the time. But there was another difference. While Norm had been there from my first day, showing me the ropes, Byron wasn't so quick to fit in. He was mouthy, famous for saying, "Magic who? I'm better than him!" Now, believe it when I say it, we were shocked at that, and we knew we would take it out on the young fella in training camp.

For the young shooting guard, his Lakers orientation would be a trial by fire. During the first three or four practices, we snubbed him teamwide, never passing him the ball. On defense, we all got our cheap shots in. I guarded him most of the time, and each time he cut, I hit him with an elbow or shoulder, or Magic or Kareem got him with theirs. We'd shout at random times, "Byron who?" But to his credit, the rookie took his lumps and responded. Slowly Scott started to earn his Lakers stripes through toughness and by not backing down. He showed that he could carry the load the team required, and not just be a trash-talking kid.

Over time, we got to be so close that Magic, Byron, and I became known as the new Three Musketeers, which reminds me—on the Lakers, we had a ton of nicknames. Byron became Baby B. Earvin was Magic or Buck. McAdoo was 'Do. Kareem was Cap. Kurt was Rambo or Superman, because he looked like Clark Kent (he even had kids dressing like him who called themselves the Rambis Youth). I was Coop or Scoop (because I knew the stories). Jamaal Wilkes was Silk. Norm was Mr. Big. Worthy was Big Game James. Spencer Haywood was 'Wood. Later when he came to the team, the Bible-carrying A.C. Green was called Ace or Junior.

But *some* nicknames I can't say because I'd have to share their illicit backstories! As for Baby B, Scott turned out to be just what we needed. After all, a race car doesn't need five engines. It needs a steering wheel, chassis, wheels, and a battery. Jerry West knew how to build engines, not just find them. And if we didn't understand his methods, he could sit us down and show his reasoning. It was special. Today, the best teams win like we won, with teamwork. Just look at the 2023 Denver Nuggets. Nikola Jokić had that team playing like Showtime with the way he passed. He's got a bit of Magic and Bird in him too. He wants to make the other guys better.

DURING THE 1983–84 SEASON, there were lots of good teams. In the East, there were the Celtics, Bucks, 76ers, Pistons, Knicks, and Nets. Out West, there were the Mavericks, Jazz, Blazers, and Seattle. All of them were above .500, winning more games than they lost. And there were other historically good teams lingering beyond those, such as the Nuggets, Spurs, and Warriors. No one was really a pushover. Not even the Clippers with their new point guard. Yes, seeing Norm in an opposing uniform was hard to swallow. He'd been an All-Star for us in 1982, and now his home was San Diego (though the Clips would move up to L.A. ahead of the 1984–85 season).

But no matter how it felt, in the end, he was our opponent now. He hadn't liked the trade out of town, and so now things were contentious. Our first game against Norm came on November 2, 1983, in San Diego. Norm's team won that one by four points, and he scored 25 and dished 12 assists in 38 minutes. You could tell that he wanted to take his feelings out on us and prove to West and Buss that they were wrong in getting rid of him. He got his vengeance. After that, we took four out of five from the Clippers and Norm didn't score 25 on us but once more. I knew his game well, so I made it my mission to hold him down as best I could.

I knew size affected his game, and while Norm was one of the quickest guards in the league, I also had some speed and athleticism to throw at him. When he came to play against us in the Forum, the fans cheered him. They loved him and what he did. No matter what happened, he was still a two-time champion with the Lakers. Next year, during the 1984–85 season, Norm was named an All-Star again, but sadly, not long after that, he tore up his knee and his Achilles tendon, and he was never the same player. As for Byron, he had a good season for us his rookie year, averaging 10.6 points, 2.4 assists, 2.2 rebounds, and 1.1 steals, and it was only up from there.

Both Byron and James Worthy were starting to understand their roles with us as they integrated into the team and our sense of camaraderie. James, who practiced as hard as he played and got healthy again, averaged 14.5 points, 2.5 assists, 6.3 rebounds, and almost a steal and a block per game in his sophomore season. We were starting to build the second era of Showtime. By now, I was 27 years old and just coming into my own as a player—the sweet spot of my career. I was also in the middle of a streak when I played hundreds of games in a row, which included five seasons of never missing one.

THE ONE GAME I thought about missing came late in 1983, when Kareem put Nair in my hair and made some of it fall out! What happened was, on Cap's 37th birthday earlier that season, when he was in the shower, we played a prank on him. A few guys and I got his clothes while he was washing up, and we cut up his shirt, jeans, and jacket so that when he got out of the shower, he had nothing to put on. That made him fume. Then another time, in the locker room, I told Magic I'd give him $100 if he knocked Kareem's newspaper clean out of his hands. When Earvin did it, Kareem looked up and said, "I heard that, Coop."

I should have known, but Cap systematically got us all back over the next few weeks, which included waiting until I fell asleep on another plane ride. He snuck up on me and put Nair in my hair and on my eyebrows. I woke up screaming! And a big, round, hairless hole appeared on my head that never came back! But that was just one of the stories from our trips. Some days we had to be up at 5:00 AM to fly commercial. We were zombies then. It wasn't until the late 1980s when owners, the values of their franchises rising, flew teams on charter planes (the Pistons were the first in 1987). Can you imagine Magic and Kareem walking through an airport?

Showtime just missed out, though it was our success that built the league. That's irony! Either way, that season was a big one for Cap, as he set the all-time NBA scoring mark. On April 5, 1984, the big fella hit a 12-foot shot over Utah center Mark Eaton to score his 31,421st point, passing Wilt Chamberlain as the league's all-time scorer (while never shooting a single three). It would be 40 years later when another Laker broke Kareem's record. On February 7, 2023, the 38-year-old LeBron James scored his 38,388th point to break Kareem's number, which the big fella set when he finally retired in 1989. Today, I'm happy the record stayed in L.A.

DURING THE 1983–84 season, I averaged 9 points, 1.4 steals, 5.9 assists (a career high), 3.2 boards, and nearly a block per game, playing almost 30 minutes. More than anything, I worked and was determined to improve my outside shooting. As we played more and as Kareem dominated inside and Magic orchestrated from the perimeter, I knew I had to be a threat from beyond the three-point arc. It was a way to stretch the floor and a way for me to score beyond the Coop-a-Loop plays Earvin and I had perfected. So I raised my three-point shooting percentage from 23.8 percent to 31.4 percent, which was a big jump in an era not as focused on it like today. (Utah's Darrell Griffith led the NBA at 36.1 percent.)

Soon, I would get so good from distance that I would be asked to participate in the league's second-ever three-point contest at the All-Star Game in 1987. But during the 1984 All-Star Game, I did participate in the league's dunk contest (wearing my Air Force 1s). Let's just say, however, that I didn't win. In fact, during the competition, which was held on January 28, 1984, I finished ninth out of what felt like eight, including the great Dr. J. It was embarrassing, especially for someone with good athleticism. I guess I was just nervous. But you can't win them all. So I kept practicing my shooting. That year I finished with 9 points, 5.9 assists, and 3.2 boards per game.

As a shooter, I increased my number of three-point attempts from 0.3 per game to 1.5. Despite this, I didn't let my defense slouch a bit, and I was named to the NBA's All-Defensive First Team. I was tenacious, offering the Lakers gritty, hard-nosed defense. In the games, I was often where the action was, mirroring my opponent, working closely to pressure him or strip him of the ball. Whenever there was a loose ball, I dove for it, either on the court or in the stands. I got my fair share of "beer baths" from fans, whose cups of ale I spilled while hustling. In film study, I worked so hard, I developed a hoops hatred for some players, from Bird to other All-Stars.

Getting an emphatic chase-down block or big steal—both of which were my specialties—makes the crowd roar, and I knew that was often the fuel we needed to get our juices pumping. I checked guards, forwards, centers. I led the league in blocks at the guard spot, thanks to my agile and active hands. I took charges. It was what led Magic to call me maybe the best athlete in all of sports. I loved shutting guys down. But while Bird was the 1984 MVP (his first of three in a row), Earvin, who never talked shit about Bird (or anyone, really), led the league in assists at 13.1 per game. It was quite the year for our rivalry. So when we met in the Finals in June, it made sense.

TOGETHER, MAGIC AND Larry brought the NBA to new heights. The Boston Celtics were founded in 1946. The Lakers were founded the same year, but as the Detroit Gems; they moved to Minnesota and changed their name to the Lakers a year later. Back then, the Lakers employed the great George Mikan, the first transcendent big man the game has ever seen and a five-time NBA champion. Today, Boston and L.A. share the lead in total NBA titles with 17. Each boasts a lineage of players, including Mikan, Wilt, Jerry West, Kareem, Magic, Shaq, Kobe, and LeBron on the Lakers and Bob Cousy, Bill Russell, John Havlicek, Larry Bird, Kevin McHale, Paul Pierce, Kevin Garnett, and Jayson Tatum on the Celtics.

But in 1984, with the world watching, we faced our biggest challenge: playing against each other—finally. All we did was think about each other. Sure, there were other teams in the NBA, but it was Boston and L.A. all that year. It was so bad that I didn't talk to old friends like Dennis Johnson, who joined the Celtics for the 1983–84 season, during the year. He was the enemy. During the regular season that year, we'd beaten Boston both times we played. In the first game, on February 8, 1984, we beat them in their gym by two points. Two weeks later, we won in L.A. by eight. It was a promising prelude to our Finals matchup.

In the playoffs before the 1984 Finals, we were the No. 1 seed in the West and Boston was No. 1 in the East. We swept the Kansas City Kings 3–0 in the first round as Boston beat Washington 3–1. In the second round, we beat Dallas 4–1, and Boston barely beat the Knicks 4–3. We moved past the Phoenix Suns 4–2 in the Western Conference Finals, and the Celtics knocked off Milwaukee 4–1. Something else I remember from this time: I can't remember which game, but the league was trying to institute an on-court dress code (Pat had already started his off-court one). It went in contrast to how I liked to dress, with my armbands, high socks, and drawstrings out.

By now, others had started to emulate my style (including my teammate Bob McAdoo). But I'd been wearing high socks and my strings out since high school. Still, Commissioner David Stern came into our locker room one day during the playoffs and said he wanted everyone in the league to dress alike, that I couldn't wear my signature style (and McAdoo couldn't either). Of course, we appeased him, but after that game, I started to pull my strings out again. I never wanted to lose my style (today, other guys, such as Kevin Durant, rock it). That was the thing about the Lakers—within the team concept, we all had our own individuality.

Anyhow, the much-anticipated 1984 NBA Finals began on May 27 at the Boston Garden. In the opening game, we won 115–109, with Kareem, who was dealing with a painful migraine, scoring 32 and Magic dishing 10 assists. Boston's gangly forward Kevin McHale scored 25. I started the matchup and made Larry work; he scored 24 but shot only 7 of 17 from the field. But Game 2 was a different story. Boston won by three in overtime, and Larry scored 27 to lead a balanced attack from Beantown, which had eight players in double figures. Magic also had 27, Kareem had 20, and James Worthy scored 29. Jamaal Wilkes had 13 off the bench, and McAdoo got 16.

Despite McHale missing two big free throws near the end, we just couldn't take that game. If we had, we might have swept the series. What still kills me from that day was the mistake James made at the end of the game. But really, it was on me. After Magic called a timeout rebounding McHale's second miss, Pat elected to take the ball out in the backcourt instead of advancing it up court, which he calls his biggest mistake as a coach. As for me, I'd fouled out of the game. So when we took the ball out, it was James, not me, passing it in. He got it to Magic, who was double-teamed and threw it back to James.

But young Worthy, almost underneath the Celtics basket, made a bad decision. With 13 seconds left and us up two, he threw a lazy looping pass to Byron Scott, who didn't run to get the ball. Out of nowhere, Boston's Gerald Henderson picked off the floating pass and barreled toward the hoop for a layup that forced OT. To this day, I don't blame Byron, James, or Pat for that; I blame myself for fouling out. Byron and James were young, both learning what championship basketball was about. I needed to be in the game, and I let us down. To this day, that hurts the most out of any other play (even more than it would hurt in 1986 when Ralph Sampson hit his crazy shot—but more on that later).

As for the rest of Game 2, we didn't even get a shot off at the end of regulation, and in the overtime, with Boston's angry, vitriolic fans spitting and screaming, the Celtics won thanks to a Scott Wedman score with 14 seconds left. Well, in Game 3 back in L.A., we killed Boston 137–104, making up for our overtime performance in the previous game. Bird scored 30 on 9-for-16 shooting, but no one else played well. Wedman, who'd hit the clutch shot in Game 2, was Boston's second-leading scorer with 16. I was our second-leading scorer with 17 points, behind only Kareem's 24. Magic had a triple-double: 14 points, 11 boards, and 21 assists in Game 3 (a Finals record).

But Bird was his team's leader. While he was often encouraging, after that game he called his team out in the locker room, saying to reporters, "We played like sissies." That word lit a fire under the Celtics, who went on to beat us 129–125 in L.A. in Game 4. All five Celtics starters scored double digits, including Bird with 29 and 21 boards. Parish got 25 and 12 boards. Dennis Johnson had 22 with 14 assists. For us, Worthy got 30 and Cap scored 32, while Magic had another triple-double with 20 points, 17 assists, and 11 boards.

But more than any stat sheet, Game 4 will be remembered more for McHale's clotheslining of Rambis. The cheap shot of all cheap shots. After McHale upended Kurt, I lunged at M. L. Carr, and that sparked a bench-clearing brawl. Kurt was stunned, but the foul only led to two free throws for him. Later, in the third quarter, Kareem threw an elbow at Bird and they began to jaw. Then Magic and M. L. barked at one another. At the end of regulation, Earvin turned the ball over to Parish, and in OT he missed two big free throws. James missed two more, leading Maxwell to make his famous choke sign walking across the lane. Then James threw away another inbounds pass for a Boston bucket. We had zero composure. They just pushed our buttons. Again, Boston won it 129–125. That's when the Celtics started calling Earvin Tragic Johnson.

Game 5, the infamous Heat Game, was back in Boston. Throughout NBA history, in a 2–2 series, the Game 5 victor almost always wins the series. Because Boston had a better record in the regular season, they hosted it (and would host Game 7 if necessary). This led to another Riley line: "Championships are won on the road." In that catastrophic Game 5, we lost 121–103. Bird had 34 with 17 boards, and 15,000 Celtics fans were relentless, yelling every name and epithet their little minds could muster. Worthy had 22, Cap got 19, and 'Do had 18, but we just couldn't outdo Boston. They had five guys in double digits.

Why is it called the Heat Game? The pace was so fast in that game that referee Hugh Evans passed out. The Garden had no air-conditioning, which was likely planned by legendary jerk, team president Red Auerbach. It got so exhausting with 100-degree temps that Kareem needed oxygen. People were smoking in the stands while our jerseys dripped with sweat. But the series wasn't over, and we took it back to L.A. for Game 6.

We won Game 6 119–108. In the game, Worthy got his revenge on his childhood idol Cedric Maxwell by pushing him into the basket support on a layup attempt. Cornbread wasn't happy about that. Kareem had 30 with 10 boards. Larry matched him with 28 and 14. I had 23 with 8 assists, and Magic had 21 and 10 assists. After our win in Game 6, it was *back* to Boston for the deciding Game 7.

We needed a police escort to take us to the Boston Garden, a place that was home to rats and cockroaches. This time, temps got to about 91 degrees. But whatever the heat index, Boston won 111–102. Maxwell had 24 with 8 boards and 8 assists. But Boston got a steal off Magic with a minute left after we'd come back from being down 14 points to cut it to three thanks in part to my big block on Johnson. Game over. While we should have swept Boston if we had just won Game 2 on their parquet floor, we didn't. These were the results we had to live with.

IT WAS DURING the 1984 Finals when Larry told me, "Coop, I'm gonna wear your ass out." That was strange, because Larry rarely talked to me during the game. He knew trash talk didn't affect me. But I have to admit, he was incredible the entire series. There was even one play in L.A. in Game 4 when I went by him on offense for a layup, but as he got the ball to inbound it, while I was behind him, he stuck his big butt out and I went flying into the cameraman under the hoop. Of course, no foul was called on White Jesus. Bird was several inches taller than me and weighed

40 or 50 pounds more. He knew how to use his size down low. But I was his shadow.

During the 1984 Finals, there was a great deal of chicanery from Boston. Fire alarms went off in our hotels in the middle of the night before the games, and we got crank calls on our phones, even though Pat switched our hotels each time. The local newspapers always found out where we were. We brought our own water to practices, just to guarantee it hadn't been tampered with. It was a heated series, with fights and near-fights galore. People pushing each other into the basket support, elbows flying. Not to mention the Heat Game, which felt like running in sand. After the series, Boston fans threw bottles and who knows what else at our bus as we tried to leave. It was madness, built day by day over years.

In the end, due to their team history, the Celtics knew how to win just a little bit better than we did. And losing to them marked the eighth time in a row that the Celtics had beaten the Lakers in the NBA Finals. Disgraceful. But iron sharpens iron, and we knew this wouldn't be the last time we'd see them. They were more physical than us, they were sharper than us, but we were more talented. Boston had shown they were more mentally tough—they'd dubbed us the L.A. Fakers. From an incredible high of a series came the incredible low for us. But it was our turn to improve, to learn some very important lessons. We knew we'd be back.

I HAVE A TRADITION. Before every game, I say a prayer. It goes like this: "Dear Lord, give us the strength and courage and stamina to endure the game tonight. And if we win, let us win like men. And if we lose, let us lose like men. Amen." Well, my constitution was tested after losing to Boston—a team of goons—in the 1984 Finals. We had always dreaded the possibility of not only losing to the Celtics but of doing it in Boston. At the end, their fans rushed the court even before the final buzzer. Because of that, during every practice in the summer, we repeated the same mantra: *Keep those motherfuckers off the floor.*

As the fans stormed the court after Game 7 in 1984, I was on the other side of the floor from the locker room tunnel. So I had to fight my way through hundreds of people. They were rabid. Kareem got his signature goggles ripped from his head. Kurt Rambis threw a punch at a fan who was trying to rip his jersey off his back. (Kurt broke the guy's nose, which he was later sued for. Well, the guy shouldn't have tried to take Superman's cape!) The Boston fans were shouting, "L.A. sucks! We hate L.A.!" We heard everything they said, and I soaked it all in—we all did—knowing to use it for fuel the next year. Somewhere, Norm Nixon was smiling.

To reporters, Red Auerbach said after the series, "Whatever happened to the Los Angeles dynasty?" But in our locker room, Magic kept saying, "We can never let this happen again." In fact, Magic and I stayed in the shower for some 45 minutes after everyone else had left. "These fucking fans," he said. We could hear them outside. "We can never let them do that shit to us again." We made a commitment. We were the backcourt. The offense and the defense relied on us. He was the star; I was the glue. We sat in the corner of the showers, water falling on us (I cried). "You know what, Coop?" Earvin said. "We'll never lose to these motherfuckers again."

It was the way he said it—when your leader talks that way, you believe him. It makes you sit up and pay attention. We stayed in the shower and talked about the entire 1983–84 season—everything that had led us to that moment, when we were losers. The reporters were waiting on Magic—they wanted his quotes after the loss—but we just kept talking. Magic told me what I needed to do better, including shoot more threes. We said we would take a week or two off and then be back to work. The next day, when we finally got on the plane back to L.A., Magic addressed the team. "This can *never* happen again!" he said. "Boston can *never* beat us again!"

Teammate Testimonial

Bob McAdoo

Michael Cooper was a defender. He was our best defender. We put him on the opponent's best offensive player every game. He was our stopper. We put him on point guards, shooting guards, small forwards—he could guard the three positions on the court equally well. Coop was slippery. People would try to set picks on him, and they couldn't do it because he was just . . . his footwork was just impeccable. He could get through screens or get around screens so well. The thing about it was, he could also jump! You'd have small forwards that were 6'8" like Larry Bird. We even put Coop on Larry Bird, who outweighed him by 30 pounds. He could just guard anybody.

When I got to the Lakers, Coop was the first one to give me the lowdown on what was going on. The Lakers when I got there were going through some changes because the coach had just gotten fired. Mitch Kupchak had just injured his knee. That's when the team came and got me. The Lakers weren't functioning well at the time. They were playing slow-down basketball, which they didn't really like. They wanted to get up and down the court, and when I came, they changed the dynamic a little bit.

I've always been a fast-break type of guy, and when Mitch went down, I was a different type of player than him, so that helped speed the game up, which made people happier. Magic could run the ball up and down the court. Norm Nixon could get up and down the court. It wasn't just post up to Mitch and Kareem. That's when everybody started talking about Showtime. It just changed everything. We started to play fast-break basketball.

Of course, nobody wants to come off the bench, but Coop and I would notice when we were playing that if the team was down or tied, our bench was so proficient that we'd come in and we'd get a 10- to 15-point lead, and we'd get pissed when Pat Riley would take us out. And then practicing, we'd always play against the first team, and we beat them all the time when we had scrimmages. We beat them *all* the time!

We went to four straight Finals together when I was with the Lakers. We were disappointed because in 1982 we won, but in 1983 and '84, we just had too many injuries. We thought we could have won it every year. We just had too many injuries. In '83 and '84, that cost us championships. So that was disappointing. When you get to the championship, you want to win, and when you lose a championship, it feels like you lost in the first round. When we played Boston, there was so much hype for the Lakers because the Lakers had never beaten Boston in a championship series. And when we finally pulled through in '85, that was probably our most satisfying win.

Chapter 10

No One Forgets a Champion

I USED TO LIE AWAKE AT NIGHT THINKING ABOUT LARRY BIRD, the one they called the Hick from French Lick. We'd now lost two Finals in a row, and in the process Bird had gotten his second ring, to match Magic's two. As I lay awake thinking about Bird's every move on the court, I wondered if he was up at night thinking about me. At home, I watched hours of film, every game we played, watching them over and over, seeing what I could do differently against him. Wanda had to pull the VCR plug many nights. Later, at Bird's retirement in 1992, he told reporters that out of everyone in the league, I gave him the most trouble. "I'll take that to the grave," he said.

Watching video is the key to success, even if I did obsess about it a bit (I had 130 tapes of Bird). But I got that from Pat Riley, who was equally focused on watching people's tendencies. You have to know your own weaknesses as well as you know your opponents'. They're watching your film; you can believe that. So ask yourself, "Am I predictable on defense? On offense?" Watching tape helps you imagine the game playing out. Who will move where, how? When I played Bird or Danny Ainge or Dennis Johnson, I had a plan. For Bird, I learned to overplay him, but I had to fight if he took me down low. I played up on Ainge since he didn't like to dribble before he shot.

Study and think positive, that's the key. But Larry was so good that he could set up a great play in the fourth quarter with something simple in the first. With him, a move in one direction one second could lead to another that might win the game at the buzzer. He was so smart, so skilled, and he never rested. You had to worry about him with the ball and without. He was the game's best shooter (before Steph Curry) and one of its best passers (along with Magic). He could rebound like a center and he was an excellent defender (just ask Isiah Thomas about the 1987 playoffs). Bird was competitive, he wouldn't quit, and he did whatever it took to win.

I think enough years have gone by that people like me, guys like Magic and Kareem and James Worthy, are all finally willing to admit that Larry Bird is the most complete player the NBA has ever seen. His fundamental game was basically flawless, and on top of that, he was like a savant out there.

How hard is it for people to admit that he's the guy? I don't know, but I was just talking to my Lakers comrades last week. All of us were in a room—Kareem, Magic, James Worthy, me—and we got to talking about Bird, and we all agreed he's probably the greatest player ever to play the game.

There's not much he wasn't the best at. Larry Bird is probably the closest thing to GOAT as there can be. Kareem even said that Wilt Chamberlain said Bird was the best player ever. I mean, why are all these Lakers guys saying this stuff, man? It's probably taken us all years of hindsight, but there's no doubt in my mind.

Wilt knew it before all of us did. I think in 100 years from now, artificial intelligence robots will probably factor in all the data, and Bird will pop out as the answer to who was the best.

Bird, for as good as he was, wasn't a loud trash-talker like Chuck Person or Rick Mahorn, but when he talked—at least to me—it was quick and concise. Preparing for him was fun but tedious. His skill was the kindling that helped build the fire of the greatest rivalry in basketball. I worked hard guarding him. Kareem said of my effort, "[Coop] would play Larry's right hand. Larry was good with using his left hand. He would make great passes with his left hand. But he didn't shoot with his left hand very often. But Coop would have his notebook out. When it got serious, that's what he prepared to do."

Today, teams and players aren't going at each other like we did. Today, everyone knows each other and there is camaraderie among guys. But when we played the Celtics, it was all-out war. By the time the 1984–85 season came around, we thought we knew everything they were going to do, and vice versa. The Celtics were coached by K.C. Jones, who had played for Boston in the 1960s and won eight rings, so they were prepared.

I knew Larry so well that I felt like I knew when he went to bed and when he got up to use the bathroom! And he probably knew everything about me—how I prepared, my tendencies. But I also had to learn how some other players on the team played, including Dennis Johnson, Danny Ainge, Cedric Maxwell, even Kevin McHale. In practice, Riley—the Armani suit model with slicked-back hair—was a taskmaster. He ran the shit out of us, driven by the images of Kareem and others sucking oxygen in Boston in 1984. His attention to detail was obsessive. But when Boston called a play like four-down or zipper, we knew what it was, where the ball would go.

By the time the 1985 playoffs came, Purple-and-Gold blood would have dripped out of each and every Lakers player if you'd cut us. Throughout the regular season, we followed each of Boston's 63 wins and 19 losses. Unfortunately, the Celtics got home-court advantage in the 1985 Finals because we'd won 62, one fewer. Well, Riley did say championships were won on the road. While we prepared for that, the NBA continued to rise in the public eye. Commissioner David Stern, who'd taken over in 1984, was capitalizing on the Lakers-Celtics rivalry with the fans. And over the summer, the league's future—Jordan and Hakeem—were drafted. *Uh-oh.*

BUT IT WAS still our time now. And the Lakers were close-knit. Sometimes for reasons outside of ball. Over the years, one of the things Kareem Abdul-Jabbar and I bonded over was our love of music. But on January

30, 1983, Cap experienced one of the lowest moments of his life. We'd lost to the Celtics that night, but Kareem had it worse than the rest of us. That night, his million-dollar L.A. home burned to the ground from an electrical fire, which took 90 percent of his possessions with it. Thankfully, Kareem's girlfriend, Cheryl, and their son, Amir, were able to flee the house through a window, but it was terrible nonetheless.

With that fire went 3,000 jazz albums Kareem had collected over the years, turned into a smoldering pile of vinyl. But in the wake of that, something incredible happened. Lakers fans from all over began sending him their records, including ones he'd lost in the blaze. The gesture warmed Kareem's heart. From tragedy came compassion. It opened up Kareem's spirit to the fans too. Born in New York, Kareem's father, Ferdinand, was a jazz musician, a trombone player, who performed in Harlem during the bebop era with the likes of Dizzy Gillespie, John Coltrane, Miles Davis, and Charlie Parker. So the music held a lot of meaning to the big fella.

Of course, basketball itself is a lot like jazz—free-flowing, improvisational, smooth at times but also wild at others. Often composed of quintets, guys who blended together but also stood out on their own—those are some of the reasons I loved it too. Miles Davis, Nina Simone, John Coltrane—these were our icons. (My favorite album ever is Miles's *Kind of Blue*.) I've loved jazz since I was 10, when Tom, my uncle, turned me on to it. Tom had served in Vietnam, and it was there where he learned about the music's history. He brought albums back from war in his duffle bag, and he shared them with me on our old record players in the house. That's how I learned about Miles.

Later, I got a chance to meet Davis during what ended up his final show, at the Hollywood Bowl in 1991. That will stay with me in my heart forever—the notes, his timing. Kareem is one of the biggest jazz enthusiasts I know. He turned me on to the great Herbie Hancock; the two of them were close friends. Cap, who grew up with the greats in his home, and I would have conversations about the music. He would show me things he listened to and loved, and I would do the same. We'd trade records. It's these kinds of bonds that build lifelong friendships and the

I was so skinny as a kid, my grandmother called me Sticks. Here I am in my school picture at age eight.

Even though we weren't always living together, my mother, Dezzie Jean Cooper (shown here in 1976), was always with me.

My grandmother, Ardessie Butler, was the glue that held our big family together, and one of the most important people in my life.

I got cut not once but twice from the varsity squad at Pasadena High School.

I wore jersey No. 42 because of Connie Hawkins and football player Paul Warfield.

Starting my collegiate career at Pasadena Community College wasn't an obvious fast-track to the NBA, but it was the right decision for me. Not only did I develop as a player but I learned some serious lessons about accountability.

In 1975 I transferred to the University of New Mexico, where I had a great two years with the Lobos.

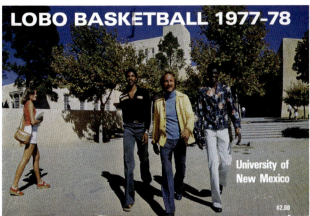

Coach Norm Ellenberger (center) was a shrewd recruiter who took a good look at JUCO All-Americans like me (right) and Marvin Johnson.

I was honored to be recognized by UNM in 2024.

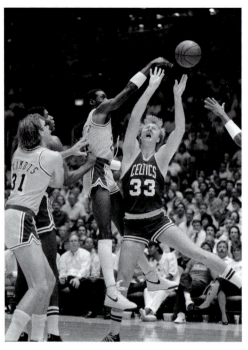

Iron sharpens iron, and nobody made each other better than the Lakers and Celtics during our championship rivalry in the 1980s. Courtesy of Getty Images

Sure, Magic and I had our Coop-a-Loops, but I also worked hard on my three-point shot. Courtesy of Getty Images

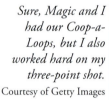

Pat Riley was known for his Hollywood swagger, but he was a detail-oriented coach whose discipline and preparedness left nothing to chance. Courtesy of Getty Images

Known to basketball as the Logo, Jerry West was my guardian angel. Courtesy of the Associated Press

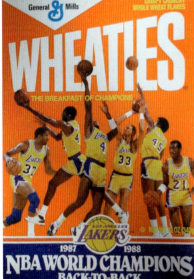

Kids, work hard and eat your Wheaties. One day you might be on the box.

1987 was a very good year. I won Defensive Player of the Year and the J. Walter Kennedy Citizenship Award, and the Lakers notched another world championship. Courtesy of Getty Images

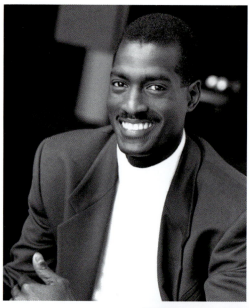

My second act as a model and actor wasn't quite the "showtime" my basketball career had been.

In the WNBA, I saw more success. As head coach, I was fortunate to have Lisa Leslie as a player on an L.A. Sparks team that won back-to-back championships in 2001 and 2002. Courtesy of the Associated Press

I even got a shot at coaching in the NBA, as interim head coach for the Denver Nuggets in 2005. Courtesy of the Associated Press

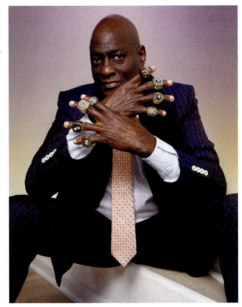

*Winning five championships
was sweet, but the
lasting brotherhood
between us is sweeter.*
Courtesy of Hernan Rodriguez,
https://hernanphotography.com/

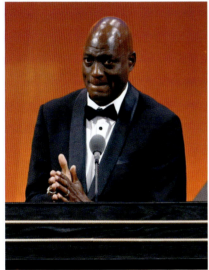

*Being inducted into the Naismith
Memorial Basketball Hall of Fame in
2024 was the honor of a lifetime.* Courtesy
of the Associated Press

*Magic was on hand
when the Lakers
retired my No. 21
in 2025.*

Being a grandfather is a new, wonderful experience.

I've been fortunate enough to have coached all my sons; here I am coaching Nils on his Two One Elite AAU team.

My entire family was there when I was inducted into the Hall of Fame: (left to right) my son Michael II, daughter Simone, daughter-in-law Princess, son-in-law Brandon, daughter-in-law Lisa, son Miles, me, son Nils, and wife Yvonne.

deep connection that teammates need to win on the biggest stage in sports.

Thinking about the Showtime Lakers in the mid-1980s, we were a lot like a jazz quintet. Magic was our Miles. The person around whom we all followed and flowed. The bright trumpeter. Kareem, who called me the Lakers' "defensive stopper," was like upright bassist Ron Carter. Wise, stoic. Like Cap, Carter is prolific. He's the most recorded jazz bassist in history. James Worthy would be Herbie Hancock, an underrated genius, as entertaining as he was fundamentally sound, as much a joy to be around as he was to hear. Then there's Jamaal Wilkes, who'd be drummer Tony Williams. Part mystery, part dynamo. And I would be Wayne Shorter on the sax. The X factor.

ALONG WITH WINNING, losing can be important. And that was very much the case for us after 1984. We were angry. While we never wanted to fail, losing to the Celtics in that series, which was one of the NBA's greatest Finals ever, was illuminating. It taught us how to win—that's what losing can do, if you listen and learn from it. As for me, the new 1984–85 season was when I solidified myself in Lakers lore for good as far as I am concerned. That was the year when I became the ultimate sixth man, the Platonic ideal of the position.

Jerry West and Pat Riley talked to me about my role, and while they didn't say I'd never start on the team, my job was clear. They said that for the Lakers to win, they needed me to be the best possible sixth man off the bench the league had ever seen. I thought back to Havlicek and how his example in Boston would let me build and become even better. So it was 1984–85 when I became *Michael Cooper*. I cherished my role with the Lakers, as the league's best guard defender, and as Magic's backup point guard. I was our bench "igniter," as Riley called it. Although the role limited me in terms of what awards I might receive—the league doesn't often make bench players formal All-Stars or retire their jerseys—all I cared about was the ultimate prize: winning another championship.

Ahead of the 1984–85 season, I also signed a new multiyear contract with the Lakers in which I earned not some $30,000 for the year but more than 10 times that, garnering $325,000 for the season. While that's not nearly what players get today—some get more than $30 million!—it was a huge deal and a big upgrade in the moment. (In 1987–88 that number would double again, and I'd make about $676,500 for that season. Good money!) As far as my basketball ability, I was getting stronger by the day, physically and mentally. And I challenged teammates such as Byron Scott and James Worthy in practice to be better right along with me.

The whole goal was to never, ever, ever lose to the Boston Celtics again. You know who else had seen enough from Boston? Julius Erving. The man even punched Larry Bird during a game on November 9, 1984, in the Boston Garden. Apparently, Larry had said the wrong thing to Dr. J, calling him old and over the hill, and Julius had just had enough. A scuffle ensued, and then Charles Barkley and Moses Malone held Larry from behind when Erving punched him three times in the head. As good and well-respected as Bird was, I think he learned a lesson not to cross the line with a basketball god. But that was the NBA for you in the 1980s.

If that happened today, Dr. J would be suspended for 50 games! The NBA doesn't want that behavior now. But in the 1984–85 season, things were different. It was a different league. And, well, we loved it. During the year, Riley used to tell us something that actually surprised me. He would address the team and tell us to remember to stop once in a while to "smell the roses." That's when I was sure we were going to win in 1985, though I'm not sure why. Pat said one day all of this would go away in a flash. Maybe he was thinking about his own life, his own father, who'd played minor league baseball and whose career ended before he made the majors.

Riley told us to appreciate the fans, that they'd be gone, and no longer cheering our names, before we knew it. We were all in our twenties (except for a few of us, including Kareem), and we weren't trying to hear about the future or stopping to smell any roses. But he was right. Occasionally, it would sink in, and I'd steal a look at Magic or Byron and think, *Man, am I lucky I landed on this team in my hometown!* Today, I know how fast

28 turns to 38 and even 68! So I'll always be grateful to the fans in L.A., all those millions of people who embraced me. Who cheered for us. Who were there for our lowest lows and highest highs.

PART OF GETTING older in the league is seeing young guys come up. While my biggest challenges up until then had been George Gervin, Andrew Toney, David Thompson, Dennis Johnson, Gus Williams, Larry Bird, and some others, a new guy had come in through the draft: Michael Jeffrey Jordan. He was a player who tried to win games single-handedly, and while I knew I could take a break on him when he didn't have the ball, when he did have it, he was maybe the best ever. And he knew it too. Michael was arrogant as all hell—to a fault, if you ask me. But that's also what made him so great, the fuel he fed on. He didn't ever think he should lose. And in the 1990s, he rarely did.

Magic and Bird showed the world what basketball could be. But for the most part, they played below the rim. Jordan was the first star after them who took the game above it. He did so in the flashiest of ways. The way I tried to defend Michael was to push him to a side of the court. He loved to go down the lane, hang in the air, and score. It's what made the Detroit Pistons years later create the Jordan Rules, where they knocked him down and roughed him up in their fight for Midwest supremacy. But I worked to stay in front of him and push him to a side. For the most part, it worked well enough. He was young, though—still developing as a player.

THE NBA CAN be an unforgiving league. The best example of that in 1985 was Silk. Jamaal Wilkes's last game for the Lakers was February 1, 1985. He'd lost his starting spot to James Worthy during the year; Worthy had filled in for him well early in the 1984 playoffs when Silk missed games due to a stomach virus. But Jamaal missed the last 40 games of the 1984–85 season after tearing up his left knee, and the team waived him in August 1985. While he played for the Clippers the next year, he was never the same, unfortunately. Let me say, Jamaal is and forever will be a Lakers legend. But the game can be cruel. We all find that out one day or another.

His injury started the second era of Showtime. The first began in 1979–80 when Magic was a rookie. He, Norm, Jamaal, Kareem, and I helped the team win two rings. Now, the second with Magic, Cap, Byron, James, and me was unfolding. Not only that, but the league was getting stronger. Teams such as Jordan's Bulls, Isiah Thomas's Pistons, Terry Cummings's Bucks, and later Mark Price's Cleveland Cavaliers were powerful. That was the East, along with Bird and Boston. Out West, we had the Twin Towers in Houston, Stockton and Malone in Utah, Gervin's Spurs, Clyde Drexler (whom I feared) in Portland, Alex English's Nuggets, and the rising Phoenix Suns.

But the Celtics defeating us in 1984 made it harder for all. We were *determined*, and no person or team would stand in our way. We'd see the schedule weeks ahead of time and mark down games we knew we'd win. We marched to the playoffs, earning a 62–20 record without a doubt of what the season's outcome would be. We easily traversed the few ups and downs of the year. We had no internal turmoil, and all of our roles were defined. Byron fit well at shooting guard, and James was perfect as the starting small forward. Kurt was a tough power forward. Magic and Cap were All-Stars at point guard and center. And I was our versatile sixth man.

That season, I earned votes for Sixth Man of the Year too, finishing fourth for the award. It was the third season in a row that I got votes for the Defensive Player of the Year Award too. If there was one accolade I did secretly covet, it was that one, but it wasn't something I talked about. I also finished the year scoring 8.6 points per game to go along with 5.2 assists and 3.1 rebounds. But more than anything, my teammates and I were focused on the playoffs. That would be the true test of our abilities, and we wanted revenge when it came to playing Boston. We were practically salivating.

TO BEGIN THE playoffs, we swept the Suns 3–0 and then beat the Blazers 4–1. In the Western Conference Finals, we took down the Denver Nuggets 4–1. Boston, here we come! After losing in 1984, we knew we had to be better, mentally and physically. Thankfully for us, the 1984–85 season was the year our legendary trainer Gary Vitti entered the picture. Over the course of his career, Vitti would be a part of 12 Lakers Finals teams, earning 8 rings. Vitti had worked with the Utah Jazz a few seasons prior to coming to L.A., and now, with us, he instituted new strength training, which Coach Pat Riley also embraced. With him, we evolved from finesse to fitness.

We had been getting beaten up in 1983 and 1984 by the more physical Eastern Conference teams, and Vitti helped us put some muscle in our running game, especially for our frontcourt players. But in Game 1 of the 1985 Finals, nothing could help us. The Celtics were looking to repeat as champs for the first time in nearly two decades. And they had home-court advantage since they'd won 63 games to our 62. The series, which for the first time since 1955 went back to a 2-3-2 format, opened in Beantown. Boston had a big front line with two-time reigning Sixth Man of the Year Kevin McHale (then a starter), Robert Parish (a tough matchup for us), and Bird.

They also had a great backcourt with guards Danny Ainge (a former MLB and NFL prospect), Maxwell, and Dennis Johnson. But to us, it didn't matter who they had. We were finally seeing our nemesis again in living color. We were certain we were going to win. Personally, I wasn't afraid of anything walking in green during that series. Both Magic and Bird had two rings each (though Magic had the college championship), and this was for all the tiebreaking marbles. We just *had* to beat Boston. Yet Game 1 went about as bad as it could have. Today, it's known as the Memorial Day Massacre for how badly Boston beat us up.

We lost—but can you guess the score? Well, it was 148–114. They beat us like a drum. If you believe in signs, this wasn't a good one. Kareem was only able to muster 12 points with 3 rebounds against Boston's big front line. He was 38 years old, ancient for the NBA, but that was no excuse.

For Boston, Parish outplayed him and Scott Wedman went 11-for-11 from the field for 26 points—that's how good (I mean lucky) Boston was. Bird, Parish, McHale, Ainge, Dennis Johnson—they all had great games. M. L. Carr was wearing out his wrist waiving his towel in celebration. The fans went nuts.

Afterward, Pat Riley tore us to shreds. But he did it in an especially unique way. After the loss, we were in the locker room, and no one said a word. We were expecting a speech from Riley, but he just said, "Put your clothes on; we're going back to the hotel." We got on the bus and thought we were going to get torn up in practice the next day. But Riley said, "Go to your room, drop your bags off, and come back down to the conference room for a meeting." When we got to the conference room, Pat had the video all set up, with chairs around, and he said, "Have a seat." No one said a word. Riley made us sit there and watch Game 1 twice in a row. When it was done, he rewound it again. And when you made a mistake on film, he rewound it.

Once the tape was done the second time, Riley put the lights on and walked over to this big green chalkboard. We thought he was getting ready to write some words of wisdom. By now, we'd been sitting there for two hours *after* the game. But he just walked up to the board and said, "This fucking shit will *never happen again*!" And he punched the board. He put a big hole in it. "This will *never* happen *again*! You guys better get your fucking jobs done and win this next game!" He threw the chalkboard down and just walked out. We were left sitting there. That was it for us. Magic, who'd taken 1984 so badly, got *that* look in his eye again.

Thankfully, it was only Game 1, and we weren't lost. Despite the horrible showing, we had been sharpened over the course of the season, and we still had a chance to win. We were mentally and physically tough. Kareem had been in the front row at our team film session. He never sat up front, but there he was. That's when he spoke up, echoing Riley, saying he would never play as poorly as he had in the Massacre. It was rare for Cap to make a statement like that. So we knew he really meant it. Usually, it was Magic who talked. Kareem was the strong, silent type. But he said the loss was on him and that he'd never let us down again.

The rest of us had a chip on our shoulder now too. It was time to come out like champs for Game 2. Beforehand, Cap asked Riley if his dad could ride on the team bus to the game. Pat, who loved rules, forbade family on the bus. But he made the exception for Kareem, even talking about his own father to inspire us. In Game 2 in Boston, Cap, who everyone had called too old, had 30 and 17 with 8 assists and 3 blocks. I added 22 points, shooting 8 of 9 from the floor. And we won 109–102. Game 3 was no different. We delivered a smackdown in L.A., winning 136–111. Cap broke the all-time playoff scoring record (held by Jerry West).

In Games 2 and 3, I kept Bird from taking flight. In those, he shot 17 of 42 from the field. For us in Game 3, James Worthy scored 29, Cap had 26, McAdoo added 19, and Magic was a rebound shy of a triple-double. But Game 4 was closer, with Boston scraping out a two-point win. McHale had a good game, scoring 28 with 12 boards. And Dennis Johnson hit a buzzer-beater for Boston, netting two of his 27 points. But we had resolve. We won the crucial Game 5 by nine points, 120–111, for the third and last game in L.A. before we went back to Boston. The Celtics had five players score 20 or more, but James and Cap each had 30-plus.

In Game 5 I also added 10 points and 7 assists. Now, headed for Boston, we had one goal: win Game 6. Magic told us, "Pack one suit." We weren't staying for two games. We didn't want to see what the Celtics leprechauns had in store for us if we went to a Game 7 *in there*. And you know what? We did it. Worthy had 28; Magic had 14 points, 14 assists, and 10 boards; Cap scored 29; and I added 9. We beat the Celtics 111–100 on their home floor, stunning the Boston faithful, who had to watch us celebrate there. Bird dropped 28 points and McHale had 32, but no one else for Boston helped. And Red Auerbach couldn't light his famous victory cigar.

The score was tied at the half, but coming out of the break, we held Boston to 18 points in the third quarter, proving our strength and our defensive ability, two things glitzy Showtime was often criticized for. The only real scare, for me at least, was when I got hurt during the game. It was so bad that I couldn't walk, and I had to be carried off the court and into the locker room by my teammates Larry Spriggs and Mike McGee. If there had been a Game 7, I'm not sure if I would have been able to play in it (but I darn sure would have tried!). Thankfully, we didn't need one. We won that night in Boston.

To the local fans' credit, they cheered me as I got carried off. Some might think the locals would have thrown popcorn at me. But instead they gave me a (brief) standing ovation. Even the TV announcers noticed it and said something about the city's class. After the game, Kareem earned the Finals MVP, showing it's not how you start but how you finish. As for those other fans who were so ready to storm the court the previous year—those who called me Cooper the Pooper and worse in the heat of battle, those who secretly energized me with their trash talk—we sent them home.

One reason we prevailed, along with the play of our stars, was our bench. Larry Spriggs, 'Do, Mike McGee, me—we held it down in the series. It made sense—during practices, we often beat the starters in scrimmages. Now, on the biggest stage, we showed that we were the best bench in the league, and that the Lakers were the best team in the world. The star of the bench, offensively, was McAdoo (Boston and Detroit fans called him McAdon't when he played there), who felt he could start on half the teams in the league. But he wanted that ring, and now he had two! We all had skills, and we all covered up for one another—that's what a good bench does. We were so good that our starters couldn't take days off or else we'd take their jobs. (Today, it's not like that in the NBA, but I digress.)

ONE QUESTION I get a lot today is whether I would trade the rings I won with the Lakers for a giant payday like even bench players such as Ben Simmons get in the NBA today. While I drool at the money, I know that champions live forever while money is easily spent. Especially when you consider that Finals win over Boston *in Boston*, snapping a streak of losses by L.A. against the Celtics. Before, our franchise had been 0–8 against them in the Finals. But our win was what we were *supposed* to do. It was a workmanlike atmosphere all season preparing for it. Yeah, we'd had a little fun here and there. But we knew our mission: *Revenge. Revenge. Revenge.*

For the season, I made the All-Defensive First Team. That was sweet but not as sweet as the win. Growing up, I'd watched Boston beat L.A. over and over, with Elgin Baylor and Jerry West losing year after year. But 1985 was *our* year. The dominance of Boston over the Lakers was dead. It felt so good to squash that in Boston—to leave those dopey fans slack-jawed, wondering what happened. From there, we were the only visiting team to win the Finals in the Boston Garden. They won because Red knew all the tricks, from dead spots in the floor to keeping the locker room frigid in winter and sweltering in summer. All Bird could do was say they'd get us next year.

ON A MORE serious topic, it's important to note the influence of race in the Boston–Los Angeles rivalry. Not only did the matchup pit East Coast versus West Coast and cold Boston against warm L.A., glitz and glamour against Beantown's so-called blue-collar mentality, but it pit Larry and Magic against one another. While both were from the Midwest (Magic from Lansing, Michigan, and Larry from French Lick, Indiana), and while America got to know both in the 1979 NCAA Finals, what was most stark between the two was that Magic was Black and Larry was white. Feeding into all this was that Boston, a very white city, was known as a racist one.

Boston was the city that Celtics great Bill Russell left and never returned to. He was a former MVP and 11-time champion for the Celtics, and still white people in Boston would break into his house and defecate on his bed and walls while he was away (until he told newspapers he owned a gun). Later, Black players in the NBA rarely signed with Boston if they were free agents. Of course, many of the people there were good, hardworking souls, but the angry, racist minority was very real.

The flip side of this coin wasn't pretty either. Meaning the Black players on Boston would often get painted with an Uncle Tom brush. The thinking was—and this was wrong on our part—that because they played for and repped what we saw as a racist city, they were then only feeding into that. This is something Cedric Maxwell has since spoken eloquently about, wishing we didn't portray him like a subservient person. While it was okay to trash-talk, sometimes that stuff went too far, and today I'm not proud of how we acted at times. Another problem was that the Celtics were thought of as this collection of players who were the Great White Hope in a majority Black league. Bird, McHale, and Ainge, three of the team's biggest names, were white as vanilla ice cream.

While Bird had earned the respect of Black barbershops across the country, we felt the NBA and its refs favored the Celtics and their lily-white roster. We felt like the refs called more fouls for Boston, that we couldn't touch their fair-skinned players (though I was never one to jaw at the refs). And the media made it all worse. It was clear the Boston-L.A. rivalry was as much about race as it was hoops, as much about the playground style versus the traditional NBA. But that's life. You have to survive it. Today, most of us—from Cedric Maxwell to me—are pals, thank goodness. In the end, I'm just happy we freaking won in 1985.

Teammate Testimonial

Byron Scott

When I hear the name Michael Cooper, I think just what an unbelievable person. He's really the salt of the earth. When I think about him from a basketball standpoint, I think about one of the best defensive players I've ever seen in my life. That goes back to playing with him, that goes back to watching him in college, that goes to the present day. I haven't seen anybody over the last 10 to 15 years who can guard people the way he guards people. He was just phenomenal. So for me to also be able to play with that Lakers team and learn from him on that end of the floor, it was amazing.

Magic, him, and me—we always hung out on the road. We always went to dinner and the movies together. So we had a lot of time together. We also spent time together when we weren't playing because his wife, my wife, Cookie, they all were friends. So we spent a lot of time together. One of my favorite memories of Coop was the Michael Cooper Backyard Boogie! They would have everybody over, and Wanda, his ex-wife, would cook. We just had an unbelievable time, spending time together, the whole team. He would invite the whole team. But that was Coop. He was always very, very much a team player. Very team-oriented, very family-oriented. But those were some of my favorite times, just being able to spend days with him and the family.

It's crazy, because my first year, obviously, they weren't real excited about me being there. So he and Magic both were testing me and hitting me and all that stuff during practices. And I think after about a week, I think Coop hit me with an elbow and I told him, "All right, next one of y'all throw a 'bow, I'm punching you! I'm tired of this!" I think just gaining that respect from them was beneficial. I had huge respect back then for Magic and Coop because I watched them and I knew how great they were and I knew what type of players they were. I didn't yet know what type of people they were, but I knew what type of players they were.

But I think our bonds continued to grow because of our work ethic. All three of us were maniacs in the gym. We all wanted to be great. We all wanted to win. So we had those things in common, and we didn't care who got it done. We just wanted to win. We wanted championships. I think that was part of our biggest bonds—we had the same DNA. We wanted to win, and we were going to go out there and do our best every single night. And I think with us three, the one thing we had in common was that we just didn't want to let each other down. We made sure we had each other's backs every single game, no matter what. That meant in the '80s if Coop got into it, I was going to be right there and Magic was going to be right there. If I got into it with somebody, then they would have my back.

It was just a beautiful relationship on and off the court. And I think the thing that speaks so highly about that relationship is that we're all still so close to this day. We call each other; we try to spend time with each other as much as possible, even though we know all of us are busy doing this and that. But our relationship to this day, our bond, is still really tight. I look at the Chicago Bulls—Scottie Pippen and all these guys—and that would never happen with us. We're just that close; we love each other that much and we care about each other that much.

In terms of our Finals appearances, I think the biggest one for me is being able to go back to Boston and close out a series and beat the Celtics in the Boston Garden, where no team had done that, including no Lakers team. And being the first team to win back-to-back championships in almost 20 years. Just that memory in the locker room. And then that night afterward. Pat Riley was so great. We had a big party in Boston in our hotel at a ballroom, and Pat had a tuxedo on, so obviously he had planned this! The memories of that team and winning a championship in Boston that year are probably the biggest and fondest memories I'll ever have.

Chapter 11

Houston, You Are a Problem

In the summer of 1985, Jerry West did it again. This time he struck gold late in the first round of the 1985 NBA Draft. At the top of the list was Georgetown's Patrick Ewing, who was selected first by the New York Knicks. Wayman Tisdale went second, Xavier McDaniel went fourth. Chris Mullin went seventh. Detlef Schrempf and Charles Oakley followed. Karl Malone got picked 13th, Joe Dumars went 18th, and Terry Porter went 24th (Lithuanian Arvydas Sabonis went 77th). But just ahead of Porter, the Los Angeles Lakers selected A.C. Green, a senior forward from Oregon State University. With that, West hit another home run.

The late 1980s was the golden era of the NBA. That's when the NBA boasted the most Hall of Famers in its history. But sometimes it's the role players who make the biggest differences. For us, that was embodied by A.C. Green. Jerry West knew the two most important parts of team-building. He could identify talent and he could see how it fit into a team—specifically ours. From Byron to James to A.C. to me, we were all people he selected for the Lakers roster, likely to the surprise of many. Today, A.C. remains one of my favorite teammates. In the 1980s rookies were to be seen but not heard. He picked up on that quickly at first before impressing us all.

Green has told the story of seeing Kareem for the first time in training camp. He likened it to *Jurassic Park*, seeing Cap eclipse the sun like a T. rex. But he didn't let that intimidate him. He'd block guys' shots in practice (including mine) and he'd hit his midrange jumper. At that time, though, the NBA was changing. It was getting faster. Rosters weren't built like they had been, with the big seven-foot center and 6'11" power forward. It was more about athleticism, speed, and agility. You had to be strong, but you couldn't be a Frankenstein. In college, A.C. could score (notching more than 19 per game as a senior). But in the pros, he would have to fit a role.

With A.C.'s emergence, Kurt would soon be part of the bench. But that wouldn't be for another year. For now, it was the 1985–86 season, and we were hoping to repeat as champs. But we weren't the only team retooling. On the other side of the country, Boston made its moves. As images of Larry Bird rewound and fast-forwarded in my dreams, Red Auerbach, who had built the Celtics through deft trades, was dreaming of more roster changes. Losing to us didn't sit well. So what did they do? They got bigger and whiter (I kid!). On September 6, 1985, Boston traded the 1981 Finals MVP Cedric Maxwell, who'd been hurt, to the Clippers for Bill Walton.

A star at UCLA in college in the early 1970s, Walton led the Portland Trail Blazers to the 1977 NBA title, earning the MVP award the next year. But lower-body injuries destroyed his career. He was a two-time All-Star who could've been a 10-time All-Star had he been able to stay healthy. Now, after six disappointing years with the Clippers, he came to Boston, set to be the team's sixth man with McHale now in the starting lineup. (Though I heard L.A. could have gotten him first.) It was a risk, but if it worked, it would be a victory for him and Boston.

While Beantown was happy, Maxwell wasn't. I remember him telling me a sad story about the Clippers. He'd complained to a ref in a game about a call, but the ref turned to him, unhelpful, saying, "You don't play for the Celtics no more!" That summed it up for Cedric.

Back in Beantown, the Celtics had an incredible season, I'm sorry to say. They'd won 63 games the year before, and during the 1985–86 season, they won 67. Bird got his third of three MVPs in a row. The guys in green also went 40–1 at home in the regular season and 10–0 in the playoffs. That's a record that's never been broken. Their one home loss came December 6 against the athletic Portland Trail Blazers with Clyde Drexler, Terry Porter, and Mychal Thompson. Boston lost 121–103.

Two months later, Larry beat them in their gym, scoring 47 using only his left hand. But while Boston worked on itself collectively, I continued to work on myself individually. I'd gotten into the craw of Boston fans for my tight defense against their hero, Bird. So much so that I was getting "fan" mail from Boston zip codes—cards written by Celtics fans that said things like, "Hey, Mr. Cooper, I appreciate and respect what you do. But I don't like you because you wear a Lakers uniform." That was fine. I felt the same way about them. The truth is the rivalry was perfect. If Magic had been on Boston and Larry had been on L.A., it wouldn't have been the same.

In the gym, I practiced 500 to 1,000 shots a day. And for the 1985–86 season, I increased my three-point percentage to 38.7 percent, which is excellent even by today's standards. The year was also the fourth in a row that I played every game (the following would mark the fifth). I needed to be a weapon for the team every season—or else risk getting dealt. I dribbled a ball everywhere I went. Around the house, outside, from my car to the gym. I like making practice fun, and so I made myself dribble in my daily life. You can't stay the same and expect to win. I needed to be better as a backup point guard, shooter, and defender against bigger and smaller players.

So I worked. At the same time, the NBA was working us hard. Ahead of the 1985–86 regular season, the league had us play the Celtics a whopping four times in the preseason. By this time, we all just plain hated each other. And that feud even led to a brawl during the second game of those four. It was at the Forum when bruising bench big man Maurice

Lucas, who'd been brought in to replace McAdoo but never quite fit in, got into it with Robert Parish and both benches cleared. On the bottom of the pile of players, Celtics coach K.C. Jones and I were wrestling. But that's what our rivalry did—even the coaches got in the scrum.

BASKETBALL WASN'T ALL about determined focus. We had some fun too. The Lakers were a family, and so bus rides were particularly memorable and jocular. Most of the things we talked about there in the back seats, I can't talk about today. Some secrets can't be said out of school. Riley sat up front, but Byron, Mike McGee, James Worthy, Magic, and I were in the back. Kareem was a few rows up from us, apart but still connected to the chatter, always within earshot. We told stories and laughed at each other's exploits with women (and at strip clubs). We talked about games, how to defend certain guys. We talked big dunks, roaring like bombs going off.

Magic talked about wanting to be a billionaire. Byron talked about wanting to coach in the NBA. And I talked about wanting to coach women, which I ended up doing later in the WNBA. It was wild to discuss those things and years later to see them come to pass. (Okay, Magic may not be a billionaire, but he's pretty darn close.) But when it comes to the stories people told about their exploits with the fairer sex, it felt jovial. We were the Lakers, surrounded by groupies throwing themselves at us. I remember one woman, chest all out, handing a homemade pie to my *wife* to give to *me*. Wanda just looked at her and said she could make her own pies.

Still, though, those were tough times. It's not easy being in a marriage and on the road half the year, especially when you're a young, famous athlete. But the Lakers wives were an important group. At our best, going back to 1984, they were an extension of us. We were the generational team we were in large part because of them and the family atmosphere they created at home. The Lakers wives started charities, they hosted get-togethers, they took care of the domestic life, raising children while each of us focused on our profession—from Wanda to Linda Rambis to Chris Riley to Anita Scott to Angela Worthy to Charlina McAdoo and more.

There are a lot of stories about the Lakers, the Forum Club, Dr. Buss, Magic, and all the women around us. But the wives were essential, and everything they had to deal with wasn't easy along the way. Magic famously slept with thousands of women, sometimes picking them out of the stands. But he wasn't married. Shoot, I may have lived like that too if I weren't married. Still, though, I wasn't always respectful to my wife at the height of Showtime and my celebrity, which I regret.

Wanda was a blunt talker from New Mexico, and she had her limits. She once was asked if she worried if I were fooling around on the road, and she responded, "One less blowjob I have to give at home." *Oh, boy.* Some other time, a woman gave Wanda a perfume-scented note that was meant for me. It read, "I like your moves on the court, like to check them out off the court." But she never gave me that one. Like I said, it wasn't easy, even if it was a lavish lifestyle. While we were on the road, the wives would set up sleepovers at home, even bringing the kids. They were close, thankfully. They'd sip wine and start telling stories, commiserating. Some said they found other women's underwear in our suitcases.

One road trip, after playing the Hall of Fame Game in Springfield, Massachusetts, I remember someone knocking on my hotel door and saying, "Hey, Coop! You've got to come down here to see this!" I said, "What's going on?" I looked out and saw a teammate standing in his doorway. So I knocked on Earvin's door and we went to check it out. The room where everyone stood was dark except for a dim red light. And there was this woman in there on her knees going from guy to guy. While some like A.C. carried a Bible 24/7, that wasn't everyone's bag. Some would have women lined up for them after the game. They'd just point to them in the stands.

BUT WHEN IT came to the best way to take care of your body as an NBA player, Kareem is the perfect example. He did yoga, focused on stretching, and ate right, and he lasted well into his forties before it was fashionable. But the NBA at that time was drenched in drugs, sadly. My pal and former four-time NBA All-Star Michael "Sugar" Ray Richardson was banned from the NBA in 1986 for cocaine use. The league had just instituted its three-strike system, and Sugar Ray had gotten his third. Others in the league just fell out from the deterioration that comes from drugs. More players were suspended too. It was ugly.

In 1980 Spencer Haywood succumbed to the allure of drugs, and he was dismissed from the Lakers before we won the Finals after he fell asleep in practice. He was our only casualty of the drug war. In Los Angeles, between actors and musicians too, things like cocaine were everywhere. People smoked, drank liquor. But the Lakers largely abstained. Instead, it was always women. There were certain clubs guys would frequent. Magic liked this one in Hollywood on the Sunset Strip. People knew he'd be there. Women, as beautiful as they are, can be sharks too. On the rare occasions I went out at home in L.A., I tried to stick to my second love: dancing.

Some of the guys I hung out with even called me the Disco King. I have just always loved to dance, and I still do. It makes me happy. If you see me at a wedding, I'll be on the dance floor. When I was a kid, my mother and her three sisters formed a little gospel singing group called the Butler Sisters. And when I was eight or nine, I'd go around with my mom when she cleaned houses. She would sing or put music from Aretha Franklin on the radio. I'd dance the whole time, always bouncing around the vacuum as it sucked up dirt. That love of music and of dancing translated to my time with the Los Angeles Lakers.

We were called Showtime for a reason: we knew how to make it look good, smooth, and effortless. Not to mention the jazzlike quality of basketball and the balletic moves we had to do at times to block a shot or finish a dunk. It's all music and dance. With the rise of Showtime, hip-hop was also coming into play. We started listening to it as a team. We would dig those disco break beats as people rapped over them. In the clubs, I'd show off moves. My teammates even went so far as to start calling me John Travolta. There was once a point in my life when I thought I'd never run or dance again because of my knee. So I never took it for granted.

IN THE 1986 playoffs, we started off strong, sweeping the San Antonio Spurs in three games. While in the East, Boston swept an up-and-coming Bulls team with Michael Jordan, who scored 63 in an overtime Game 2 after scoring 49 in Game 1, leaving Bird saying, "That wasn't Michael Jordan out there. It was God disguised as Michael Jordan." (I remember not sleeping ahead of some games against MJ—he was that good.) In the next round, we dispatched the Dallas Mavericks in six games, winning 4–2, while Boston beat Atlanta 4–1, a series that featured Dominique Wilkins and Bird going back and forth, scoring a combined 66 in Game 3.

We were poised and ready for the Celtics. Now we were just two series away from winning back-to-back titles, knowing that Boston—with Walton, Bird, McHale, Parish, and the boys—would be at the end of the journey. If we kicked their ass again like we did in 1985, we'd be the first team to go back-to-back since 1969. We were drooling at the thought. I didn't think we were going to lose to anyone. We'd won 62 games again in the regular season. We were on fire. And in the first game against the Houston Rockets in the Western Conference Finals, we won easily at home, 119–107. Magic scored 26 and dished 18 assists. Kareem added 31. On to Boston, right?

Then the unthinkable struck. We lost the next four games—a run that culminated with Hakeem Olajuwon punching Mitch Kupchak in Game 5. Dominated by Houston's Twin Towers of Olajuwon and Ralph Sampson, we lost Game 2 112–102 in L.A. Then we lost Game 3 117–109 in Houston, and Game 4 there too, 105–95. Game 5 back in L.A., we put up a fight but fell 114–112. In that, Sampson scored 29, Olajuwon had 30, and Rodney McCray had 11 points and 11 boards. I was one of five Lakers in double digits, scoring 15 points with 5 steals,

7 assists, and 7 boards, but it wasn't enough. We went from being 110 percent sure we'd win to devastated.

What made Game 5 worse was that we lost on a lucky buzzer-beating shot from Sampson. With less than a second left and the game tied, Houston had the ball out of bounds. Sampson and his 7'4" butt stood in the lane. When his teammate threw the pass, he jumped in the air, caught it, and flicked the shot over his head in one move in a fraction of a second. The ball bounced around the rim and fell through, and we lost the series on our home court. As I saw the ball go through the net, my legs buckled and I fell to the floor. Houston had beaten us again, five years after they had knocked us out in the 1981 first round with Westhead as our coach.

But that was just it—Houston simply beat us. We'd make big runs in the game, and they'd just hang with us. It was hard to swallow. The only consolation prize was thinking that Houston was going to go on and destroy Boston, keeping them from earning their third ring. After Sampson's shot fell, I got up and went up to Hakeem "the Dream" Olajuwon and said, "Y'all go and kick Boston's ass." But that didn't happen. The sicko Celtics fans who hung Ralph Sampson from the Boston Garden rafters in effigy got to celebrate their heads off yet again. Houston fell to the Celtics in six games and Bird got to enjoy his third ring. Disappointing, to say the least.

AFTER THE SEASON, during which I averaged 9.2 points, 5.7 assists, and 3 rebounds, we had to retool again, just like after 1984. We had to come back after the summer in tip-top shape; Riley and Magic demanded it. Training camp wasn't about conditioning; it was about planning for war. We took two weeks off and then came back snarling. Byron, A.C., Magic, James, and I started our own mini-camp even before training camp began for the 1986–87 season. Back then it was something Magic and the rest of us invented on the fly. Earvin rented out the UCLA gym, and we'd play pickup against other NBA guys or the top local talent, such as UCLA's Reggie Miller.

There, we ran wind sprints, scrimmaged, ran more sprints, did individual drills, lifted weights, stretched a ton. We were single-minded. I continued to concentrate on my outside shooting. Earvin and I put up 1,000 shots a day. Going into the 1986–87 season, we wanted zero weaknesses. I'd played fine in the Western Conference Finals against the Rockets, scoring 15 points with 5 steals, 7 assists, and 7 rebounds in the deciding Game 5, but I knew I could have done more. Their big guys outdueled us, including our bench. We all needed to be better heading into the defining new season.

Chapter 12
The Dynasty's Official

EVEN THOUGH I'D BECOME A MUCH BETTER SHOOTER over the years, there were still some moments when we played Boston when Bird would throw me off. He'd say, "Shoot it! Coop, shoot it!"—trying to bait me and get in my head. There were times when I wasn't a confident shooter, looking to pass it to Kareem or Worthy in the post. But the 1986–87 season wasn't one of those times—that year I made 89 threes, second only to Bird. My confidence was through the roof. The previous year, I'd also made the NBA All-Defensive Second Team. That was nice, albeit below my standards. So for the new season, all bets were off. Time to achieve hoops nirvana.

Each summer was all about improvement. From my jumper to the team's conditioning to Jerry West's tinkering. But his biggest move came during the middle of the 1986–87 season when he traded for Mychal Thompson from San Antonio. Not only did it make us better, but the move made Larry Bird ill. In Portland with the Blazers, Mychal averaged about 17 points, 9 boards, and more than 3 assists per game. A 6'10" center (and father of Klay Thompson), Mychal was traded to the Spurs in the summer of 1986, and Jerry traded for him in February 1987.

We needed another significant piece, and Thompson was it at backup center for Cap. A great teammate, funny guy, and quintessential legend in his own mind, Mychal didn't need a ton of shots. He did the dirty work, had a great basketball IQ, and best of all, as a former teammate of Kevin McHale's at the University of Minnesota, he knew how to guard the gangly, long-necked Boston player better than anyone. Hungry to win a ring, Mychal fit right in—that was another point of Jerry's genius.

Jerry was tough, and he could even be rigid at times, but he was always true and truthful. He knew an important secret to team-building, and that was that to keep a team hungry to win, you had to bring in a new player who was hungry to win. He did it almost every season, from Bob McAdoo to Mychal Thompson and more. Today Mychal, who is originally from the Bahamas and is a big boxing fan, remains one of my favorite teammates ever, and even though he only spent a few years in L.A., he's a Laker for life as far as I'm concerned. It's a title you get when you win with the team. But one of the reasons I love Mychal is because he was always talking. He was a funny guy who said whatever was on his mind.

In the locker room, as Magic would quiz us on our defensive assignments, Mychal and Byron used to talk trash to one another over who was the better fighter. Byron, who was from Inglewood, said he had natural fighting skills, while Mychal, the boxing aficionado, said he was best. Well, one day the two squared up after practice, and I was the ref! It wasn't all that serious, but when Byron got Mychal on his chin, well, Thompson went down and I got to a three-count. Then Mychal opened his eyes. But there was no real beef between the two—just guys being guys after playing ball. And even though he couldn't take a punch as well as he thought, Mychal was essential to our team.

A bench player like me, I was sixth man A and he was sixth man B. He could score in the low post, shoot 15-foot jumpers, and play great defense. But of course it was always about us against the Celtics. A former standout, Mychal was on a great high school team in Miami, and he flourished in college and the pros. Why San Antonio gave him up, I'll never know. But it drove Bird and McHale—who I hate to this very day—mad. That made me smile. Jerry also picked up the standout defensive point guard Wes Matthews as a backup for us that season.

As usual, Boston was trying to retool right along with us. But there was a giant, unfortunate problem. In the summer of 1986, the Celtics drafted the 6'8" forward Len Bias out of the University of Maryland with the second pick (from Seattle). But sadly, two days after he was picked, Bias died of a cardiac arrhythmia, which came from cocaine use. It's one of the biggest losses in the NBA of the past 50 years. If Bias had lived and had Boston been able to integrate him into their system, it's easy to imagine the Celtics could have had the upper hand and been in the driver's seat well into the 1990s. Later, in 1993, Boston experienced another tragedy when Reggie Lewis collapsed on the court against the Charlotte Hornets in April and died three months later of heart failure.

Bias could jump out the gym and shoot the midrange jumper. He was just as good as James Worthy. He could defend, score, and intimidate. With Bird, McHale, and Parish—*oof*, that would have been tough. I'm not sure we would have beaten Boston with Bias in the lineup in his prime. And I would have had to check him. It feels crappy to say that I'm glad it didn't happen, because I would trade that tough assignment every night if it meant Bias had lived. But the truth of the matter is that he didn't. He wasn't there for the 1987 playoffs and wouldn't be there any other year. It was horrible luck and a horrible reality for a proud franchise.

THERE WAS SOME levity in the 1986–87 season, however. But still, even that was connected to the presence of drugs in America. In 1987, after the season, the Lakers team—including Kareem, Magic, Pat Riley, and me—shot a rap music video called "Just Say No!" And while the message is excellent—don't abuse your body with drugs—the execution was silly. (Why do ballers always want to be music stars, and vice versa?) My line went, "My name is Michael but they call me Coop. My main hangout is up around the hoop. We play hard, but we still play smart. We never let drugs tear us apart!" The whole team wore shades and tank tops. It's quite a time capsule.

The summer before, Magic and Larry had filmed a commercial themselves, for Converse sneakers, in which Magic pulled up in a limo in Bird's rural Indiana hometown of French Lick. The two prattled about who was the best and who deserved the signature shoe more, and then played one-on-one. It was a good commercial, and one that actually brought them closer as friends. But it was also something Pat Riley hated. "I was not happy," he later said. But then Pat thought about it more, wondering if maybe it was Magic going into enemy territory to defuse some of the disdain. *That could work in our favor*, Riley thought. Time would tell.

Another wild event from the season came during the 1987 NBA All-Star Game in Seattle. While Magic, Kareem, James, and Pat Riley were there representing us in the actual game, I was there repping the team in the three-point contest. Larry Bird had won the inaugural contest in 1986, the year before, and now he was there defending it. Participating in the shootout were Bird, Danny Ainge, Dale Ellis, Craig Hodges, Detlef Schrempf, Byron Scott, Kiki VanDeWeghe, and me. While it doesn't bother me (much) that I was never an All-Star, I was glad to be repping L.A. in the three-point contest at least.

Here's how it went: In the locker room before the shootout, an official from the NBA came in to tell us the rules. We were looking around while he was talking, wondering where Bird was. Then Larry walked in, and the official told him he'd be shooting last. "I don't care when I'll be shooting," Bird said. "I hope all you guys are here deciding who comes in second, because I'm winning this motherfucker." Then he walked out. Everybody's jaw dropped. Did he really just say that? (I heard he did the same thing the following year too.) Sure enough, he went out and won the thing. That was Larry's nature. Magic's too, truth be told. Straight killers.

Larry kept his warm-ups on for the contest. He was *warming up* while he was kicking our asses. Back then, guys in the league weren't friends unless they were on the same team. You could be friends after you retired. I hated Dale Ellis during that time, but now we're the best of pals. Larry won $12,500 for his work. Detlef got second and won $7,500, and I got $5,500 for third. Not bad for an hour's work, huh? Once the weekend was over, though, it was back to the job. For the season, the Lakers finished 65–17, our best record in years. On top of that, Magic—who Pat said needed to take over the lead from Kareem—earned his first MVP.

THE PREVIOUS SUMMER, in 1986, I'd taken home the NBA's prestigious Walter Kennedy Citizenship Award for community service for my basketball camps, my Reading Is Fundamental campaign, and for a program I'd worked on with Lakers PR rep Rhonda Windham that aimed to help young kids increase their attendance in school. We knew that if kids couldn't get to school, if their parents were unable to help, then they most certainly couldn't learn from their teachers. So we worked to make sure they made it to class. I went to all the schools in the Los Angeles school district, and I'd be there in the morning to talk about the importance of attending class. I'm very proud of that. That's the benefit of hard work.

And now for the 1986–87 season, I received the hallowed Defensive Player of the Year trophy. To get it as someone who came off the bench made it that much sweeter. When the NBA handed me the award, I pointed to my family in the stands to acknowledge them. The award was a result of my teammates too. They'd taken to calling me the Minister of Defense! While I wouldn't have minded getting the Sixth Man of the Year Award too, with past winners such as Bill Walton and McHale (heck, around this time, Bob Cousy wrote that I was the best one in the league), accolades weren't my motivation. Rings were. And we were gearing up to get one of those too.

TO WIN, WE knew we had to defend, rebound, and run the break. We had to cover each other's backs, take away players' sweet spots, and make our opponents uncomfortable. Rambis said I had a "sickness" for defending.

McAdoo said I was like "a rat" getting through screens, putting my body through the smallest openings. Riley said, "There isn't a more important player on this team than Coop." I won the Defensive Player of the Year award by playing on the wing and guarding individuals and in the post. Back then, there was no zone defense. Footwork was key. So were your eyes: Focus on a man's chest and hips, nothing else. Trace the ball. If he pulls up his dribble, put him in a cage.

We would have to put our best foot forward in the postseason now. To start, we swept the Denver Nuggets. We blew those boys out 128–95, 139–127, and 140–103. Then in the Western Conference Semifinals, we beat the Warriors 4–1. My task in that one was Sleepy Floyd. He was their best player and shooter. But I talked a little too much trash that game, getting on him after we won Game 3 133–108. We were up 3–0 after that one. But All-Star Sleepy went off in Game 4 in Oakland, scoring 51 points. His team won 129–121. That taught me a lesson: don't motivate guys if you don't have to. We could have swept them if I'd kept my mouth shut.

After beating Golden State in five, it was on to Seattle, where I matched up against Dale Ellis. It was a close series, even though we swept them. In Game 3, I had a big block on Dale, getting a fingernail on one of his jumpers in the final seconds, tipping the ball to Magic for a fast break. We won that game 122–121. Not necessarily *because* of my play, but that extra effort helped. Keep fighting, keep hustling. Be the rat getting through the smallest of spaces. After Seattle, it was time for the real guys in green: Boston. By now we had our PhD in Celticsology. We were confident. They couldn't run with us. They could only hope to save a little face.

THIS IS SOMETHING Pat Riley may get mad at me for saying, but with the Lakers, we practiced two kinds of defenses. The first was a more traditional helping-style defense. With it, we'd jump to a teammate's man if he needed assistance or a double-team. It's something they teach you at the grade school level. But we also had another style where Pat would tell me not *ever* to leave my assignment. If it were Bird, Andrew Toney, Isiah Thomas, whomever, he said to just deny the guy and not to worry about what was happening behind me. This confused teams, even the smart ones. They were so used to a guy helping that when I didn't, it blew a fuse in their brains.

Riley was smart—down to the last detail. He used to hand out 10- to 12-minute videotapes with our assignments on them. But he knew it was unlikely most would take them home and throw them in the VCR, so he started putting code words in the videos' beginning, middle, or end—"Larry Bird," "Fly Like an Eagle," whatever. And he'd quiz you on yours the next day to see if you'd watched it. If you didn't know the password, you'd feel like an asshole—and Riley would fine you $1,000. (The money from fines would go into a big pot for an end-of-the-year party.) Pat was sharp as a tack. He got everyone on the same page with his little tricks like that.

Going into the 1987 Finals, we knew we were going to win. Even more so than we'd known in 1985. Boston was getting older. Bird and McHale were both hobbled—with a bad back and bad foot, respectively. But that's part of the game. We knew that if we ran, they would be dead meat. Not to mention we had defenders such as Mychal. The biggest reason they'd even made the Finals was that they'd beaten the Detroit Pistons in the Conference Finals thanks to the famous "Bird steals the ball" game. With only a few seconds left in Boston, Isiah Thomas just needed to get the ball inbounds and his team would have dribbled out the clock and won.

Out of bounds to the left of Boston's basket, Isiah stood demanding the ball. The ref asked if he wanted a timeout, but Thomas said, "Give me the damn ball." But Bird faked him out and Isiah threw it into his open hand. Falling out of bounds, Bird got the ball to a smart, streaking Dennis Johnson, who laid it up for the game winner. Boston went on to beat the Pistons in the series. After losing, Isiah called up his close friend Magic and cried to him over the phone. Isiah was there for Magic after we lost in 1984. He'd hung around the Lakers whenever he could, especially in the postseason while his Detroit team was out of it.

After that loss, though, a shitstorm rose up for Isiah when Detroit's rookie defender and future NBA irritant Hall of Famer Dennis Rodman called Bird overrated, saying he'd only earned praise because "he's white." Following that, Isiah, still hurting from the loss, echoed Rodman, saying to reporters, "I think Larry is a very, very good basketball player, an exceptional talent. But I'd have to agree with Rodman. If he was Black, he'd just be another good guy." To his credit, Bird didn't feed into the maelstrom. But reporters everywhere made Isiah out to be a villain, which he never quite recovered from, all for having the nerve to talk about race. It was sad.

IN GAME 1 of the Finals, we finally had home-court advantage. And the celebs were out, including Whoopi Goldberg, John McEnroe, Jack Nicholson (who actually mooned Celtics fans later in the series, in Boston), Dyan Cannon, Johnny Carson, Henry Winkler, Denzel Washington, John Travolta, Bruce Willis, and others. We won the opening tilt 126–113. James scored 33; and Bird had 32, but no one else on Boston shined. In Game 2, I scored 21 off the bench and added 9 assists. In fact, I hit six big three-point shots in that second game, setting an NBA Finals record! It made all those thousands of shots I'd put up in the summers worth it. The Forum gave me a standing ovation.

Yes, I made threes from all over. "He's the best at what he does," Pat said of me. "He was blazing hot," Kareem added. But I also defended. Writer Jack McCallum likened me to a piece of flypaper on Bird. And while Larry and I hardly ever talked trash to one another, I made sure to tell him once in a while, "You're getting nothing tonight, Larry." I never thought I got into his head, but I still had to poke, make him think for a second here and there, right? We won Game 2 141–122. In Game 3 back in Boston, we lost a close one 109–103.

But Game 4 was the ultimate classic. With just minutes left, Earvin drove to the hoop and then kicked it out to me. I hit a three and cut the lead to 103–100. Then, with the Celtics resorting to their old dirty tricks, they went up on us 106–104 with just 12 ticks left after Bird hit a three from the corner. Next, we came down and Kareem was fouled. He hit the first free throw but missed the second. But McHale, busted foot and all, lost it out of bounds—poor baby! Down one, it was our ball, and Magic made magic happen. With just seconds left, I took the ball out and got it to him. He had it near the left sideline. He was some 20 feet from the hoop, then he made his move with a hesitation dribble. Magic got in the paint and threw up one of the most famous shots in NBA history.

It was later called his Junior Junior Skyhook, which he'd learned from Cap. From eight feet out, Earvin got his shot up just half an inch above the outstretched arms of the greatest front line in NBA history: Bird, McHale, and Parish. The ball swished through the net like God himself had dropped it in. But Boston still had a chance to beat us. Down 107–106, with two seconds left, Boston got the ball out of bounds near halfcourt, ready to make a play. Blanketed by Worthy, Bird ran to the ball but then broke back and faded to the left corner right in front of our bench. Dennis Johnson had the ball out of bounds, and he rifled a pass to him.

In a flash, Bird, who never let up and was somehow more dangerous without the ball, threw up a fadeaway jumper in the corner. That shot from him went in 90 percent of the time; he'd just made one like it seconds before! Watching it, his shot was perfectly on line—"Straight as an arrow," Riley later said—but it was just a fraction of an inch long. After the miss, Bird looked at Riley like, *You left me that open?* He'd missed, though, and we'd won Game 4 107–106, getting the road win we'd need. The shot clanked, and the hostile Boston Garden crowd, which was practically spilling out onto the court, let out a giant moan. Everyone knew that was the series.

Even former Celtics great Tommy Heinsohn saw it. He was broadcasting the games for CBS, and he knew as well as anyone what had just happened. Tommy was in the Hall of Fame as a coach and a player—that's how good he was. And he was one of the guys, along with Bill Russell, who helped make me a household name in the 1980s. His gruff, rough voice saying "Michael COOOPAHH" with his thick Boston accent helped turn me into a world-famous Laker. Yet even after that miss by Bird, Boston was somehow able to save face and bounce back in Game 5 to beat us 123–108 in their last home game of the Finals, denying us a second win on their court.

But now we had two tries to win the series back at home. Turned out we only needed one. Kareem came to the game with a freshly shaved head and was ready to seal the victory. He scored 32, Mychal added 15, Worthy dropped 22, and Magic notched 16 points, 19 assists, and 8 boards. We won Game 6 106–93, and, along with it, the series. We also took the lead in the NBA's defining rivalry. Our favorite song, "I Love L.A." by Randy Newman, played and our fans stormed the court. *Bye, Boston!* For Magic, who'd had his own end-of-game miscues in past playoffs, he was vindicated. It was an incredible end to an incredible season, maybe the best ever.

BUT THE STORY of 1987 is as much about what happened *after* our win as during it. Directly after the series, Bird said, "Magic is a great, great basketball player. The best I've ever seen." The win over the Celtics would be the last time we'd face Bird in the Finals. The NBA was changing. The Celtics were getting older. And behind them in the East were Isiah and his Pistons as well as Michael Jordan and his Bulls. Knowing this, Riley put the screws to us for the following year, literally as soon as he could. With champagne flowing in the locker room after our 1987 win, Riley guaranteed we'd win it all again the next year. And from that moment, he never backed off that idea.

After we won, there were parties. For several days, at least. One was at a private club on Sunset, a favorite of Magic's. We had events at the Forum as a team, giddy as ever. My voice went hoarse from all the cheering we did in celebration. Some had called us too old to start the year, and we showed them experience was a requirement. We needed it during all 100 games, from October to June. Magic, who just got better every year, earned the Finals MVP after getting the regular-season MVP award too.

Now, I was 31 and I wanted more rings, just a little bit more of the glory. I could taste it. So could the rest of us. In the championship celebration days later, Riley kept at his promise. The Celtics were slow, built to survive in the East against physical teams. Now with them out of the way, the squads they had helped sharpen were gunning for us. While Riley had nicknamed us the Greyhounds, knowing we had to race to outdo Boston, we now had to run with some new dogs—Detroit and Chicago were coming. When you win, it's just a fact that it's harder to come back the next season and have the same razor-sharp edge you had before you won. It's human nature to let up at least a little bit.

So during the championship celebration in the giant parking lot of the Fabulous Forum—as the fans went nuts; as they expressed their love for us; as Inglewood was again the city of champs; as Earvin thanked the crowd in the hot sun, saying, "I can't *hear you*, Laker fans!"; as Chick Hearn hosted the day; as the fans yelled "*Cooooooooppppp!!!*" when I got to the microphone; as I yelled, "The Celtics suck!" instigating them—Riley had a plan. He stepped to the mic and thanked the fans. He said the trophy was for them. Then he said to the ocean of fans, "I'm guaranteeing everybody here, next year, we're going to win it *again!*"

When he did that, I thought tens of thousands of heads were going to explode, including mine. The crowd went berserk, cheering. No team had gone back-to-back since Bill Russell's Celtics before the dawn of time. We all looked at each other. Then Riley looked back at us. *What?!* But it was on, officially. What that did was tell us, collectively, that 1987–88 started *right then*—not in a few months. When we got back into the locker room, Pat barked, "Did you guys hear what I said?" We all nodded. "So," he continued, "what are we going to do now?" Then he walked out. We got together for one last huddle, *"1, 2, 3, Lakers!"* But we were officially on notice.

EVERYONE WENT HOME for a few weeks. Wanda and I went to Italy for a brief vacation, then out camping with the kids. I also wrote a book on the art of defense, *No Slack*. My teammates and I knew we had to work out even during our time off, that we had to be in better shape than we ever had been. James went back to North Carolina, A.C. went back to Portland. But soon we were all back on the court. Magic, who always tried to improve, rented out a UCLA gym again, and we sharpened our skills playing against young guys. Some of us ran the Los Angeles sand dunes. I ran the hills in Valley Ridge.

Then came the treadmill test, something Gary Vitti had brought to us. Each year before camp, we had to take physicals. Part of that meant running on the treadmill. For that, Vitti got each of us on the machine going eight miles an hour, and every two minutes he increased the incline. The best on the treadmill was A.C., who ran it 23 minutes *straight*. I got to about 20, which I was proud of. We all did better than we had in past training camps. Even Cap got to 12. It was like the last season never ended—we were so *dedicated*. Pat got all the numbers from our physicals, and he was thoroughly impressed by his so-called greyhounds. With us displaying that effort, we began to think maybe we *could* do it again.

Teammate Testimonial
Gary Vitti

In my 32-year tenure as the head athletic trainer for the Los Angeles Lakers, I've had the distinct opportunity to work with many champions. I started my career with the likes of Kareem Abdul-Jabbar and ended it with the great Kobe Bryant. There were also many in between, and one of those greats was Michael Cooper. Coop is most known for his defensive prowess, for which he so rightfully earned that great reputation. But there is much more than his ability to play defense that makes up his championship heart.

Of all of the great Hall of Famers who wore the Purple and Gold that I had the honor of working with, there is no one who personifies being the quintessential professional more than Michael Cooper. From an athletic trainer's perspective, Michael gave 100 percent of himself every single day.

When I think of someone I could rely on, Coop always comes to mind. He was always prepared, never missed a bus, plane (okay, maybe once!), practice, or game. In fact, he was the ultimate iron man at a time when playing all 82 of an 82-game schedule meant something.

To give you an idea of how Michael approached the game: from the 1979–80 season to the 1989–90 season (11 years) he played in 870 regular-season games and 168 playoff games. That's an average of 94.4 games per season. Those are *iron man* numbers, and they were achieved while playing the most physically brutal part of the game: defending every team's best players. Michael Cooper can play on my team any day of the week. I am so happy for his induction into the Naismith Memorial Basketball Hall of Fame, and I am proud to call him my friend.

Chapter 13

Rewriting History

ISIAH THOMAS HAD WATCHED EVERYTHING WE DID. He was a sponge, soaking up each lesson the Lakers and Magic could teach. He and the Pistons had lost to Bird in the playoffs in demoralizing fashion, which had been his fault in the final seconds. Now, he wanted revenge on the entire NBA. Their roster, assembled by "Trader" Jack McCloskey, looked startlingly like ours, down to the trio of star guards (Isiah, Joe Dumars, and Vinnie Johnson), wiry defensive stoppers (Dennis Rodman and John Salley), and its coach with the slicked-backed hair (Chuck Daly, aka Daddy Rich). It was eerie. Isiah had been with us to support Magic after 1984, our most brutal failure.

Magic stayed in a hotel room that June 1984 evening, up all night, watching the city of Boston party after his loss, up and down every street. With him were Isiah and Mark Aguirre. Magic wept as his friends comforted him, trying to take his mind off the game. I was disconsolate in my own room with Wanda. Then, after Isiah threw it away to Bird, he wept to Magic, the two sharing the same pain. Through Magic, Isiah learned the secrets of the game. Namely, that it's not about the sport as much as it is about team chemistry. In the league, we're all great athletes. Winning demands more than just talent. There has to be drive, trust, and joy.

It's why the Lakers didn't win until Magic arrived. And why Detroit didn't until Isiah got there and learned from Earvin. But don't get me wrong—Isiah was one of the best players in the NBA on top of all that. The shortest greatest player ever. An All-Star 12 years in a row, he led the league in assists in 1984–85. And in 1987–88, he'd just come off four years in a row averaging 21 points, 11.5 dimes, 4 rebounds, and 2.2 steals per game. While the Lakers were winning series after series in the early and mid-1980s, Zeke, as Thomas was known, was often in our locker room, watching every high and low. He likened the experience to going to Harvard.

He learned how to be a champion. Like us, the Pistons were built for speed and tough games. But even rougher, rawer—the so-called Bad Boys of the NBA (a name inspired by *Scarface* and the Oakland Raiders). In the 1980s, after all, championships were won in the paint, not with threes. Though Isiah had his bright smile (like Magic), he grew up hard. His mother used to sit on the front stoop of her house with a shotgun telling the Chicago gangs that her son Isiah was off-limits. It wasn't easy for his family. When he got to the NBA, his life changed. Part of that was his closeness with Magic. Zeke even had his own room in Magic's mansion.

AS FOR MY own life, it was going through changes. When I was five, my dad had left at Christmas. Then, when I was 23, I started looking for him. My mom wouldn't help. She wouldn't tell me where he was. But during the 1987–88 season, I found him. He lived in L.A., in Watts. In fact, he lived in perhaps the most dangerous housing project in the city: Nickerson Gardens, the largest public housing development west of the Mississippi River. The place was named after the founder of Golden State Mutual Life Insurance, ironic because it's also where killers like the Bloods originated.

I remember driving to Nickerson Gardens—this was before Google— and just asking if anyone knew Marshall Cooper. I had to ask people to help me even find the projects. Then I found them and him. It took a few people to get me to the right area, block, and room. But then I knocked on his door. This man had a whole new family there. My father was a true rolling stone. He came from 23 brothers and sisters, and he fathered 21 kids with 5 different women. To his credit, he'd never reached out to me, even as I became a famous basketball player. Then when we made contact, he started to be a part of my life here and there.

We didn't hang out regularly or anything. But we were in contact, and I was happy about that. A person wants to know where he comes from, who he comes from. My mother, who'd moved back to the Los Angeles area in 1984 before settling in Chatsworth, about an hour outside the city, wasn't happy about me connecting with my dad, but I told her that it was my decision. She did say, "Well, he is your father." It wasn't necessarily life-changing to have my dad in my world again, but it didn't hurt either. It was good that we could have even a little relationship. It remained good until the day he passed away.

WITH THE LAKERS, each season was about a championship. We followed the Malcolm X credo: by any means necessary. Good was the enemy of great. We had intensity from the huddles to the games. That season, we finished 62–20 (again). The season before marked my fifth in a row playing all 82 games (which made 556 in a row). I'd averaged 10.5 points and 4.5 assists. I'd looked to score more to make sure fans and writers remembered me. After missing almost my entire rookie season, I'd only missed seven more games through 1986–87. But in 1987–88 I missed 21 games. My streak ended not for injury but due to a one-game suspension for fighting during a game against the Knicks.

A.C. Green would later pass me and set the all-time record in the league with 1,192 straight regular-season games played (though he only played a few minutes in some of those!). Take *that*, 2024 load management! After my suspension, I badly sprained my ankle in March 1988. Then I missed some games after Karl Malone tossed me into a press table and I bruised my foot. We'd gone to the Finals so many times, my body was breaking down. I couldn't heal like I used to. Magic also missed 10 games that year with injury. But in a game on December 11, 1987, he hit a three-pointer in Boston at the buzzer and won the game. It was that kind of year for us—highs and lows.

By now, the Los Angeles Lakers team was one of major celebrity, from our GQ coach to our style of play to our Hollywood fans. Even anonymous guys became famous around us, such as Dancing Barry, a corny-looking chestnut-haired white guy who would dance through the aisles during timeouts. Not only did we have the Laker Girls shaking their stuff during timeouts (or washing fans' cars pregame) and Chick Hearn yelling into the mic, but there was Dancing Barry. First he just wore street clothes, but then he started wearing tuxedos, even coordinated yellow-and-purple ones. That stuff was as much a part of the circus of Showtime as a no-look pass.

Today, security would stop someone like Barry. But I think Dr. Buss told them to let him go and do his thing. He got the crowd hyped. And when we won, that Randy Newman song "I Love L.A." would punctuate the night. It's what Dr. Buss always wanted, how he designed it. People would spend an hour at the Forum Club before the game, then three hours at the game, then more time at the club after. Jack Nicholson and Dyan Cannon, who was my favorite celeb, would sing along and stoke the fires. Those two *still* come to games. Jack was great to hang out with. He'd often sit next to Lou Adler, a music producer who owned a few L.A. clubs.

Lou wore a funky-looking hat and was always next to Jack. We'd go to his clubs after wins, including On the Rox. The wives would come too. And sometimes I'd find myself talking with Jack Nicholson (who is now enshrined in the Basketball Hall of Fame as a fan). He loved talking basketball, and he knew a lot about it. He knew the opposing teams, who to watch out for. It was fun to mingle with him, with stars. During 1987–88, we felt very confident. We knew it would be hard, but we all believed we could make sure Riley kept his promise. But little did we know our collective little brother Isiah Thomas was lurking, waiting for us. We really had no idea. It was always Boston on our minds. Or *maybe* Philly.

But along with their talented guards and wings, Detroit had some game-changing big guys, such as James "Buddha" Edwards, who'd played in Phoenix and knew us well, enforcer and trash-talker Rick Mahorn, and everyone's most hated California rich boy Bill Laimbeer, the big white jerk who could shoot from outside. Like us, they could play multiple ways, fast and slow. Pat made sure we were versatile. It seemed like with every year, Riley became more and more detail-oriented, obsessive. Kareem at times called him Norman Bates behind his back. He was so intense, crazed. Pat would tell us, "There's winning and then there's misery. That's it."

The whole team was bent on being the first to repeat as champs since the 1969 Celtics. While Pat had made his guarantee, he also talked to us privately, saying winning again was going to be the hardest thing we'd ever done on the court. Coach Riley, for all his maniacal tendencies, was insightful, profound. He was a walking book of aphorisms. He was right too: it was the hardest thing we'd ever done. To have the target on our back, to play another 100-game season, and to do it with so many miles on our legs already, having just trounced Bird and his Boston Celtics, we knew that if we were able to win again, we'd let out a big, exhausted sigh of relief.

THE PLAYOFFS BEGAN against San Antonio. But we quickly dispatched the Spurs in a sweep, even though the final game was close. We won—but just barely—in Texas 109–107. After that, the most grueling Finals run in NBA history began. Moses had his "Fo' fo' fo'." Well, we went through sev', sev', sev'. Yes, three straight seven-game series. It was excruciating, just as Riley had predicted. In the conference semifinals, we matched up against the Utah Jazz, with their budding two-man game between Hall of Fame point guard John Stockton and burly Hall of Fame forward Karl Malone. That series started normally enough, with a 110–91 win for us.

But then danger struck. We lost the next two games, one at home in L.A. and the next in Utah. It was rare we were ever down in a series, even rarer if it wasn't against Boston. But Utah didn't care about legacy. In Game 4 in Utah, however, we got the road victory we needed, winning 113–100. It's hard to beat any playoff team three times in a row, and we took advantage of that. In Game 4 Magic scored 24, Worthy had 29, and Byron and Kareem each had 20. Next was the all-important Game 5, with the series tied 2–2. Whoever won would likely win the series. We opened Game 5 back in L.A., coming out with our signature chant, "1, 2, 3, it's *Showtime*!

At first we had the game in hand. We were up by five after the first quarter, but the Jazz (a team that used to be in New Orleans but moved to Utah in 1979) tied it at halftime. We were up by eight after three quarters, but then Utah came roaring back. John Stockton was masterful; the small, white point guard from Spokane, Washington, put on a clinic, making shots and dishing tons of assists. While Malone scored 27 points with 16 rebounds, Stockton scored 23 with a whopping (and playoff-tying record) 24 assists. Utah's Thurl Bailey added 28 points. As stars such as Mel Gibson, Jack Nicholson, and Billy Crystal watched from the stands, we were in trouble.

Over the airwaves, Chick Hearn said things such as, "No lead is safe with Stockton out there." With just a minute left, the score was 106–105 when Magic brought the ball up, but out of nowhere Stockton got a steal and fed it to Malone for a dunk (and Stockton's 24th assist, tying Magic's record). With 12 seconds left, the Jazz were up by a point after Bailey hit a baseline jumper. Out of timeouts, I inbounded the ball from about halfcourt and got it to Magic. He dribbled into the lane and then threw a no-look pass out to me, and I was suddenly wide-open.

I'd made buzzer-beaters before, including opening night in Seattle in the 1980–81 season, but this was big. Yes, this was different. This was the playoffs. I caught the ball, and Stockton—who had doubled Magic—seeing me open, busted right to me. But in one fluid motion, I put up the shot with nine seconds left, time ticking down. "Out to Coop!" Hearn said into his microphone. "Eighteen-footer. *Gooooooodd!*" Yes, I'd come through. The Laker Girls, who were known to distract visiting teams during timeouts, went wild. The crowd chanted "*Cooooooopppp!*" It was my first and only basket of the game. We ended up winning by just two points after a James Worthy free throw. *Phew!* Afterward, Magic called me "the man of the hour" to the reporters.

It felt great. But we were exhausted in Game 6, and the Jazz, who were 47–35 on the year, beat us 108–80. That didn't matter. We had Game 7 back at home in L.A., and we won that by 11, 109–98. Malone scored 31 with 15 rebounds, and John had 29 and 20 assists. But we had three guys with 20-plus, and Kareem added 11. Now, it was on to Dallas for round three of these grueling playoffs. In some games we might have thrown in the towel, consciously or not, since we had won the year before. But it was Pat's diabolical guarantee that kept our minds sharp. Funny how that worked.

RILEY KEPT US in our roles, no "disease of more" for us. That was Pat's concept, coined after watching some players want more money or more playing time after winning. He thought some guys would forgo the sense of the team for the sake of green, and that was always to be avoided like the plague. So he warned us and told the world about his philosophy: *the disease of more.* He cautioned us and made sure the players on the Lakers never got too big a head, never put themselves ahead of the team. And he let it be known that if we did, we risked losing our place on the roster. Tough love sometimes is the only kind.

In the Western Conference Finals, we played the Dallas Mavericks. They were 53–29 on the year and boasted players such as Mark Aguirre (25.1 points per game and Magic's dear friend), Rolando Blackman (18.7 ppg), Derek Harper (17 ppg, 7.7 assists), Sam Perkins (14.2 ppg), Roy Tarpley (13.5 ppg), and up-and-comer Detlef Schrempf. That's an underrated, great lineup. For us, things went according to plan for the first two games. We won both—113–98 and 123–101, respectively. In the Lone Star State, the script flipped. Dallas won their two home games,

106–94 and 118–104. The crucial Game 5 was back in Los Angeles. Thank goodness for that home-court advantage.

Thirsty for a victory, we won by 17 at home. They beat us in Game 6 by two points back in Dallas, and we won Game 7 two days later in L.A., 117–102. Worthy, Magic, and Byron again each scored 20-plus. It was quite the trio. Back East, the Detroit Pistons were getting through their playoffs. They beat Washington 3–2 in the opening round and the Chicago Bulls, with newly minted NBA MVP Michael Jordan, 4–1. Following that, Detroit got back at the Celtics for their series the year before by beating Bird and the guys in green 4–2. After that, before leaving the court, McHale whispered to Isiah to crush us. He said we couldn't play physical ball. Yeah, right.

All of a sudden we had a new Finals foe. We'd put the 76ers down in the early 1980s, beating them 2–1 in the Finals. Then we beat Boston 2–1 in the Finals in the middle of the decade. Now it was time to match up against Detroit. Then again, be careful what you wish for. The storyline leading up to the 1988 Finals was the friendship between Magic and Isiah. The two even kissed before tip-off, which Pat hated, thinking it made Magic look soft. It was something they'd continue to do through the series. Isiah explained it by saying the two were family, brothers. When you see your family, he said, you don't shake hands. But during the game, it was a battle.

In Game 1 in L.A., we dug a big hole. Former Laker (and one of the guys whose laundry I used to do) Adrian Dantley scored 34 on us, and Isiah dished 12 assists. A.D. must have been drooling to get back at L.A. for trading him. We lost the opener 105–93. Before Game 2 in L.A., Magic had the flu (he lost eight pounds in a matter of days). Yet we were able to win 108–96. Our defense dug in, and no one on Detroit scored 20. Whereas James, Earvin, and Byron each had 20-plus. Kareem got 15, and A.C. Green scored 12 with 13 boards. In a slump, I got 5 points and 4 assists, with lockdown defense against their guards.

Back in Detroit at the cavernous Silverdome, the Pistons thought they were going to win Game 3. But we surprised them with a 99–86 victory with Magic's dad sitting courtside, spoiling their Finals opener. Now we were on cruise control, right? Well, Detroit won Game 4 in a bruising blowout 111–86, despite Magic knocking Zeke out of the air with a forearm at one point. With the series tied 2–2 we *had* to win Game 5, Detroit's third and final one at home. But we didn't; the Pistons won 104–94. Despite Kareem's 26, we couldn't do much else as a team. Dantley had 25; Dumars had 19; Isiah, whose wife had given birth the night before, had 15 with 8 dimes.

Vinnie Johnson, who people called the Microwave for how fast he could heat up off the bench, added 16. We headed back home to L.A. for Game 6. That's when one of the strangest stretches in NBA playoff history took place. Detroit was winning the series 3–2. With one more victory, our hope of repeating was over. The Pistons led 26–20 after the first quarter of Game 6. And we were up seven at the half. Then they were up by two after three. But in that third period, Isiah landed on my foot after he took a shot, and he rolled his ankle. In severe pain, he went to the bench. But knowing the stakes, Isiah somehow only stayed out for 35 seconds.

To say he was hobbling around would be an understatement. Yet he was also possessed. He got into *the zone*, he wanted to win so bad—to beat us, to beat Magic. He'd been through so much in his life to be there at that moment. He'd seen people murdered, had his mother holding a shotgun on his stoop, dealt with that turnover to Bird in 1987. Now this bum ankle. He could taste the win. He scored 25 points in that third quarter alone. But in a tight fourth, with us down a point, Kareem got the ball on the right block with 14 ticks left, and he turned to shoot his signature skyhook when Pistons center Bill Laimbeer bumped him and the ref called a foul.

To this day, the Pistons call bullshit on that whistle. Isiah said it was cheating! He said Kareem was not fouled and that if Laimbeer didn't have a reputation for being a physical (dirty) player (and a jerk), then he wouldn't have been whistled. That's karma for ya! Kareem went to the foul line and calmly sank two free throws. We won Game 6 103–102.

Isiah finished with a bum ankle and 43 points. After, it was reported he called Magic up for help finding doctors to treat his ankle, but Magic never called him back. While I don't know about that, if Isiah had called me, I don't think I would have picked up either. This was the Finals, baby!

Game 7. We were again at home, thanks to Detroit's 54–38 record against our 62–20 season. In the locker room, Riley played a highlight tape from the season, which got us hot. On the floor, it was war. The Pistons, with Isiah diminished, went up by five at the half. In the third, we made our move and pulled away, outscoring them by 15. They came back in the fourth but could only outdo us by seven, and we won 108–105 as the fans stormed the court in the final seconds. Isiah had 10 points; Dumars got 25. But that was it for the Bad Boys. Worthy scored 36 with 16 boards and 10 assists, Byron added 21, and I had 12. I heard Laimbeer was crying in the locker room.

WITH HIS GIANT stat line, Worthy became "Big Game" James (some had thought of him as Little Game after some prior playoff miscues), and we'd won our second title in back-to-back years. James got the Finals MVP. We'd beaten the Bad Boys, and we proved to be one of the greatest teams of all time. Byron thinks the 1987–88 team is the best ever. We were immortalized on a Wheaties box, our entire team on the front. *Have breakfast with the champs!* After the series, we had another parade outside the Forum. Everyone was having fun, but as soon as Riley got up to the microphone, Kareem ran up and put a big towel in his face to shut him up.

If Cap hadn't done that, Pat might have gone out there and guaranteed a three-peat (a term he'd trademarked). Though we knew we had the chance now to go back-to-back-to-back, there was no sense guaranteeing it. After our Finals win, we got a chance to meet President Reagan. It wasn't the first time—we'd been to the White House so often in the 1980s that they probably could have named a wing after us: the Lakers Lounge. During one of our appearances there with him, he famously said, "Does

America believe in Magic? You bet we do!" Visiting the White House is just one of those nice perks you get when you win it all.

Dr. Buss, Pat Riley, and Magic even got some alone time with the president, but the rest of us hung out on the front lawn, taking in the moment. Today, people ask me if I think the Lakers would have won as much if McKinney had stayed with us and not been hurt. And my answer is that I don't think so. Pat had so much energy and was so resilient and innovative. He fit his system to the players, not the other way around. Heck, we might have lost in 1981 if we'd had Pat. He, along with his assistants, including Bill Bertka, were just excellent. But even Pat didn't have five rings. That honor remains reserved for three 1980s Lakers: Magic, Kareem, and me.

BEING A LOS ANGELES LAKER means carrying yourself with a lot of heart and doing whatever it takes to win. After the 1987–88 year, scoring 8.7 points with 4.7 assists, 3.7 boards, and a steal per game to go along with 5 rings in my pocket, I was named to the NBA All-Defensive First Team again. That marked my fifth time to go along with three Second Team nods. While all of that's tremendous, I've always felt its more important to be connected to my higher power. It may sound strange, but I've long had faith that I was put on this Earth to understand my faith through the game. That's what I'm supposed to do, in the vocational sense of the word.

God gives us all talents, but it's up to us to see Him in them. For instance, growing up, I had an uncle who liked sports. But what he was best at was drawing. I believe he could have been great. His pictures were so vivid and lovely. But he worked against his talents. He fought his skills. All he wanted to do was play basketball. I'd tell him, "Ricky, you can draw so well. Get into that!" It wasn't like he was going to make the pros. But all he wanted to do was play ball. So he quit drawing, left his gift. That was a sad day. If the shoe were on the other foot, if all I wanted to do was draw but I was a world-class athlete, I would have been using my gift wrong.

But I always knew I was supposed to be a basketball player. Fulfilling that meant I was doing what God wanted. He gave me another gift too: the ability to communicate. I understand that now just as I did 30 years ago. It's the basis for my Five D's (to refresh, they are determination, desire, dedication, discipline, and decision-making). Anyone can use those in their daily lives. You don't have to take advantage of all of them in every scenario, but one or two can be a part of your repertoire. I used them in my career, and they helped me become a great player. Today, that's the benefit of celebrity. If a kid hears me talk about hard work, he or she just might listen.

Teammate Testimonial

James Worthy

My first memory of Michael Cooper comes from when I first saw him at Loyola Marymount, where our practice facility was with the Lakers. He had a black Trans Am with the T-bone at the top, and I was just like, "This brother is so cool." Because I'd watched him on TV with the high socks, and I couldn't wait to see the high socks in person. Those were my first two visual impressions—that black Trans Am with a little tan stripe he had when everybody else was driving Mercedes. That car looked like him.

Then when I got around him personally on the basketball floor, there was no one tougher. No one tougher. To get all that out of that body and to have Larry Bird say he was the toughest guy that ever played him—I saw that day in and day out. I don't know how he could take it. He could take punch after punch after punch and still stand. But his defense was second to none. He was a menace on defense.

When I first saw him in practice, I'd never seen anybody flat out—until A.C. Green came—be a flat-out assassin every second on the court. His work ethic was second to none. And then off the court, he was the kindest guy. He always invited us young kids to his house for dinner. To this day, he's the same person.

Before I came to the Lakers, I was watching them play the Celtics in Boston in 1982. Magic was out of the game, and if I'm not mistaken Coop dropped 31 points in that game. That just goes to show you how much he gave up coming from New Mexico just to become a champion defensive stopper. I remember that, and I remember numerous Coop-a-Loops. He knew how to set you up for it. On defense—people think LeBron James is the guy who tracks people down from behind, but Coop was one of the best at that.

I just remember when we played the Celtics, I always started on Larry Bird at the beginning of the game, but I was so happy to hand him over to Coop in the fourth quarter because we needed him. I just remember him taking a lot of physical beatings, and just—you couldn't move him. He was strong as an ox. One of the things I also remember from '88: I think they wanted him to try out for the Olympics that year as a high jumper!

When I got to the Lakers, everyone was already used to winning. And usually after you win a championship, you celebrate and party for the next couple of months. But when Riley made that guarantee [about winning back-to-back championships] in 1987, we wanted it subconsciously. We didn't know he was going to guarantee it publicly, but even if not, we probably would have gotten together as a group and made a promise. But Coop was one of the first guys I remember saying, "Damn right."

He agreed with Pat immediately. He said, "I'm tired of winning one; we're good enough to win two." A lot of people think Magic was our leader, and he was. But Cooper was just as much a leader as anybody. He was vocal, and he led by example. Today, the one thing about Coop is that he'll never let you float away. I just got a call from him maybe a few weeks ago. We get together from time to time—he, Byron, Gary Vitti, and me.

So Coop's always around. He went and picked up Kareem a few weeks ago after he was in the hospital. Coop is a big mama! He loves people. He loves people! He's got feelings, you know? He can cry. He's just full of all of that. So that's my favorite memory of Coop. That's what I'll always think of most when I think of him.

Chapter 14

Three-Peat?

WE'D DONE WHAT SEEMED IMPOSSIBLE. Now everyone wondered what the 1988–89 season would have in store for us. At the same time, the NBA was changing. The 1980s were almost over. The golden era of the league was about to meet its dusk with a new dawn down the road. The only question was, could we hold on for another year? Could we win a third Finals in a row? Well, we were about to find out. But one thing I was happy for during this journey was that I had someone like Magic at my side. One of the greatest competitors in sports, Magic was undaunted. He had highs and lows like everyone else, but he never worried about failure.

That was one of his best skills. He also had that Midas touch, where so much of what he was involved with—from the occasional craps game in Vegas to business deals like his theaters to his play on the court—turned to gold. Sure, he had an ego at times. We all had our egos. But the thing was, Pat Riley didn't mind that. Instead, it was about fitting those egos and talents together like puzzle pieces. Could we do it one more time? Could we bring home one more ring? Well, it would be another slog. To three-peat, we'd have to find strength we didn't know we had. Even to get to another Finals would be a miracle.

The one thing we knew was that the Boston Celtics wouldn't be at the end of any Finals run for us. Larry missed all but six games during 1988–89. His last game that season was on November 15. Over the past two seasons, the NBA, thanks largely to the success of the Lakers and Celtics, had grown a lot, and over two years, four new teams arrived in Miami, Charlotte, Orlando, and Minneapolis. It was against Miami in 1988 when Bird left the game early and didn't come back for the entire season. He had surgery for bone spurs in both heels. He also had severe back pains. We were all getting older, and the NBA is relentless.

FOR THE YEAR, we finished 57–25. Somehow, I was able to play 80 games, finishing with averages of 7.3 points, 3.9 assists, 2.4 rebounds, and 1 steal per. It was a grind of a season, like the Lakers organization's gears lacked oil. It was also filled with internal drama, which hurt the team. There was a kind of power struggle between Pat Riley and Jerry West. Pat wanted control of everything, but he wasn't about to take the reins from one of the greatest general managers of all time (and someone he'd learned from). Later, Pat would go on to new teams, such as the New York Knicks and the Miami Heat, taking both to the Finals and winning rings in Miami.

But now, he was still our coach. His hope for greater control had begun in 1988–89. And as we tried to three-peat, he put the pedal to the metal. Our practices were harder than ever. I was 32 years old, and Magic, who'd won his second MVP that year, was 29. Kareem was 41. To get some new blood in, the Lakers had added forward Orlando Woolridge, who'd averaged nearly 21 points per game over the previous four years with the Bulls and Nets. He was a boost off the bench. He learned how tough it could be on a winning team. We'd been a young team, but now we had a lot of mileage on us. Playing high-pressure 100-game seasons, one after another.

On top of it all, it was Kareem's final tour. After the season, he planned to retire. He'd told us that ahead of the year. But it was still a sad thing to see and experience. I'd played with Cap my entire career with the

Lakers. He was on the team my rookie season, and we had a special bond between the two of us, listening to jazz music in his house—his favorite tracks from growing up in the 1950s and '60s. Our birthdays were just a day apart, mine on April 15 and his the next day, on April 16 (both Aries). Our children were close too. I didn't want to think about the day we'd be without him in the middle, his big skyhook gone. We wanted to win for him, to get one more ring.

The Pistons also made roster moves. Out was the high-scoring Adrian Dantley, and in was Isiah's close friend Mark Aguirre from Dallas. That was big. To start the 1989 playoffs, we faced the up-and-coming Portland Trail Blazers, but we made quick work of them, sweeping the guys from the Pacific Northwest 3–0. Next we took on their northern neighbors the Seattle SuperSonics, and we knocked them out without losing a game, sweeping them 4–0. Then we flew to the desert and played the Phoenix Suns, sweeping them 4–0 too. Maybe a three-peat *was* in our destiny! We'd barely broken a sweat.

Detroit was running through their opponents too. They swept an injured Celtics team 3–0 in the first round. Then the Pistons swept Milwaukee 4–0. Then in a much-anticipated matchup, the Bad Boys played the Chicago Bulls for the right to face us in the Finals. Detroit, with their famous "Jordan Rules," beat up the Bulls, using every dirty and cheap trick in the book. Violence *was* a solution when it came to Detroit's tactics. They played like a desperate team. The thing was they were also talented. That's a dangerous combination. Literally. Jordan and his Bulls won two of the first three against Detroit, but the Pistons won the next three in a row to take it.

THE FIRST GAME of the 1989 NBA Finals began on June 6 at the Palace of Auburn Hills. A week before, though, since we'd swept our way to the playoffs, Riley took us to Santa Barbara to train. No break for us. Riley wanted to practice hard ahead of the Finals. He pushed us really, really hard. We were used to it, but some wondered why he made us go 110 percent just days before Game 1 of the Finals. Then, after arriving in Detroit early, Riley's strategy found new scrutiny when, during a routine drill, Byron tore his hamstring. Now he was out for the series. Without him, our rotation and bench would be severely affected.

I'd have to come in to start, and untested guys such as rookie David Rivers and former Piston Tony Campbell would have to pick up the slack, which was a tall order. We lost Game 1 to Detroit, 109–97. Still, we felt we could bounce back and handle Byron's absence. But then in Game 2, Magic, who'd suffered leg injuries during the year, pulled *his* hamstring and had to leave (even though he didn't want to). Still, we came close on Detroit's home floor, bringing the game within two points. After getting fouled on a drive to the hoop, Worthy stepped to the free throw line with seconds left but only made one of two shots, and we lost by three.

We gave that one away in the fourth. We'd been up 92–84 after three quarters, but Detroit outscored us 24–13 in the final period. Detroit's nasty superfan Leon "the Barber" Bradley was ruthless, berating us. We were a team running out of gas, driving with less than a full set of tires. The same thing happened back in L.A. We were ahead after three quarters in that one, 88–86, but the Pistons outscored us by six in the final frame and we lost 114–110. In Game 4 we tried to avoid the sweep, but we just couldn't. Worthy scored 40, keeping us close, draped by Pistons big man Rick Mahorn, but it wasn't enough. We lost 105–97. It hurt bad.

IT WAS STRANGE for me to be the only one of the Three Musketeers left playing. I felt alone—Byron, Magic, and I had synergy, camaraderie. We'd talk on the court, giving each other pointers on what to do in certain situations. Those two not being there to have my back, and me unable to have theirs, I didn't like it. Our team was strong—we were in the Finals, after all—but it felt off without them. The silver lining was I got to play more with Worthy. We'd talk nonstop. He'd tell me where he wanted the basketball, when to look for him on certain plays. I got closer to other teammates too, built more trust. But we knew we were missing our two top dogs.

At the end of the series, Pat subbed the 42-year-old Cap out, and the Lakers crowd gave him a standing ovation. It was his final game. Kareem, who'd won rings with Oscar Robertson and Magic Johnson, was hanging it up after a long career (which included almost losing all his NBA earnings and suing his business manager). He'd enjoyed a retirement tour the whole season, with gifts along the way at each city, including a giant rocking chair in L.A. We'd tried to win one more for him, but we just couldn't. We were too beat up and Detroit was too focused on beating us and "eating our liver," as Isiah later put it. In a way, with that, Showtime was over.

It was the end of the era when the Lakers could do it all. We could run on the break with the greyhounds. Or hold up and get the ball to Kareem—the greatest scorer ever, and just a brilliant man—for a bucket down low. For my money, we had the two greatest players of all time on the roster in Magic and Kareem. I was just lucky that I fit so well with both as a shooter, as a dunker, and most of all as a presence on defense. The good Lord had put me in that position, and I was lucky enough to capitalize on it through spirit, hard work, and attention to detail. It's not talent that takes you to the top; it's heart. But now, we'd come to the end of our road.

Detroit got their revenge on us from the year before, and you can best believe Isiah didn't care about our injuries, given his ankle issues the year prior. When Magic went down, Isiah and his team wanted to kill us. I remember telling Worthy we were about to get our ass beat. Pat's dream for a three-peat was over. We lost, and while some blame his tactics for our injuries, I put no blame on him. We had full confidence every step of the way with Riley. We knew he knew what he was doing. How you practice is how you play. Details matter; practice makes perfect. Conditioning matters. What he put us through was hard, but it wasn't traumatic.

We never doubted Pat. Heck, we'd *made* the Finals, and you can't win *every* year. Though, of course, every Laker from that era feels that if we were at full strength, we would have beaten the Pistons. But no Byron?

No Magic? It was too tall an order. That's why Detroit's guards went off on us (Dumars got the 1989 Finals MVP). Sadly, we weren't the first team to three-peat since Russell's Celtics; that honor would later go to Jordan's Bulls in the 1990s. Still, it was an amazing run. Life-changing. Every NBA Finals of the 1980s included either the Lakers or the Celtics. We'd won five; they'd gotten three. Only the 76ers and Pistons won outside of us.

We'd faced all-time Hall of Famers in every series and come out on top more often than not. What more could you ask for? For my Finals career, I averaged 10.3 points, 3.9 assists, and 2.9 boards in 46 games. But more than any shot, it was the number of points I'd prevented in those championship series, whether from Larry Bird, Isiah Thomas, Julius Erving, Joe Dumars, Dennis Johnson, or any other great. If you could compute those, I'd have affected the game like a 30-point scorer. That's what being a team player is all about. Achieve in the spaces that don't always make headlines or the marquees. Leave it all on the hardwood.

Chapter 15

One More Shot

THERE WOULD BE NO PARADE AFTER THE 1989 FINALS at the Fabulous Forum, the Roman Coliseum–esque building in Inglewood, California. No packed parking lot with thousands of fans wearing Purple and Gold, yelling "*Coooooopppp!*" Yet as a franchise, we knew we didn't want to give up just yet. Towels were for M.L. Carr, and we surely weren't going to throw ours in just yet. While we hadn't won three rings in a row, maybe we could get three out of four? As a team, we decided to give it one more shot. Even with Kareem gone from our storied locker room, maybe we could squeeze one more ring out from the Showtime era fumes. Maybe.

To replace the hole at center—though Kareem himself could never be replaced—the Lakers looked overseas and drafted Serbian center and Olympic silver medalist Vlade Divac. Today, everyone knows Vlade, the smooth-passing big man who used to smoke cigarettes in the locker room's bathroom stalls before games (like Bob Lanier used to). But back then he was an unknown quantity, one of the first European players to come into the NBA. To start the 1989–90 season, he was also one of three foreign-born players on our roster, along with British-born Steve Bucknall and Bahamas-born Mychal Thompson. The NBA was changing. And so were the Lakers.

We'd had our run throughout the 1980s. Going into the new decade, people were just getting older. Pat kept pushing us, trying to make sure we were the best we could be as individuals and as a team. But the squad needed new blood. A.C. Green was taking on a bigger role. We'd gone from Mitch Kupchak to Kurt Rambis to A.C. in a matter of years. Basketball is about evolution, and we were in the middle of it again. The whole time, teams such as Boston, Detroit, Philly, Utah, Portland, and more had been loading up to beat us. Change was inevitable after all the success. The conference was getting younger while our legs were only more worn out.

For my part, I didn't feel hateful or spiteful about the changes. How could I fight them or ignore them? It was the end of an era. And that reality really made Pat Riley's words sink in deeper. His whole thing about "Don't forget to stop and smell the roses. This will be over in a minute" rang truer and truer. That minute was here. Vlade, another diamond in the rough found by Jerry West, was another example of that. He was a seven-footer who could play outside. Prior to him, whenever a center came to the perimeter, it was for a pick-and-*roll* to the hoop. But Vlade, who was also tutored by Cap, could pick-and-*pop* to shoot it from outside. He was an innovator.

During the 1989–90 season, we had to adapt to him and he had to adapt to us. He could put the ball on the floor too. And he was a funny guy on top of it all. When he got to L.A., he couldn't speak English all that well. But I thought he hid behind some of that too, so I'd call bullshit! Whenever he didn't want to do something in practice, he'd shake his head, like, "I don't know what you guys are talking about!" But it was a front. That aside, he was a wonderful guy to play with. He brought different skills, a different energy. Later, he'd go on to a decorated playing career in the NBA and then as an executive (one of many former Lakers who did so).

REMEMBER ALL THOSE YEARS when we went 62–20? Well, we did that one game better during the 1989–90 season, somehow, going 63–19. Magic led us in scoring at 22.3 points per game and James was close behind at

21.1. For that and for his 11.5 assists per game, Earvin earned the MVP for the season, edging out Philly's Charles Barkley. We had a lot of success that year. Even A.C. Green earned an All-Star nod and a selection to the All-Defensive Team. As for me, my minutes went down. I played in 80 games and started 10, but I only averaged 23.1 minutes. The year prior, it had been 24.3, and for my career, I played about 30 minutes a game. Father Time, man.

I was happy for A.C. We'd put him through the wringer. He was a devout follower of the Bible, and guys would send over liquored-up women to sit on his lap in the Forum Club, which was a lot like Hugh Hefner's Playboy Mansion or Studio 54, as he drank his orange juice or ice water. A.C., as close a follower of the Bible as he was, was a virgin, which was something he wasn't shy about talking about with the world. He focused all his energies into rebounding and defense for the Lakers. The rest? The women, the booze, the drugs—which were all at his disposal—well, he disposed of them. He didn't want anything to do with those temptations.

I admire him to this day for that. The Bible thumper was the only guy on the team not having sex. He was saving himself for that special someone. And in 2002, after leaving the league (and winning one more ring in 2000 with Shaq and Kobe), he married his lovely wife, Veronique, adding a wedding ring to his three championship ones. With the Lakers, A.C. brought a different dynamic to the team. He carried his faith strong and stuck by it. He was our preacher and pastor on the road and in the locker room. He curbed our cursing, curbed a lot of things we did. But he added such joy and energy. He was great to be around.

A.C. was also one of the strongest guys I ever played with, which includes the likes of Maurice Lucas and Artis Gilmore. A.C. was *built*. We used to say his strength was infused by God, that he was unbreakable thanks to the Lord. But even with A.C.'s strength, we couldn't get over the hump during the 1989–90 season. We'd started by winning 10 of our first 11 games, and we ended up winning 16 of our final 19. Riley earned his first Coach of the Year Award for that. But the playoffs were a different story. Back East, it was all about the Pistons and Bulls. But in the West, it was about succumbing to our fate. Pat kept pushing, and it just got to be too much.

At one point during the season, Magic, Worthy, and I went to Jerry West. He'd been asking what was wrong. Despite the wins, we just didn't seem happy. We were all breaking down from a decade of incredibly hard work. And while he had the best intentions in mind, Pat was pushing us too hard now. More than that, more than the work, which we could take in the end, he was closing off to us. We had once been able to go to Riley about anything and everything, but now he'd put up a new wall. He began to separate from us. I don't want to speculate, but maybe it was an emotional thing, like he knew it was the end.

Previously, Pat used to ask us in practice, "What do you guys want to do today?" That's one thing I ask my own players now when I coach. But there was much less of that open dialogue with Riley at the end. It felt a little bit like the old era with Paul Westhead, who wouldn't budge from his system. I guess it was inevitable. It was harder to run like we had before, harder to keep up that mystique. Riley thought he knew what to do, but we wanted to give our say too. He had tunnel vision. Pat was so busy preparing his game plan that he didn't stop to listen to anyone. We needed a break. But he thought that was letting our guard down.

In the end, it became something of an "us versus him" thing. Pat was mad we'd gone to Jerry, and I think he blamed me especially. But by now, that's all water under the bridge. When you're close with someone and work with them for years, you're bound to have ups and downs. Breakups can be hard. Today, I love Pat Riley and thank him for everything he did for us and for everything he saw in me. I wouldn't have been the Laker I became if it weren't for him. It all has to end sometime. For us, that came in the second round of the playoffs that season.

Opening the postseason, we beat the Houston Rockets 3–1. But in the Western Conference Semifinals, we stumbled and lost to Phoenix 4–1. The Suns had players such as Tom Chambers, Jeff Hornacek, Eddie Johnson, Dan Majerle, Kevin Johnson, and two former Lakers, Mike McGee and Kurt Rambis. They were fast, and they knew our weaknesses.

But more than that, we just collapsed. While the Suns went on to lose to Clyde Drexler and the Trail Blazers, who went on to lose to the Pistons in the Finals, the final NBA game of my career came on May 15, 1990, in a 106–103 loss at home to the Suns. My stat line read: 5 points, 3 steals, 6 assists, and 3 boards. Magic had 43 points, refusing to let us lose. But we did.

AFTER THE PLAYOFFS, Dr. Buss took me out for dinner. I'll always be grateful for how he handled my situation. He took me to a nice place in Beverly Hills, and after we ate, he gave me three choices. Pat Riley was leaving (he and Magic cried together at Earvin's house when the choice was made), and would go on to broadcast for a year before signing with the New York Knicks. Pat, who wouldn't have coached if there had been no injury to McKinney, was now an icon. But with the change (L.A. was bringing in Mike Dunleavy), Dr. Buss said the team was going in a new direction. As I said, he gave me three choices. He said the team could trade me, I could retire, or he could just cut me.

But he added, "Whatever you decide, I want you to know there is a five-year coaching contract waiting for you after you finish playing." That, to me, is why Dr. Buss is the greatest owner in sports history: his ability to take care of his people. I knew I didn't want to be traded, because I didn't want to play for another NBA team. After winning five rings with Showtime, I didn't want to deface or destroy that legacy and memory, even though my agent said Boston (ha!), the Spurs, and the 76ers were all asking about me. But I also knew I wasn't done playing. So I decided that I'd leave the Lakers and head overseas.

Not only were the Lakers changing, but the idea of the NBA's sixth man was changing. Before, it had been a do-it-all position. I'd come in to guard the best player and play backup point guard. I'd come off the bench to start the games, but I darn sure finished most of them. Now, though, the role was becoming one more of "instant offense," one for quick scorers such as Detroit's Vinnie Johnson. To replace me, the Lakers picked up Terry Teagle from Golden State, who'd averaged 14 points for the past 5 seasons with the Warriors and 16.1 in 1989–90. But I understood. As a guy who grew up in Pasadena who never thought he'd make the NBA, I'd done just fine.

WHILE WE DIDN'T win any more rings after 1988, we knew that we'd established a lasting culture for the Lakers that would remain for a long time. We set a tone by winning thanks to our "All for one, one for all" mentality. Being a part of the Lakers was one of the greatest feelings I've ever had. And though the team hasn't won since the 2020 bubble season during the COVID–19 pandemic, the culture continues, instilled by our squad in the 1980s. We'd gone to eight Finals and won five of them. Few teams can boast those credentials. And that I was named eight times to the league's All-Defensive Team, winning Defensive Player of the Year once, was the cherry on top.

I also finished my career ranked in the Lakers' all-time top 10 in three-point field goals made (428), games played (873), minutes played (23,635), steals (1,033), blocked shots (523), assists (3,666), defensive rebounds (2,028), and free throw percentage (.833). These aren't things you ever plan for as a kid. You can only work toward them one day at a time. It's humbling to see those numbers written out in front of me. I can't believe I did all that—truly. Not to mention the five championship rings that fill up an entire hand. Pat Riley once said, "Coop could've started for any team in the league." But then I might have missed out on all this.

I read recently that I had the most wins out of anyone who played in the 1980s. Can you believe that? But sports is ultimately about failure. Only one team wins their final game at the end of the year. And no one beats Father Time. Thankfully, I know what it was like to win big. And as I look back on my Lakers days, I made more great memories than I can count. Some I'll be able to tell my grandkids while they're young, and some I'll have to wait to tell them when they're older! But in the end, I'm proud of my career. Even though we're 30 years removed from it today, I'm still close to many of my teammates. And I can remember beating Boston like it was yesterday.

Chapter 16

Lo E L'Italia, a Friend in Need, and Back to L.A.

WHILE SOME PLAYERS IN THE NBA now make $50 million per year (and counting), back in the 1980s and early '90s, salaries were much different. During the 1990–91 season, only one player earned more than $4 million (Patrick Ewing), and the league minimum was $120,000. But overseas in places such as Italy, there was bigger money to be made. You could make 10 times the NBA minimum over there, even at the tail end of your career. You could see the world and hear new fans cheer in new languages. As I left the Lakers, knowing my time in the league was done, my agent told me he could get me another gig overseas.

That summer, young guys such as Danny Ferry and Brian Shaw were leaving Italy to start careers in the NBA, and so their team Il Messaggero Roma of the Italian League needed Americans. Days after that news, my agent said that team now wanted my services. At first I thought I'd play closer to home, in a Mexican league maybe. But when it was Italy, my gears began to turn. The job paid well, and my family could see Europe. I thought about it for a day or two and talked it over with Wanda. We knew it would be a big change, but if I were going to accept the job, I knew I didn't want to tear myself away from my family. And she was in!

185

Wanda and I took our three kids with us, and we braved a new world. I signed a two-year, $3.2 million deal and made a commitment to Rome. There was no returning to the United States for 12 months. I wasn't about to spend any of my money to travel after we landed in Rome. And it turned out to be one of the greatest decisions I ever made. My mother used to tell me that traveling abroad is a very special thing. A lot of people don't get the opportunity. When I was a boy, she used to push me to read, to travel in my mind, because no one in our family (except her) had been to Europe—and she'd only been for a weekend in Florence with her church.

To live in Rome was exciting. It's a historical city and a biblical one. But it's also enough like home. I'd get the chance to do something I loved, be paid for it, and travel the world. I signed on the dotted line and was prepared for some fun. While I was set for the first year, I could renew my deal for the second season if both the team and I liked where we were at, if they thought I was giving full effort. As far as my jersey number, I chose 16. In high school, it was 42 for Connie Hawkins and Paul Warfield. At New Mexico, I wore 22. And with the Lakers I'd chosen No. 21 because No. 22 was hanging in the rafters for Elgin Baylor.

THE HIGHLIGHT OF my year there was the 1990–91 All-Star Game. Held on December 1, 1990, the affair was in our home arena in Rome. There were some 16,000 people at the game. The local crowd was great. The fans were getting into basketball in serious ways. Past MVPs of the game included Americans such as Joe "Jellybean" Bryant, Michael "Sugar" Ray Richardson, and my former teammate Wes Matthews. And on December 1, I was named the game's MVP! Before the game, I remember an international reporter coming up to me, saying, "Michael Cooper, in order for you to win MVP, you'll have to put on a show!" I said, "Okay, let's go!"

I knew what he was saying. The Italian League, especially the referees back then, favored the home team and home players. When you played at home, there seemed to be around a 95 percent chance that you'd win. It's not that things were crooked; it's just that the home court swayed a lot. So during the game, I put on a personal show. I threw some between-the-legs passes, got a couple of big-time dunks. People started jumping up and down, screaming. I didn't score a lot, but I took everything I'd learned from my good friend Magic and lit up the night. My teammate Roberto Premier was on the All-Star team with me, and I made sure he got his looks too.

We won the All-Star Game 182–176, and I hoisted my MVP trophy afterward. It was my second award of the star-studded event. I'd already taken home the three-point contest trophy that weekend, something my friend Bob McAdoo did during the 1986–87 affair. I'd been Magic in the game and Bird in the shootout. I'd truly learned from the best. (Now, if only there had been a skyhook contest later in the day!) All in all, the All-Star experience was fun and validated my choice to go overseas and test my skills abroad. The Italian League was good, one of the best leagues—if not the best—outside of the NBA. Europe cared about basketball, and they'd soon impact the NBA.

Some things I had to get used to, though. The ball was live as soon as it hit the rim, the three-point line was a few feet closer, the lane was a few feet wider, and the refs never called traveling. Other than that, it was pretty similar. My coach, Valerio Bianchini, was a lot like an NBA coach (though he didn't dress as well as Pat). He was a former Italian National coach, and while he allowed me to play all of the positions at various times in games, I was mostly our point guard. I played nearly 40 minutes a night and was our team's best player, which made me understand what Kareem and Magic had to take on every game.

If we won, it was expected. If we lost, it was the American's fault. But that's what I got the big bucks for. The league's competition was strong, including guys such as Dino Radja, Mike D'Antoni, and Vinny Del Negro. But our team was good. At one point we were 16–6 before a skid. I scored 25 points in our third game and 24 three games later. And I got my season-high 26 not long after. But at the end of the year, from February 17 to April 3, we sputtered, losing five of our final seven games. Today, some still ask when or how I knew it was time to hang up my professional sneakers. For me, I knew it with three games to go that season.

In Italy, we only played one game a week. But we practiced hard. (The floor in Rome somehow felt even harder than the courts in America. It was like New York City blacktop.) It wasn't easy stuff, despite the light game schedule. One day, I walked into the gym and just looked around. There were a lot of young guys on the floor, with only two or three veterans around my age. Premier was in his late thirties. I'd always said I was going to leave basketball when I wasn't having fun at practice. That day, as I laced up my shoes, I just didn't want to be there anymore. I knew right then it was time to retire. So I played out the final three games and hung 'em up.

IN MY SHORT Italian career, I averaged 15.8 points, 6.1 rebounds, 1.9 steals, and 1.8 assists. Not bad for a 34-year-old with about 34 million miles on his old Showtime legs. Virtus and I agreed not to renew the second year of the contract. Though I was glad for my time abroad. Most people in Rome spoke a little English, and I did my best to speak a little Italian. Wanda and our three kids were able to see some of the world outside of Los Angeles, which was something they could keep with them for their entire lives. And because there was less traveling for the season, I was able to spend time with them, which I cherished.

Many NBA players had already gone overseas to play in Italy, from Sugar to Earl Cureton to McAdoo. Certain parts of the country were Americanized, including Rome and Milan. They were cultural hubs. Wanda, who hated the "mad dog" Italian drivers, enjoyed shopping in Rome. And we loved all of the cuisine. Italy was slower than L.A. back then. Rome shut down for several hours in the middle of the day, which was good for everyone's well-being. And while I know it existed there, I didn't see any racism. The fans called me a "Black king." But we missed home. So we went back to Los Angeles, and I was officially retired.

ONCE I GOT back to the States, I wondered what my next move would be. Dr. Buss had promised me a contract for the Lakers. So I soon took him up on that offer. But I wanted to try my hand at a few other things first. One of those was a couple modeling gigs for Aramis cologne. Those even required me to put on a suit! I'd always wanted to try modeling (my time in Italy furthered that interest). People in my life had suggested I do it. But I didn't necessarily believe that I could, even though I was tall, slender, and handsome. So I tried it and was successful. It was fun to act all important during the shoots, putting on my "Blue Steel" face.

Speaking of acting, I tried that too. Once I got modeling out of my system, I knew I could do okay in front of the camera. So I thought acting might not be too tough. I knew a thing or two about entertaining, and I lived in the capital of the business. So I went out for a few roles. Unfortunately my efforts did not come to amount to an acting career.

But I like to think that the popular 1990s sitcom *Hangin' with Mr. Cooper* with comedian Mark Curry, which was about a retired basketball player in California, was loosely based on my life. There'd even been some talk of me playing the lead role, but I didn't quite have the acting chops, which was understandable since I'd never done it before. Mark was hilarious and played a credible former Golden State Warrior. (There was even a character on it named Earvin Rodman!) My only regret was that I never had a small role on the show, like a neighbor or something. It would have been nice to have a cameo on that show, either way. But my name was still in the title! Outside of the show, there was still a lot happening in my life. After coming home from Italy in the spring of 1991, the Lakers were back to their winning ways in the playoffs. The team had a 58–24 record under Coach Dunleavy.

The Lakers still had Magic, A.C., Byron, Mychal, and Worthy, along with Vlade and newcomers Sam Perkins and Elden Campbell. In the first round, they swept our old foes the Rockets. In the next round against the Run-TMC Warriors, they won 4–1. Magic and co. won 4–2 against Clyde Drexler and his Trail Blazers next. Now there was a new foe in the Finals. No longer was it Boston or Detroit; now it was Chicago with

Michael Jordan, Scottie Pippen, and Horace Grant. While they were formidable, I believed the Lakers would win. This was the Bulls' first time in the Finals and Magic's ninth. You had to lose before you could win—at least most of the time.

I REMEMBER GOING to those Finals. It was the one where Michael Jordan, the league's new golden boy, flew through the air, down the lane, and changed the ball from one hand to the other midair. He went up soaring for the layup, and as Perkins jumped with him, Jordan made the move, bringing the ball from his right down and back into his left. On TV, famed announcer Marv Albert screamed, "Ooooh! A spec*tacular* move by Michael *Jordan*!" It's one of the most famous play calls ever. But more than anything he did, it was a trip for me watching my old teammates in the final series again without me. I felt like I wanted to jump onto the court.

Magic was still great, though he was older. Byron still had it too, and so did Worthy. But there was no Pat Riley roaming the sideline, and no Kareem in the post, either. While I didn't know Mike Dunleavy well, he'd played with Houston in his younger days, and we'd faced him in the playoffs a few times. He brought the big man–oriented style to L.A. And as I got to know him later as a person, we got along pretty well. Our kids even played basketball together at Brentwood High School, and his eldest son played in the NBA. Mike Dunleavy Jr. now works for the Golden State Warriors as their GM. But Mike Sr. was just a young NBA coach back in 1991.

The Lakers won the first game of the series. Chicago looked scared and unready. But they'd discovered something crucial late. They put the long-armed Pippen on Magic, and in subsequent games, he wore Earvin down, cutting off passing lanes. It turned out to be the key to the series, other than Michael's brilliance. The Bulls won the next four and earned their first ring. Later Magic said to me, "Coop, if we'd had you, we would have won." Those were kind, flattering words from my close friend. Part of me wished we'd been able to find out. (Personally, though, I believe he's right. I could have helped.) But today I have no hard feelings.

WHILE LOSING IN the Finals to Jordan, the guy whose sneakers everyone was wearing, hurt my friend Magic, the next few months would be an even bigger gut punch, to say the least. After a routine physical for a life insurance policy, his doctors found something. When his docs found out what was wrong, the Lakers were out on a preseason road trip. The team was in Utah, and an exhausted Magic got a phone call at his hotel. He was told to return to L.A. right away. Magic had expressed a wish not to attend the road trip in the first place but gave in, knowing it was good for the team. So to be called back home before the Utah game was a shock.

Utah, where he'd requested to be traded during the Paul Westhead debacle in 1980, would be the site of another significant moment for Earvin. He flew back to L.A. and got the bad news. His bloodwork indicated that he was HIV positive. All most people knew about HIV and AIDS in the early '90s was that it was sexually transmitted and that it was a death sentence. But beyond that, we had no idea what the disease was or how to fight it. Now we knew that our friend had contracted it, and it floored us all. It also impacted the world at large a great deal. Suddenly, Magic was the spokesman for the illness.

And since Magic had it, that meant anyone could. It was a diagnosis that would have crushed anyone—except him. While it scared him at first, leading to some pretty dark thoughts, his longtime agent Lon Rosen said, Magic resolved to face it head-on. He told the world about it in a press conference on November 7, 1991. For me, that was one of the darkest times of my life. When you have a loved one share that news, you immediately think they are a goner for sure. Society, including the NBA, was just beginning to talk about HIV and AIDS, but now they would both be talking about it much more. Magic became the face of the illness.

Back then, when a team played on the road, it would stay in hotels. And in those hotels, parties and women would be present. That's one of the major reasons teams started to charter planes, to get their players out of cities directly after games. The NBA also began holding seminars about safe sex. Every player who learned Magic's news got tested. But before he told the world, Magic called me. It was a few days after he left the Utah game, and he'd asked me to come to Dr. Buss's office. James Worthy was there. So were Pat Riley, Mitch Kupchak, Gary Vitti, and Magic's doctors.

At one point, Magic pulled me aside into another room, and we spoke privately. "Coop, listen. I want you to know what's happening," Magic said. He wanted me to know I was a special person in his life, one of his closest friends. "I contracted the HIV virus," he told me. At the time, I didn't know much about it at all other than what I'd seen on TV. When he told me the news, when I heard the words come from his lips, the first thing I did was start weeping. "E, are you serious?" I said through my tears. It's an exchange I hold especially dear to this day. But what he said next nearly floored me. I still get chills when I think back on it. He said, "Hey, Coop, I'm going to be all right."

He looked me in the eye and he told me that in his heart, he knew he would not only live but beat the illness. All I can say today is that God puts things on people's shoulders—heavy burdens at times—but He doesn't do it unless He knows you can carry it. Magic could carry this one. He would beat it like he beat the Celtics and 76ers. This was Magic's burden. Prior to him finding out, he'd already slowed down his life and married his longtime on-again-off-again girlfriend, Cookie Kelly. She was the best thing to ever happen to Earvin. And thankfully, neither she nor their unborn baby had contracted the illness.

I WAS THERE in the room on November 7, 1991, when he told the world his news. The reporters were all crying. Today, I hold the chance to be with him that day high in my heart. When Larry Bird heard the news back in Indiana, he nearly crashed his car. Larry, who retired after that season, was one of the first people to call Magic to express his love for Earvin, to say if he needed anything, Larry would be there. Magic also made sure to tell Jordan, Arsenio Hall, Kareem, and a few others. When he called his father, the news made Earvin Sr. curl up in bed in tears. But Magic's mother, Christine, knew God was in control.

It's hard to underestimate all of this. Magic was so famous that he once signed a pair of ballet shoes for a woman who, moments later, had a heart attack and passed away. Not to be morbid, but that was his effect. Gary Vitti told me later that Magic pulled him aside to tell him the news, and he told Gary, "When God gave me this disease, he gave it to the right person." Vitti said Magic told him that "without a hint of self-pity." Magic said, "I'm going to do something really good with this." In some languages, the word *tragedy* has two connotations: devastation and opportunity. Somehow Magic always saw the world through that second lens.

Earvin was special, and Cookie, perhaps more than anyone, knew it. She saw Magic as "the chosen one" for the illness, knew that his example would both bring awareness to its dangers and, in that way, give a way to beat it. Magic told me, "Coop, I got this." He whispered it in my ear when he addressed the Lakers team before that November 7 press conference. If an entire group's knees could buckle, ours did that morning. I thought I was losing my friend; we all did. I couldn't help by cry; my brother was in grave danger. The news devastated Dr. Buss too; he had lived a playboy lifestyle but now was resolved to do anything he could to help Earvin.

Magic, as we know now, beat the disease and removed stigma around it for others. He did the impossible. For someone who, as a freshman in high school, helped bring Blacks and whites together during the days of Michigan's bussing and integration programs and later changed the NBA at the center of the Lakers and Celtics rivalry, this was perhaps his greatest miracle. To his credit, NBA commissioner David Stern was also integral in helping to educate the public and lift up Earvin. The NBA has been at the forefront of much when it comes to society and culture. And while it's not perfect (nothing is), the league's work with safe sex education is at the top of that list.

After the press conference, Magic quit the Lakers and got educated about HIV. He threw himself into advocacy. He changed how he ate, he worked out, and he got his strength up. He appeared on a special on Nickelodeon, speaking to children about the disease. One seven-year-old, Hydeia

Broadbent, who sadly died in 2024, cried to Earvin, saying, "I want people to know that we're just normal people." Magic, the overflowing spirit that he's always been, responded gently and kindly. "You don't have to cry," he said. "Because we are normal people. Okay? We are." It's a moment that still brings tears to people's eyes today.

AFTER MAGIC RETIRED from the Lakers, he quickly got the urge to play again. He'd learned about HIV, and the fact was he couldn't give it to other people through normal basketball contact. So while he'd tried to play in a few games after learning he had the disease, he initially retired after a controversial moment when Vitti treated a minor cut on his arm without gloves. Magic, though, now wanted back in. His first real opportunity came in the 1992 All-Star Game. Stern and the league said he could play in it, and so, despite not playing that year, he was an All-Star again. The only problem was, not everyone in the league was so open.

The headliner was Karl Malone, who questioned his safety if Magic were to play, wondering what would happen if a drop of Magic's sweat went into his eye. But others also expressed worry, including Mark Price, A.C. Green, and Byron Scott. They just didn't know the truth and were scared. Others questioned Magic's sexuality. To his credit, Dennis Rodman, who was an All-Star in 1992, said he didn't think about the diagnosis. "Who cares?" Rodman said. In his own way, he made it known Magic was okay by him. Well, Magic played in the All-Star Game and earned the MVP. Six months later, he won a gold medal with the Olympic Dream Team in Spain.

IT WAS IMPOSSIBLE to live in L.A. and not hear about Magic's news. But another headline we all saw around then was the beating of Rodney King by LAPD police officers on March 3, 1991. King, who had fled when officers attempted to pull him over, was captured. And those cops nearly beat him to death. Later, they were found innocent in a court of law. That turned the city into a war zone. Black versus white, the poor versus the police. Law enforcement is supposed to protect you. But when we saw

King nearly die at the hands of police in that video, which had been shot by a bystander, it was dehumanizing for him. No one deserved that.

It opened our eyes to what police could do to you simply because they wanted to—to do what they felt like they could do to Blacks. Yes, King had been using drugs, and yes he'd fled. But they didn't need to beat him within an inch of his life. That was too gruesome. It had L.A. on edge for weeks. Then when the white officers were found innocent, the city burned. It made me sit my own children down to talk to them, to tell them how to protect themselves if cops ever pulled them over. That's not something I thought I ever had to worry about as a young person in the 1960s and '70s. But there we were. As Rodney King said, "Can't we all just get along?" Good question.

BUT NOT EVERYTHING was so dire in my world. I'd gotten back with the Lakers. Beginning in 1991, I'd come back to the team to serve as special assistant to General Manager Jerry West. I held the job for three years, and it was like a PhD program on the inner workings of the league. Being with Jerry and getting to know the team and the NBA from an administrative standpoint was eye-opening. West taught me how to scout players, giving me secret insights into his process. For example, when you're the GM of the Lakers, you have to spot talent toward the end of the draft, since we always had a good record. That was a skill in and of itself.

So Jerry, who talked fast, ate fast, and played golf fast (he wasted no time), told me that when I went to scout colleges such as UNC or Indiana, I shouldn't pay much attention to the starters. Those were the guys who the bad lottery teams would be selecting. Instead, we'd check the players who were coming off the bench. Jerry knew there was a reason they were on top 10 teams: they were talented and highly rated, and their coaches saw something in them. But if they were coming off the bench, that meant they could also play with other great players. They were part of winning programs and knew how to stay within a role. So they'd be perfect for us.

Jerry liked guys who were between 6'4" and 6'9", so I made sure
to watch out for those guys too. He also taught me about maintaining
relationships with executives in the NBA. He was always on the phone.
It was especially helpful around draft time when we might have to reach
out to a team to see about trading up from, say, the last pick to the 20th
to get a guy we wanted. It was amazing sitting around with Jerry West,
Mitch Kupchak, and Dr. Buss to talk team-building. My special assistant
role was one West uniquely invented for me. Today, special assistant to
the GM is a popular job. But I was the first in the NBA to have it.

WHEN I HAD some free time, Earvin would often call. After he became an
international star thanks to the 1992 Summer Olympics in Barcelona,
Magic wanted to capitalize on it. So he started the Magic Johnson
Traveling All-Stars. It was a barnstorming effort not unlike the Harlem
Globetrotters. He invited me to play on the squad, which toured the
globe, mostly during the summers. Other players he invited were Bob
McAdoo, Kurt Rambis, Mike McGee, Moses Malone, Mark Aguirre,
Ralph Sampson, Alex English, Earl Cureton, and Reggie Theus. The
team kept our dreams of playing hoops for big audiences alive and let us
see the world.

We flew to China, Japan, Spain, and other countries. We played CBA
teams, college All-Star teams. We faced off against players such as Penny
Hardaway and the guys from Michigan's Fab Five. We got to make a little
bit of money too. But Magic was the attraction. He demanded we were
serious about it. As long as we never lost, he said, people would continue
to see us, which they did in droves. We often drew more than 5,000
people for games. He and I even got to run our old Coop-a-Loop play
for fans. Magic was good too. At one point, I thought he might even link
up with our old coach Pat Riley and play for the Knicks in the NBA. But
that never materialized.

AFTER A FEW years on the job with Jerry West, he began talking to me
about coaching. It was an intriguing idea, and one I was grateful he

brought up. Over the years, Jerry mentored me and he groomed me. We'd talked about everything from contracts to draft picks. After three years, he thought I could be a great assistant coach for L.A. After losing to the Bulls, Dunleavy stayed around for one more season. Then in 1992–93, Randy Pfund took over as head coach, going 39–43. Randy lasted another half season before Riley's old assistant Bill Bertka took over as interim coach for two games. For the remaining 16 games of the 1993–94 season, Magic became the coach. In March 1994 I joined his staff. We won five of our first six games under Coach Johnson, but the season fell apart and we lost our last 10. Del Harris took over for the 1994–95 season, and I stayed on as his assistant. Coach Harris was an old-school guy, one of the most technical and thoughtful teachers in the game. We had Elden Campbell, Cedric Ceballos, Vlade Divac, Anthony Peeler, Kurt Rambis (he was back!), Nick Van Exel, and rookie Eddie Jones, who was my personal project. He was long-armed, quick, and talented on defense—cut from the Michael Cooper cloth!

Del, Jerry West, and Dr. Buss wanted me to help set the team culture. So over the next three years, I worked with Del, who won Coach of the Year his first season (and then gave plaques to all us assistants). I got in the trenches with the guys. As a coach on the sideline, you can tell someone how to do something, but if you can get on the court with them, as I still could, you can *show* them, not just tell them. And that's one of the reasons why Magic decided to come back to the NBA and suit up for the 1995–96 season. He wanted to teach the guys, who'd nicknamed themselves the Lake Show, how to win, how to carry the torch. He just couldn't stay away.

At 36 years old, after seeing Jordan and Hakeem win rings in his absence, Magic came back for the final 40 games of the year (playing in 32). Even before that, he'd begun coming to games, and you could see he was champing at the bit to prove he could still play. He'd sit close to the bench, talking to players. He'd had a taste of the NBA again in his coaching stint; now he wanted to wear the uniform. But the Lakers didn't quite get back to the playoffs with him. Still, Magic averaged more than

14 points along with nearly 6 rebounds and 7 assists per game. After which, at least, he could retire on his own terms and become the point guard of the boardroom.

THE SAME YEAR Magic came back, Michael Jordan won his fourth NBA title after making his own comeback the season prior. He was on his way to his second three-peat after winning rings in 1991, 1992, and 1993. Michael came into the league in 1984, and one of the things I've always loved about him was how he took what we did in the 1980s and built on it in the '90s. He changed the game. His Bulls team was built around him by Jerry Krause, and while it took seven years for Jordan to get over the hump and win, he did it. He also changed fashion. No longer did NBA players wear those Daisy Dukes; it was all about shorts as long as cutoff jeans.

Each year, Jordan got better, eventually changing his game to fit exactly what the team needed. That's what a leader does and has to do at the end of the day. To watch someone come into the league talented but untested and then leave as a legend, that's what it's all about. That's what happened to Magic and James Worthy. And Jordan too. It was trial by fire for MJ. First with the Pistons and their violent Jordan Rules and later through the Knicks and Utah as he won and won and won. I'm proud I got to witness it. These aren't stories my grandfather has to tell me; these are my memories. I saw all these guys play.

ANOTHER WHO CAME into the league untested but left a legend was Kobe Bryant, who was the closest thing to Jordan we've seen since MJ retired. Talking about Kobe today is hard. It was a tragedy when he died with his daughter Gigi in a helicopter crash on January 26, 2020. He played 20 years in the NBA, and I was there when Jerry West brought him in that first day to work him out ahead of the 1996 draft. I was still coaching for the team then, and Jerry asked me to work him out. When I walked in, Kobe was at one end of the court shooting. West asked me to play defense on him, to deny the ball, to keep him from the X's they'd put on the court, and to check him on pick-and-rolls.

But when we were introduced, he started sizing *me* up. Playing him was one of the best workouts I ever had. A lot of people say the 17-year-old Kobe kicked my ass, elbowing me and working me, but I think I held my own as a 40-year-old retired player. Either way, what impressed me the most was how Kobe was able to go wherever he wanted on the court. Even though I was older, I could still get people to go one way or the other. But not Bryant. He always got to his spot, even though it was my job to stop him from doing so. He constantly was able to get the shot he wanted. I had never sweat that hard before guarding him.

After that—I'll never forget this—Jerry West said, pointing to Kobe, "That's the one." Jerry was right again. A quarter of a century later, when Kobe, a five-time NBA champion and an Academy Award winner, died in that horrible accident, I wept. I miss him today. His death knocked the wind out of the world. In a way, we're all still recovering. Kobe wasn't a perfect person, but from every account, he was striving to be one up until the day he died. That afternoon, he was traveling with his daughter to one of her basketball games. Both were preparing to be huge influences on the WNBA. It's just so unfortunate they're gone now.

IN 1997 I had my own personal difficulties I had to navigate off the basketball court. When you retire from basketball, life can be exceptionally hard. You look for the thrills that the game once gave you at the highest level— the fame, the rush from winning, the championships, and the attention. The problem is, it's nearly impossible to find in the outside world after you retire. Still, I was searching. And I was doing so, sadly, with substance abuse. Once I'd left coaching on Del Harris's staff (he later made the Hall of Fame), I got caught up in the lifestyle that L.A. can provide, which was not something I indulged in much during my playing days.

It nearly submarined me. By then, Wanda and I had grown apart— and the parties and the nightlife drew me further in. I succumbed to their enticements and lost my way. Thankfully for me, Jerry West saw what I was doing to myself and reached out. Again he helped me in a major way. Really, I can't thank Jerry enough for the role he's played in my life over the decades. From drafting me to helping me grow on the Lakers to this moment, basically saving my life, Jerry has been my guardian angel. And one day in 1997, he came up to me and said, like the father figure he was, "Coop, you have to do something about your lifestyle."

Jerry had already set everything up for me. All I had to do was agree to it, which I readily did. So I went to the John Lucas rehabilitation center in Houston, Texas. John had been a fantastic NBA player whose life, like many players' in the 1970s and 1980s, was derailed by drugs. In the wake of his own recovery, John started his rehab facility. And now that's where I found myself for 45 days. Going there, outside of the births of my kids, was the best thing ever to happen to me. The facility provided space and time for me to reflect, to get away from the lifestyle L.A. can trick you into thinking is valuable. Thank God I got the chance to be Michael Cooper again.

Chapter 17

Winning in the WNBA

A LITTLE LATER, AFTER YEARS OF GROWING FURTHER APART, Wanda and I divorced, deciding to end our marriage. We made it official in 2000, but the choice came after years of heading in different personal directions, beginning in the mid-1990s. The life of an NBA player is hard, not only on the player himself but on his family. I didn't always make it easy on Wanda. She had done some amazing things and kept our family together as I spent weeks out of every month on the road. She'd thought about leaving before and taking the kids to New Mexico, but Norm Nixon, the longtime family man, called her and helped to talk her down from that ledge.

Strangely, it was the period after my playing days that proved we couldn't stay together. With all that free time we had, we realized we'd grown apart. Long ago were our college days and honeymoon phase. We'd brought three kids up in our family—Michael, Simone, and Miles—and we loved them dearly, but they weren't a *fix* for the issues Wanda and I had. Life after basketball can be difficult, and animosity grew. It was unfortunate, but we made the eventual right decision and acted like adults. So she went back home to New Mexico and I stayed in L.A. to get my future back in order, my life back on track.

When your personal life is failing, when you wonder what will happen to your family, whether you will see them enough, and what they might think of you. It can be easy to want to go down the wrong path. Wanda wasn't perfect and neither was I, and we'd had real issues. But the question in these situations is always about how you'll recover. Forgive the pun, but it's about how you'll rebound. Thankfully I had good friends and my Five D's philosophy. I stayed determined and dedicated to keeping my head screwed on. To this day, Wanda and I are friends, and we've done a great job raising our kids. You live and you learn and you try to do better.

BY 1997 MY time as an assistant coach for the Lakers had ended and I wanted to find more to do in the game of basketball. I was 41 years old and I'd left Del Harris's award-winning staff, and now I needed another gig. Phil Jackson would soon bring in his own group of guys to coach Kobe Bryant, Shaquille O'Neal, and the Lakers with his famed triangle system. Phil, who was in a relationship with Lakers higher-up Jeanie Buss, had won six rings as coach of Michael Jordan and the Bulls earlier in the 1990s, and now L.A. was his next project. Known as the Zen Master for his philosophical style, Phil would win five more rings with the Lakers over the next decade.

But the question I kept asking myself was, *What's next for me?* Where would my next rings come from? That's when I discovered women's basketball in a real way. I didn't want to be a GM for a team. I'd had my fun with Jerry West, but the job was too much about pushing papers. Instead, I wanted the action, to be on the court in some capacity, figuring out the game in the moment. I'd learned so much from Pat Riley about attention to detail in a game plan and the ability to adjust; I wanted to employ that. That's what I liked: teaching. I'd talked about coaching women when I was still a player with the Lakers. Maybe now was the time?

Around this time, I'd started to hear rumblings about a new league coming into existence: the WNBA. I'd also started to hear more about a women's summer league in L.A. So I decided to see about getting involved in that first. There was a woman named Rhonda Windham who played basketball at USC in the mid-1980s and who created the Say No Classic women's basketball program at USC in 1991. She always tried to get me to come up and see it every summer, so after leaving the Lakers in 1997, I did just that. I went up to the exhibition, and that's when I got a chance to see some of its great players up close—women such as Tina Thompson, Lisa Leslie, Yolanda Griffith, and more.

I got hooked and I ended up wanting to coach them. But when the WNBA started in 1997, I was still helping the Lakers out with a few things, scouting a little bit. But in the WNBA's second year, I got more involved before coming fully on board. My entry into the league started thanks to former NBA star Orlando Woolridge, a career 16-points-per-game scorer on teams including Chicago, New Jersey, and Denver. I'd played with him on the Lakers during the 1988–89 and 1989–90 seasons. Now, he was about to be my boss.

Dr. Buss owned the Los Angeles Sparks at the team's outset in 1997 (today the team is owned by Sparks LA Sports, which includes people such as Magic Johnson), and he appointed his son Johnny to be team president. The franchise's first coach was Linda Sharp. After she went 4–7 to start the opening year, Julie Rousseau took over and finished the season going 10–7. Julie stayed on to start the 1998 season but only mustered a 7–13 record. That's when Orlando Woolridge took over, going 5–5 in the final 10 games. For the 1999 season, though, which was Orlando's first full year, he brought me on as an assistant. We helped the team go 20–12 for its first winning season.

It was also the team's first trip to the playoffs. By the time I finally got to see these incredible women, I knew how impressive they were. At first, the WNBA got a bad rap because the players weren't necessarily flying through the air like Michael Jordan or dunking like Shaq. But it takes time to grow a league and a sport. People forget, the NBA started in the 1950s after two other leagues combined, but it wasn't until the mid-1980s that it really took off, thanks to the Lakers-Celtics rivalry. Here I was at the outset of the WNBA, on the ground floor.

What I loved about the women's game was that, while they played below the rim, they were incredibly skilled. Not only do women look better than men in their uniforms, they smell better too! That aside, they could really *play* the game. Their attention to detail is something Pat Riley would be proud of. They know how to dribble, shoot, run plays, and how to listen to instruction better than most men. Some guys I've coached rely too much on their athleticism, and they fail to grasp the fundamentals of the game. This wasn't the case for my Sparks players. After the 1999 season, Orlando left the team and so did GM Rhonda Windham. So L.A. appointed my friend Penny Toler to be the executive and me to coach the 2000 season.

I felt lucky to be part of such a great organization. And one of the reasons why was that the Sparks employed perhaps the greatest female basketball player of all time: Lisa Leslie. There are a lot of skilled players on that all-time list, including Cheryl Miller, Nancy Lieberman, Sheryl "the Female Jordan" Swoopes, Dawn Staley, Sue Bird, and Diana Taurasi. But Leslie would be my pick. She's an eight-time WNBA All-Star who started her career in 1997 with the Sparks. When I coached her, I quickly noticed how agile and fluid she was, so I started calling her Smooth. With her ability to glide on the court, she could score, pass, rebound, and be the hub of an offense.

Lisa grew up in Inglewood and used to watch our Showtime teams. We were her introduction to the game. What made her great was that, despite her fame on and off the court, she never missed a day working. We were morning people, and we used to get up early and put in time in the gym. I was like Riley, stressing professionalism, punctuality, and preparation. If you were on time to practice, you were late. But it was Lisa who opened my eyes to what it meant to coach in the WNBA. I knew quickly the players were good. In the NBA, if you tell guys a new play, someone is bound to mess it up. The women got it after one or two run-throughs.

Still, though, I was being too cordial with my squad. And Lisa called me out on it one day. "Coop," she said, "fucking *coach* us!" After that,

I knew what she meant, and I stopped trying to be a gentleman and we got down to the nitty-gritty. That's when we turned a corner. In my first season, we finished 28–4. I won Coach of the Year. In the playoffs, we beat Phoenix 2–0 in the Western Conference Semifinals but then lost 0–2 to the reigning champs, the Houston Comets, in the West Finals.

Houston won four rings in a row in the WNBA's first four seasons, from 1997 to 2000. They were an all-time team, but the following year, in my second season, we were *determined* to knock them off. This is again where Lisa was special. Because of her statuesque appearance, Lisa was able to make money modeling and doing commercials. It was an opportunity not everyone is afforded. But that allowed her to stay home during the WNBA off-season. She didn't have to play overseas to supplement her income. And that allowed us to work together to improve her game every day. She would tell me, "Coop! I want to get better!" She wanted to learn Hakeem Olajuwon's footwork, so we practiced it and practiced it. I was amazed by her work ethic. And it paid dividends.

In 2001 we earned a second straight 28–4 record, including an 18-game winning streak, and in the opening round of the playoffs we faced—guess who—Houston. But their time was over. We beat them 2–0. The rivalry with Swoopes, Cynthia Cooper, and Tina Thompson— the league's first Big Three—had made us better, like the Celtics and the Lakers. It had also made me a better coach. It was all about getting past Houston, and we had managed to do just that.

In the next round, we beat the Sacramento Monarchs 2–1 in a close three-game series. Then we faced the Charlotte Sting in the Finals and we overcame them 2–0 for the first championship in Sparks history. I was happy for the team, but I was even happier for Lisa, who had put in so much work to make herself into the best player in the league. For that, she was awarded both the 2001 MVP (her first of three) and the Finals MVP in the series. She also won the MVP in the All-Star Game that season. We had a great connection, so much so that during timeouts I'd ask what she and her teammates were seeing on the floor, which was an old Riley move.

Speaking of Riley, after we won in 2001—which marked the first time a WNBA and NBA team from the same city won rings in the same year—and after my tears had dried, I *almost* made a public guarantee that we would come back and win it all again in 2002. I had flashbacks to 1988 when Riley got up in front of those microphones and put the challenge to us in front of the world. But while I didn't say it out loud like Pat did, I sure acted like it. I approached the off-season as if I had. I was focused, and I talked with our players about it, putting the pressure on them behind closed doors. But I knew we had a shot—or even better than that. Because we had such a talented roster, starting with Lisa. The team brought me back to my Showtime days, for sure.

Lisa was like Magic—a coach on the floor. She'd tell me if another team was doubling a certain way and how she thought we could circumvent it. She was able to make adjustments, and so was I. It was a great basketball partnership. Today, Lisa is a coach herself in the Big3 league. They grow up so fast! But in 2002 we were ready for more wins in the WNBA. Lisa was ready to ascend even higher. In fact, that year marked the first time she or anyone else dunked in a WNBA game.

We were playing Miami at the Staples Center in L.A., and there were four minutes left in the first half when the 30-year-old, 6'5" center got the outlet all alone on the break. She leapt from a foot beyond the dotted circle, rose up, and slammed it home. Lisa had already won all those MVPs and two Olympic gold medals, but now she had that flashbulb moment that immortalized her. When she rose up all by herself, I said to myself, "She's getting ready to dunk this fucking ball!" And she did. That's the type of person Lisa is. Dunking in a game is something she and many other women had thought about. But she worked on it and achieved it as the first. It's the same mentality she brought to the game as a kid. She started playing at 12 because she was tall, but she didn't learn her skills from a brother or dad; she just put her mind to it.

Lisa was so good she could play with NBA players. She may not have been as strong as them, but she was often more skilled. As 2002 progressed, we finished 25–7, and in the playoffs we won and won. In the opening round, we beat Seattle 2–0. In the next, we beat the Utah Starzz 2–0. Then in the Finals, we beat the New York Liberty 2–0 for back-to-back rings and my seventh championship trophy! The following season, we finished 24–10 and went to the Finals for a third straight trip. I hoped we would get the three-peat, the one I missed out on with the Lakers in 1989, but we fell 2–1 to—guess who—Detroit and Coach Bill Laimbeer 2–1. I can't stand that guy.

I STUCK AROUND for the first 20 games of the 2004 season, but I left after a 14–6 record to pursue new opportunities in the NBA with the Denver Nuggets, who had been recruiting me to join their staff. But that didn't mean I wasn't grateful for my time in the WNBA. One thing I've always wanted is to coach at every level of the game, and I'm so grateful for the league giving me a chance in 2000. The Sparks were a top-notch organization, with an excellent staff and players, and they put me in the position to earn Coach of the Year, win two rings, and hone my coaching skills, from when to call timeouts to when to push someone in practice.

During my time as the Sparks' coach, I learned so much from so many intelligent and capable people. Women at that level are much more mature than their male counterparts. They've been that way since the age of five, really. So coaching them, we got things done a lot quicker, from creating on-court concepts to making sure people acted professionally off the playing floor. The only thing they didn't do was play above the rim, but most people can't play above the rim—yet the game has room for it all. Still, I liked to push the boundaries, and so when Lisa dunked, that was one small step for her and one giant leap for the league.

The player who reminded me most of myself was DeLisha Milton-Jones. She'd come to L.A. in 1999 and was an All-Star in 2000 when I arrived. A product of the University of Florida, we called her D Nasty. I also used to call her my special child. She was one of the toughest players I ever had the opportunity to coach in the women's game. She was a great young lady off the court, and during a game, there was no getting past her. Over the first decade of her career, which included two stints with the Sparks and a few years in D.C., the 6'1" forward averaged 12.1 points, 1.5 steals, and nearly a block a game, making the All-Star team twice. She was tough as nails.

Another player I loved working with was Mwadi Mabika, who was from Congo and balled like James Worthy. With the Sparks, it was all about development, and Mabika was proof. She came on to the team at its outset in 1997 and got better every year, first averaging 6 points per game and then 8.2, 10.8, 12.3, and up to 16.8 with 5.2 rebounds in 2002 as we won our second title in a row. She earned an All-Star nod that season too. As a team, we'd kept bashing our heads against the Houston wall, and then we finally beat them. But we weren't lucky. We'd put in hard work and turned the Sparks into a winning brand.

When I left the team, the league was headed in an even better direction than when I'd started. Today, the WNBA is as popular as ever. It makes me smile, especially when looking back on players such as Cheryl Miller and Nancy Lieberman, who were stars in the 1980s. But they'd had to go overseas or find other work because there was no pro league for women like the WNBA back then. Cheryl was a beast who had 105 points in a *high school* game. Nancy, who is a coach in the Big3 today, played for the Lakers Summer Pro League team. The world missed out not seeing them up close like we've gotten to see Lisa. Go back and watch clips of Cheryl's dynamism and Nancy's wizardry. They're icons.

Chapter 18

Coaching Principles

THE NEXT STOP FOR ME WAS DENVER, COLORADO. Over the past four seasons, I'd earned Coach of the Year in the WNBA and become the first person to win a championship in both the NBA and WNBA. My teams were good, my players were well coached, and I was making a name for myself among the basketball community for my ability to lead and get results on the sideline. That's when Jeff Bzdelik and Kiki VanDeWeghe of the NBA's Denver Nuggets came calling. The squad from the Mile High City had been scouting me toward the end of my tenure with the Sparks, including following me on a late-season three-game road trip, observing.

Now they wanted me on their bench. Bzdelik was a longtime assistant in the NBA with teams including Washington and Miami, and he was heading into his third year as the head coach of the Nuggets. The season prior, in 2003–04, the team had gone 43–39, and they were working to build something with young players such as Carmelo Anthony and vets such as Marcus Camby, Andre Miller, and Kenyon Martin, who was one of the toughest guys in the game. VanDeWeghe, a former two-time All-Star in the league, was now running Denver as its top executive. So they asked if I wanted to come coach. While I was excited, I was still sorry to leave the Sparks.

The Sparks were 14–6 when I left for Denver. We'd just beaten Houston (a fitting last game for me). L.A. went on to finish their season at 25–9 with an 11–3 run down the stretch. I'd done the job I came there to do, and now I had a new challenge in front of me. So I got started officially in Denver in July, working under Coach Bzdelik. I knew going into the job that the team would be something of a proving ground for me with NBA execs. They'd seen that I was a talented coach after my time as an assistant with the Lakers and as the lead dog with the Sparks. Now it was time for a new opportunity.

I KNOW IT must have been tough for Jeff to have me, his potential replacement, come in and sit behind him on the bench. But to his credit, he was willing to give it a try, which I'm grateful for. The Nuggets were good already, and the team had *mile-high* hopes. They'd drafted the NCAA championship winner in Anthony in 2003, and he was in his second year, with real talent around him. Could Jeff take Denver to the next level with him? Well, it was my job to help the roster buy into his system. But just 28 games into the year, the Nuggets fired Bzdelik after the team went just 13–15, including a 2–5 record to start the year and a 1–8 stretch that got Jeff canned.

That's when Kiki came to me and asked if I would take over head coaching responsibilities on an interim basis. The staff had other great assistants, including Scott Brooks (a future NBA head coach) and Adrian Dantley (my former teammate on the Lakers and Pistons foe in the 1988 NBA Finals). Scott had been Jeff's lead assistant, and I figured Denver would appoint him. But Kiki asked me to be the interim head coach. "Coop, listen," he said. "If you don't this job, people around the league will always wonder why, and you may never get another opportunity as a head coach again."

Was I completely ready to be a head coach in the NBA? I like to think so. But two or three more years as an assistant on a winning team could have helped. I took the job; it was almost like I *had* to take it. I think I did well enough under the circumstances. The team was in turmoil, reeling. We had three days off after Jeff was let go. In our next game against the Philadelphia 76ers with Allen Iverson and Andre Iguodala, though, we won 97–92 at home. Unfortunately, we went on a five-game losing streak after that, falling to some good teams, including the Spurs and Lakers. We won three of the next five but then hit another three-game skid.

Denver decided to hire George Karl, a longtime NBA head coach who'd had success in Seattle and Milwaukee, later in the year. George would go on to coach eight more seasons in Denver, with many 50-win seasons. One of the reasons the Nuggets brought him in was that the annual All-Star Game was in Denver that year, and the team wanted to project some stability ahead of it. In many ways, they got that with Coach Karl. For my part, I had no problem with the move, and I didn't even mind particularly when he decided to let me go after the year. I'll always be grateful to Jeff and Kiki for giving me a chance, albeit briefly, as an NBA head coach.

THE JOB OF head coach isn't easy no matter where you are. But as I see it, there are five key aspects to it. First and foremost, you have to develop players. You have to help them get to their full potential. Then once you get the person working at their maximum capacity, you have to figure out how they'll fit with everyone else on the team. In that way, coaching is like putting together a puzzle. A roster is going to be full of players with varied skill sets and with different talent levels at different stages of their careers. It's your job to make sure they all come together in a way that best suits everyone.

The third tenet is motivation. That might be the most important. Every day, you have to motivate your players to be at their best at all times within the team. You have to motivate them to accomplish goals. Next, you have to have a clear philosophy and the ability to impart that to your roster. As a coach, you have to imprint yourself on the team from a psychological standpoint. If you can get your players to see the game how you do, then you're doing well. *This is who we are; this is who we want to be!* Finally, you have to nurture personalities. My high school coach, George Terzian, was excellent at that. Everyone is different, so for people to know their roles, you have to nurture them individually.

For example, the Hall of Fame rebounder Dennis Rodman is one of the most *out-there* guys ever to lace up sneakers, but his talent was so good that his coaches would sink or swim whether or not they nurtured his role on the team, helping him feel like he fit in some way or another. Those are all tall tasks, but if a coach is able to achieve them, he or she will be well on their way to wins. When I was in Denver, the team was different than when I was an assistant with the Lakers in the 1990s. L.A. was developing a culture, and they wanted me there to stoke those flames. Guys such as Nick Van Exel and Eddie Jones were good, but they weren't quite ready to win.

But in Denver, expectations were higher. The team considered itself ready to win *now*. When they brought in Coach Karl, I had a chance to listen to how he worked and watch how he interacted with guys. He was known as someone who could grate on you after a while, but while I was there, he was someone who knew how to motivate a player and get the most out of him. A few years after he arrived, he took the Nuggets to the 2009 Western Conference Finals against Kobe and the Lakers and tested L.A. While Denver lost 4–2 in that playoff series, Carmelo proved he was a star and that the franchise could win.

MY NEXT JOB came in a place I knew well: New Mexico, the region where my basketball dreams had really started to take shape. As it happened, I was sitting at home one day in L.A. when I got a phone call. One of the owners of the Albuquerque Thunderbirds was interested in finding out if I wanted to coach his team for the upcoming 2005–06 season. "Coop," he said, "we have a D-League team, and we want you to come back to New Mexico. We have a great atmosphere and we're just one step away from the NBA. What do you think?" Back then, I knew of the Developmental League, but I can't say I was an expert. Soon, I would become educated.

Along with coaching and returning to the location of some of my best years in the game, one of the reasons I took the job was to be close to my kids. Wanda had moved to New Mexico with them, and being down in Albuquerque gave me a chance to see them more. She and I had split amicably, and I'd started a new relationship with my now-wife Yvonne. We'd met in 2000 when she was working in the marketing department at Sony Pictures and I was with the Sparks, and we've been together since. Things were friendly between Wanda and me as coparents. It was lovely to have my kids come stay with me down there, splitting time with their mom and me.

The D-League, which is now known as the G-League, acts as a minor league for the NBA, where franchises can send players down or call them up depending on their needs on a given night. It's similar to baseball's Triple A farm teams. Thinking about it, I liked the idea of going back to New Mexico. So I agreed to give the job a shot. I loved coaching, and my goal has always been to do it at every level. What's special about the D-League, I learned, is that most of its players are all capable of playing in the NBA; there is just one significant thing holding them back—an injury, a missing jump shot. So my job was to find what that was and to help them fix it.

One of my players was Chuck Hayes. From the University of Kentucky, Hayes was a top prospect, but he hadn't been drafted into the NBA. He signed as an undrafted free agent with Houston ahead of the 2005–06 season but was cut. So the Thunderbirds picked him up and I began to work with him. Chuck's issue was not so much his game but that NBA teams were worried about his ankle. They didn't think it was stable enough to endure the 82-game schedule. So it was my responsibility to prove them wrong. Chuck soon became a star for us, leading us in scoring at around 20 points and leading the league in rebounding at more than 11 per game.

But the hardest part about working in the D-League was knowing a team could pick up one of your players at any given time for their own. That's just what happened with Chuck. Before the D-League playoffs that season, with Hayes destroying teams, Houston called him up. In the NBA now, with his ankle strong, Chuck played in 40 games with Houston, and over the following five years, he played in nearly 400. Over his career, Hayes earned more than $30 million. To this day, when I see him, he says, "Coop, I want to give you a million dollars!" And he means it. But I tell him I don't want his money. "You helped me earn it, Coop!" I must say, that feels good.

His is one of those types of success stories that warms your heart. But we had our own success story to write that season. With Chuck playing so well for us during the year, we were at the top of the standings. The Thunderbirds—a team that was founded in 2001 in Alabama before moving to New Mexico in 2005, and later went to Cleveland—played in the Tingley Coliseum, which was also home to the local rodeo. Along with Chuck, we had players such as the Greek seven-footer Andreas Glyniadakis and former Syracuse shooting guard Tony Bland. Because of my background, we ran NBA plays and I pushed the guys in practice, just like I had with the Sparks.

But unlike the Sparks or Lakers, the D-League had a shoestring budget. Travel was hard on the team, but the players, who were supremely hungry, followed my direction. They all wanted to be able to make the next level, and they knew that I could help. I enjoyed teaching my guys to develop and work as a unit. We carried 10 or 11 guys at once, and when the NBA teams sent players down, we carried 12 or 13. The guys who teams would send us would always have to start, and along the way you had to juggle your lineup. It just fed into my idea that coaching is always about putting together a puzzle.

My guys bought in to what I was doing, and we wound up making the playoffs that season. Then we made it all the way to the D-League Finals. In the championship game, we played the Fort Worth Flyers. For that, the Dallas Mavericks sent the Flyers several NBA players to pad their roster. But that didn't deter us. Even without Chuck, who was with Houston by then, we beat Fort Worth and won the 2006 title. The whole team was thrilled with our success. With that, they saw why I'd demanded so much from them during the year. It can be hard to get pro athletes to listen, but I had their ears perked.

Championships are won over the course of an entire year, or longer. They're not won by flipping a switch, no matter who you are. Even as coaches—we're learning too. It takes a big amount of responsibility to win. It's on *you* to win, not anyone else. And I told my players that. I also let them know that if they were lucky enough to make the next level, they wouldn't be stars. I honed in on teaching them how to do the dirty work, to excel at the job of a role player, which was something I knew well. "You'll have to set screens, take charges, and practice harder than the starters if you want to stand out," I said. And they listened, to great success.

With our ring, I became the first person to win championships in the NBA, WNBA, *and* the D-League. Not bad! I enjoyed my time that season so much that I decided to stay another year. We wanted to defend our title. And I thought we had a good chance to do so. In my second season in the D-League, I coached players such as Shannon Brown, another guy who made millions in the NBA with teams including the Lakers and Suns. But while we didn't win a ring that second year, we did make the playoffs, losing in the first round. Oh, well. I'd had fun in the D-League and shown people yet again I could coach with the best.

ONE OF THE silliest highlights for me was when I participated in NBA All-Star weekend as part of the NBA Shooting Stars Competition. It was an event that put three players from a city together to compete against other trios. On my team were Temeka Johnson of the Sparks and Smush Parker from the Lakers. Sadly, I let us down. I couldn't buy a bucket from three, missing 13 straight. We ended up losing to a guy who was one of my biggest rivals, Bill Laimbeer and his Detroit team with Chauncey Billups and Swin Cash. Afterward, Cheryl Miller interviewed Bill on TNT, and he said I *choked*. How dare that jerk tell the truth!

But none of that mattered. You know why? Because I got engaged to Yvonne. As I mentioned, we'd met a few years after Wanda and I separated. Flash back to 2000, and both the Lakers and Sparks had won championships, and the city of Los Angeles was honoring both teams at the House of Blues restaurant. At the event, I had an open seat at my table, and when I stood up for a moment to head to the restroom, I caught a glimpse of a woman with the deepest, most beautiful blue eyes I'd ever seen. She also had long, curly blonde hair and a beautiful smile. I was struck by her, and so I offered her my adjacent seat.

She was with a girlfriend of hers, who made a snide remark, and so I thought my chance with this woman had gone. But after the event, I bumped into her again and we started talking. She told me she was a marketing director for Sony Pictures. She also apologized for her snotty friend. She told me she was heading out of the country soon but she'd love to get together when she got back. I thought she was being very nice in letting me down easy. But we exchanged numbers, and sure enough, about a week later I got her on the phone!

Well, God was smiling on me that day, because meeting Yvonne turned out to be the best thing that could ever happen to me. I never thought I would get married again—to be honest, I was still enjoying the glitz and glamour that Los Angeles and basketball were affording me— but Yvonne helped to make a real man out of me. She helped me put away that frivolous lifestyle and take stock of who I was and what I was doing. She was a strong, no-nonsense woman, and she was exactly what I was missing in my life. When she got back from her trip, we went out to dinner and just talked. A friendship blossomed, and then a romance, and then a true partnership.

Yvonne brought stability into my life. She helped me learn how to be better with money—how to save it, most importantly. And she was someone I could be in conversation with until all hours of the night. Yvonne is a dynamic person—you know how some guys say they want their woman to bring something to the table? Well, Yvonne brought the entire table! She was special, supportive, independent. If we ever have heated discussions, they're always for the betterment of both of us. She's smart and funny, and while I know neither of us is perfect, I know that we are perfect for each other.

Before we got engaged, we flew to Sweden to see her family. I wanted to do it the right way, the gentlemanly way. So I met everyone, and we hit it off nicely. Then we went to Germany and I met her father (a Swede living in Germany). That's the other great thing about Yvonne—she speaks three languages, so traveling overseas is easy for us! When I met her father, he had no idea who I was. Meaning he didn't know about my basketball career. I was just this tall, skinny guy asking to be a part of his family. And to this day, I love him. He gave me his blessing, and then at All-Star weekend in 2007, I got on one knee and proposed to Yvonne.

That was one of the happiest moments of my life when she agreed to marry me. We'd already seen the welcome surprise of the birth of our son, Nils, two years prior in 2005, and now we were cementing our relationship and making sure that we'd be together for our boy forever. Thinking about that, winning the Shooting Stars Competition was the furthest thing from my mind (even though I would have loved to shut up that former Piston Bill Laimbeer!), but you can't win 'em all. A few months later, Yvonne and I got married in Negril, Jamaica. It was a small gathering, but the event just felt huge to me. It was also one of the smartest things I've ever done.

AFTER THOSE BIG life changes, I decided to get back with the L.A. Sparks. The team needed a new coach, someone who could bring them back to prominence. After I'd left, the team had gone through several coaches, including Jellybean Bryant. During the 2006 season, Joe had led the team to a 25–9 record, but the Sparks lost to the Sacramento Monarchs in the Western Conference Finals. So in April 2007 the franchise went in a new direction and brought me in. I'd won two rings with the franchise just a few years before, and the organization, led by GM Penny Toler, hoped I could do it again.

I was happy to be back in the Purple and Gold, but there was one big problem: Lisa Leslie was out for the year. She'd married her husband in 2005 and decided to take 2007 off to have a child. Still, without Smooth, I thought I could help the team improve their situation. That was tough in the first season, though. We finished just 10–24. It was a hard year, but it's not always about wins and losses; it's about instilling good habits. I continued to push my players, coaching them no differently than men. They were hungry to get better and wanted to be taught the right way, which was easy since they didn't have oversized egos.

But the Sparks had changed since I was there. Not only was Lisa out, but so was Johnny Buss. The team had been purchased by Sparks LA Sports (which included Magic). And the only good thing about going 10–24 was that we had a high draft pick the following year. With it, we selected the impact player Candace Parker from the University of Tennessee at No. 1. She was similar to Lisa in that she could change a game all on her own. Now it was my job to teach her how to win in the pros. In the following 2008 season, we got back to our winning ways, earning a 20–14 record and a trip to the playoffs.

Lisa and Candace were both elite, and they'd achieved that in different ways. Lisa worked day in and day out, while Candace was a talented back-to-the-basket player, similar to Tim Duncan or Hakeem. Together, they were *smooth as silk*, and so that's what I called Candace: Silk. As Lisa's career was in its final years, Parker's was just ascending. So Lisa was passing the torch to her as the best player in the WNBA before my eyes. Candace had been a star at Tennessee, but the pro game is different. She had to take the Sparks franchise and put it on her shoulders as Lisa had done before, and she was willing to do just that. As such, working with her was special.

TODAY, I LIKE to think that I helped Candace develop into the star she became. After my Sparks tenure, she won a ring in 2016 with L.A. Then another in 2021 with Chicago and one in 2023 with Las Vegas (the first WNBA team to repeat since my 2002 Sparks). Today, she's also a standout broadcaster for TNT. But in 2008 she was just a pup learning the pro game. Yet on talent alone, Parker averaged 18.5 points and 9.5 rebounds with 2.3 blocks, 1.3 steals, and 3.4 assists during the season—good enough to get her Rookie of the Year and MVP honors. And she increased those numbers throughout her career in the WNBA. But it was in 2008, during her rookie year, that she tasted the playoffs for the first time.

In that first round, we beat Sue Bird, Swin Cash, and the Seattle Storm 2–1. But in the Western Conference Finals, we lost 2–1 to the San Antonio Silver Stars, missing a chance to play the Detroit Shock, coached by Laimbeer, in the Finals. In the off-season, ahead of my third year, the owners of the Sparks got more hands-on. With Johnny Buss, things had always been hands-off. He trusted me to run the team and just wanted to stay informed of the big picture. The new owners, though, were more involved, which was their right. But that made it harder for me to work. They were fine—it was just different. It required a bit of an adjustment.

In my third and final year with L.A., we finished 18–16. We made the playoffs and upset the 20–14 Seattle Storm in the Western Conference Semifinals. But in the Western Conference Finals, we lost 2–1 to Diana Taurasi and the Phoenix Mercury, who went on to win 3–2 in the Finals against the Indiana Fever. After that, I decided my time with the Sparks was done and I wanted a new challenge. It was unfortunate we didn't win a championship during my second stint with the team, but I'd helped set them up for the future and gotten them back to their victorious ways. That was a win in and of itself.

In the end, over the course of eight seasons with the Sparks, I compiled a record of 167–85 during the regular season, and we were 25–13 in the playoffs. We won five Western Conference regular-season titles and made the playoffs seven times. We won rings in 2001 and 2002 and went to the WNBA Finals for a third time in 2003. For someone who had always hoped to coach in the WNBA, I think I did pretty well. You want to win every year and you want your players to take home every accolade. But we did what we could and made our fair share of lifelong memories. I'll always be grateful for them.

AFTER MY SEQUEL with the Sparks, I was at home when another important phone call came in. This time it was for a job at the collegiate level. The University of Southern California women's basketball team needed a new head coach, and my name had come up. I was intrigued when USC's athletic director, Mike Garrett, called me. His colleague Brandon Martin, who I'd crossed paths with before while scouting USC for the Sparks, had recommended me for the job. When Mike called me, though, he said we had to meet in secret. We met a few times over the course of a month at a small but very nice hotel in Beverly Hills.

Mike said USC was going to let Coach Mark Trakh go. He said the team wasn't improving like they wanted, and they could bring me in to help change the culture and create a winning attitude. I knew I could do that, and so I told them I was into the idea. The next thing I knew, USC fired Trakh and they extended an offer to me. It was a big shock to a lot of people, but others could see the value, how I would bring both credibility and a certain star quality to the program. USC had a long history of excellence with players such as Cynthia Cooper, Lisa Leslie, and Cheryl Miller, who also coached there. Now, as of May 2009, I was going to be part of it too.

In my first season with the University of Southern California, we finished 19–12, good for third in the Pac-10. We'd beaten several ranked teams, announcing ourselves. We also achieved records such as the team's best-ever free throw percentage (.725), fewest turnovers (462), and fewest fouls (484). In my second year, we finished 24–13 and made the WNIT title game, losing to Toledo 76–68. In my third year, we had an 18–12 record, and while I felt we should have made the postseason, we fell just short. In my fourth and final year, we finished 11–20. It wasn't what I'd hoped for, but in any endeavor, there are going to be fatter and leaner years.

Overall, it was a joy coaching the women at USC. They were attentive, talented, and responsible. I never had to send an assistant coach over to one of their dorm rooms at 6:00 AM to make sure they were awake for class. While some men's programs have coaches who practically hold their players' hands to get them to their first class of the day, my players were mature and reliable. Over my four years at the school, from 2009 to 2013, I amassed a record of 72–57, for a solid .558 winning percentage. But it was in my fourth year when things changed, thanks largely to an academic scandal I had nothing to do with—which had everything to do with Donna Heinel.

Many have read the headlines by now. In 2023 Heinel was sentenced to prison after pleading guilty to helping students cheat their way into USC. And in the 2010s, before the world knew of the Varsity Blues scandal, as it was called, Donna didn't like me because I am not a rule breaker. That decision later led to her pushing me out and my resignation in 2013. I'd come into USC to help turn the program around and bring some of my Lakers and Sparks expertise to the roster. And it was working. But Donna, who was a senior administrator with the USC athletic department, began to use school rosters as places to stash undeserving rich kids.

As an academic institution, USC has a high standard to admit a student. But those standards are relaxed a bit when it comes to athletes, which makes sense. You don't ask a premed student to be a D1 football star in the same way you don't expect the next WNBA MVP to get a perfect SAT score. But Donna was using this as a loophole for kids of famous celebrities and big donors. If those kids weren't able to make it into USC on academic merit, she would say they were athletes and put them on school teams. But they *weren't* athletes, weren't participating in the programs. So I wasn't going to participate in her Lori Loughlin–like scheme.

Ironically, before this Donna had reprimanded me for bringing my eldest son, who had coaching and scouting experience, onto my staff. Still, I'd gotten USC back to respectability, and we were on the verge of winning, but she'd had enough of me and pressured me to quit. That still leaves a bitter taste in my mouth. If I'd stayed, I believe I'd still be coaching at USC. After, the school hired Cynthia Cooper, who is a great coach and former player, but she ended up winning with my players. No shade to Cynthia but a rainforest's worth of it for Donna. In the end, Donna ended up getting what she deserved: prison time. Though she got lucky and served only six months.

AS THEY SAY, everything happens for a reason, and now I was ready for a new opportunity back in the WNBA. In November 2013 I was hired by the Atlanta Dream to be the team's new head coach. I was proud to be back in the league, which had employed other great coaches, such as Fred Williams, who had also been a coach in Atlanta in 2012 and 2013. The Dream, a franchise founded in 2008, had big hopes. But there were many bumps along the way. When I got there in 2013, it was owned by future Republican senator Kelly Loeffler and Mary Brock, the wife of a big-time Coca-Cola executive.

Unfortunately, while the team had a strong roster and me as the coach, we lacked leadership. In 2020 Loeffler and Brock would sell the Dream after some controversial statements, including Loeffler's tone-deaf criticism of the Black Lives Matter movement in the wake of George Floyd's murder at the hands of police. After those statements, the Dream's players wore T-shirts to promote Loeffler's *opponent* in that year's senate race, Raphael Warnock, who wound up winning.

But even prior to that, during my time with the Dream, I could tell Loeffler wasn't the right woman to run things. During halftime of games, she would come into the locker room to analyze the first half. This is unheard of. Consider Jerry Buss—his strategy was to hire the best and let them do their jobs. That's how leaders work. But Loeffler wanted her hands on everything, and she didn't know basketball the way a head coach does. In my first year, 2014, we did well despite Kelly, going 19–15. We were the top seed in the East for the first time in team history. Our star was Angel McCoughtry. She was the best pure bucket-getter I think I've ever coached. But she had trouble meshing with the team. We lost 2–1 to Chicago in the Eastern Conference semis that year.

THE NEXT SEASON we missed the playoffs. But in 2016 we had a good year, finishing 17–17. We made the playoffs as a sixth seed and beat the Seattle Storm in the first round. Angel scored 37 points on 14–21 shooting in the clinching game. She even added seven assists. The next round we played Chicago, but Angel refused to suit up! She said she was tired. I couldn't believe it. There we were, trying to win the championship, and she didn't want to dress for the game—our best player! She quit on us. I guess she really was tired, because she sat out the entire 2017 season the next year. Needless to say, we lost to the Sky, and that was the end of it.

The following year was my last in Atlanta. Without Angel, we were 12–22. The one benefit was that I was able to coach with my son Miles, who was one of my assistants. But even with him, I missed L.A. and Yvonne. She understandably didn't want to move herself and our young son, Nils, away to Atlanta for the short season. In my first few years with the Dream, I had been able to spend two-thirds of the year in Los Angeles, but the Dream now wanted me in Atlanta year-round. Since I was homesick, I decided we should part ways after 2017. My final record with them was 63–73. Nevertheless, despite the ups and downs, I enjoyed my time in Atlanta.

Today, the team is in good hands, owned now by Larry Gottesdiener, Suzanne Abair, and former Dream player Renee Montgomery. I hope that the squad, as well as the WNBA on the whole, continues to grow. The women are so talented, and they're helping to effect change in the world in places where society needs it. The WNBA has never been more popular, thanks to people such as Caitlin Clark and Angel Reese, which has also helped to expand the women's collegiate game and showcase stars such as Juju Watkins. But after the 2017 season, it was time for me to figure out my next step, to continue my journey as a coach and a person.

Chapter 19

A Note on *Winning Time*

THE MEDIA, ON THE OTHER HAND, CAN BE A WHOLE OTHER STORY. Over the years, I've learned something about the business. It can be your best friend or your worst enemy—even more so than guys like Larry Bird. Today, I work in the media and know how it functions. Headlines are king, and salacious details too often trump the truth. It's been this way for a while in lots of places. For example, I remember the early days of my career when I was shy, especially in the public eye. I didn't talk a lot, and when interviewed, I used one- or two-word answers. That's when my friend, L.A. reporter Jim Hill, who covered the Showtime Lakers, brought me in.

He said, "Young man, you're going to be a star in this league, so you better be ready to talk to the media." Jim would always want my comments after games. He helped get me out of my shell. But that didn't stop me from putting my foot in my mouth once in a while, including after a game in 1983 in which I'd missed a big dunk. Suddenly a microphone was in my face and I was asked about the miss. I said something like, "Now I know what it feels like to be white." Well, the media didn't find that very funny. It blew up in my face. People went crazy. If I had said that today with social media and the never-ending ESPN loop, I may have been sunk for good.

But back then, the firestorm lasted only a couple of days. I learned that I'd better be careful not just about how much I talked but about what I said. I became more astute in how I used my words. I learned how the media can make or break you. Thankfully, my mother pushed me to read as a kid to explore my mind through books, so I always had a good vocabulary and a natural instinct for talking. But it needs refining at times, which can take years. Since then, I've worked television jobs for ABC here in Los Angeles and as a studio analyst for more than 20 years. I've called high school and college games, and I host a podcast called *Showtime with Coop*.

On my podcast, I like to highlight "insightful BS with my Lakers teammates and NBA legends." It's a really fun podcast and gives fans behind-the-scenes looks at history. We get hundreds of thousands of listeners too, which is fun. I say all that to say this: I understand why a TV show such as HBO's *Winning Time* was made and why people were interested in it. But it's not for me. Not only was the basketball not up to par, but I wondered where they got some of their info. My issue mostly has to do with the way it handled Jerry Buss, Pat Riley, and Jerry West. The show also seemed to imply I couldn't fix my own car if it broke down. But I get why they had to exaggerate all of us. It was a TV show made for headlines, and the result was exactly that.

That's what you have to be careful of: Entertainment is one thing, but the cold truth is another. And you learn that quickly when you're at the center of Hollywood. Can you imagine the number of articles, books, and everything else that were composed about Magic's life, about Pat Riley and Kareem Abdul-Jabbar? Do you think those got everything perfect? There's no chance. Today, people have to be clear and discerning about what they believe, and while I understand the HBO show was entertaining and people liked both seasons, it's important to remember that they took liberties with what happened along the way regarding everyone involved.

Now, if I were to wave a magic wand and create my own series, it would show everything from the locker room to the boardroom. I would ask the guys who were involved, from Kareem to Pat, Magic to West, if they wanted to be part of the process, to give their input. I would show how Boston was the iron that sharpened us. How we were the iron that sharpened the Pistons. And the Pistons were the iron to sharpen the Bulls. That's how it works. One generation shows the next how it's done, how to win. Unfortunately, Jordan and Pippen don't talk anymore. But that happens. Magic and Isiah didn't talk for decades before making up later on camera.

Chapter 20

My Modern Life

Winning cost us all a lot along the way. Sacrifice is at the center of anything great. There is no glory without it—not in the NBA at least. Thankfully, at the end of the day, we all landed on our feet, including Magic, after his major health scare. So much so that we were able to celebrate the Showtime era in Hawaii in 2022. There was a lot to honor in Maui during that handful of days, and thinking about it, I know I have a lot to be grateful for in my life. Truly, I've been blessed. There are any number of outcomes that could have transpired, but I was able to play for an iconic franchise during the greatest decade of basketball the NBA has ever seen.

Not only that, but I was able to play abroad and then come home and coach in the WNBA and at USC. But my coaching days didn't end there—in fact, they're still unfolding. After my time with the Atlanta Dream, I went on to several more opportunities. Such as in 2018, when I received a call from my old friend and new Big3 commissioner Clyde Drexler. He said that with my experience and Lakers credentials, I would be a great fit to coach for one of the teams. I agreed, and so I signed up immediately. Founded by famed rapper Ice Cube in 2017, the Big3 was making big headlines in basketball for its way of showcasing the game.

Not a five-on-five league, the Big3, as the name suggests, pits older players three-on-three. It's a genius idea. As for my team, 3's Company, Allen Iverson, the slinky former 76ers guard, had originally led the squad. But when he left after the first year, I took over. The Big3 is filled with former players, some who still have juice left to play and others who just coach. I'm in the latter category, along with people such as George Gervin and Rick Mahorn. The half-court league is fun, and it's great to reconnect with so many legends. It's on the rise too. Even the Olympics included three-on-three basketball in their summer games.

Growing up, when you go down to the park as a kid, it's about five-on-five. But if there aren't enough people to play a full game, the next-best option is threes. I remember hitting the court with my uncles, cousins, and brother on days to play three-on-three. And that's what Ice Cube capitalized on. Not only that, but it's great to see rap and basketball together. They have such a long history that continues now, in part, because of Cube's vision. As far as the Big3 itself, my star pupil Lisa Leslie is one of the other coaches. Her team is the Triplets, which is led by former All-Star Joe Johnson, and let me tell you: I can't stand to lose to her!

Although Lisa does credit me with coaching tips. She says she encourages her players like I used to encourage her, how I told her how she was better than everyone else on the court. Along with Lisa, other people who have played or coached in the Big3 include Mario Chalmers, Drew Gooden, Nate Robinson, Nancy Lieberman, Baron Davis, the late Andre Emmett, Jason Richardson, Dr. J, Stephen Jackson, and Jason "White Chocolate" Williams. It's like a great big family reunion from the NBA's golden era. I'm still coaching in the Big3 league, and while I made it to the Finals once, I vow to continue until my team wins a championship!

WHILE THE BIG3 was mostly a summer job, in 2019 I signed up to coach high school at Chadwick School in Palos Verdes. After coaching in the NBA and WNBA, I always said that I wanted to give back to every part of the game, and that's what brought me there. In a conversation with the athletic director one day, I told him that I'd just finished in the WNBA, and he asked, "Coop, have you ever thought about coaching high school?" I ended up staying there for two years, working as head coach for the boys' basketball program. It turned out to be one of my best but most challenging experiences. It also was a microcosm of the concept of student-athletes.

These kids had to be great academically even to be admitted to Chadwick, and basketball was just a part of their journey. While I was there, we got some great wins, including some against teams the school had never beaten before. We really dug into teamwork and my Five D's—heck, maybe it's six D's, when you include *defense*! Working with those young men got me ready to coach AAU too, which I've done now for many a summer, coaching my son on traveling teams and helping to get him a scholarship to Pepperdine and later UC Davis. I learned how to talk to the parents of young athletes, how to manage their expectations and listen to their concerns.

AFTER MY EYE-OPENING experience at Chadwick, I coached at another high school in Culver City. Unlike Chadwick, Culver City is a public school. There, I had some of my best coaching moments. Stressing defense, in 2023 we were 19–12 and got all the way to the Southern California Regional Division III Championship Game. Over several years, we'd developed a solid foundation, and it paid off with kids such as Connor Scales and brothers Braylon and Myles Singleton. But along with coaching at Culver City, I took my job of making sure my players were student-athletes very seriously.

I drove to the school at 8:00 AM to make sure they were in class. I went by their rooms to let their teachers know I wanted to be part of their academics, that they could tell me if someone was ditching. At first, I would get emails every day about at least one kid, but those stopped as my players began to accept my rules. If a student isn't in class, he or she cannot learn. *Being there* is half the battle. I even started walking the halls during the day to make sure none of my guys were loitering after getting hall passes to go to the bathroom. By the end of my tenure, my guys had the highest GPA in the history of the boys' basketball team.

Working at Culver City brought me back to when I was young, when I would barely make class or sit in the back, not paying attention. Now, grown up, I wasn't going to let that happen on my watch. It's funny, the school principal's last name was Cooper, and she'd actually tried out for the Sparks when I was the coach. Small world! We worked together well, and I look back on my time coaching there and at Chadwick with gratitude and joy. Now, the only level I haven't coached is juco. But you never know what God has in store. Today, I'm an assistant coach at the Division-II Cal State in L.A., bringing championship knowledge to our playoff runs.

ANOTHER PART OF my coaching life comes with my 19-year-old son Nils. A 6'7" combo guard, Nils is growing as a scorer, and I'm happy to say he is a world-class defender. He had a great freshman year at Pepperdine, and now he's at UC Davis raising eyebrows and spreading his wings now that the COVID–19 pandemic is over with. He has also been a huge contributor on the Swedish national team. An excellent student on top of it all, Nils is becoming a talented writer. He once wrote a short story about me that brought tears to my eyes. He's so perceptive and bright. The only bad thing is that I can't see many of his games since I'm coaching at Cal State (the same school where Ron Artest coached the women's team). Thankfully Yvonne can be there, supporting him for both of us. I'm so proud of my son and what he's been able to do in his life. Really, it's a testament to my bond with his mother. Yvonne is our family's rock. My partner in life, she has held us together and lifted us up.

Sometimes a ray of light just finds to you. For me, that was her. I've always felt I needed a partner in my life, and Yvonne is that person. Together for 25 years and married for 14, she's also my best friend. Yvonne is never timid about sharing what's on her mind, and today she acts as my manager and handles my scheduling and bookings. Men out there—if you ever find a person who you can talk to until dawn and who has your back every day of the week, hold on to them. Without Yvonne, my life today would be completely different. Thankfully we met and fell in love, and I'm standing on the sturdiest ground I ever have today because of her.

With Yvonne not working as much as she did when we met, that gives her time to go and watch our son, Nils, play basketball. Recently, I was able to watch one of his games live with her. Nils is long like me, but he has a more advanced skill set. I've always taught him to be patient and wait for the game to come to him. But he's talented enough now to get his own on the offensive end when he needs to. I see myself in his defense, and that's often what coaches praise most about him. But he has the chance to be even better than me. Yvonne and I couldn't be prouder. Truly, I thank God for putting them both in my life.

THINGS WERE NEVER tougher lately than on November 18, 2023. That's when my only brother, Mickey Cooper, was senselessly shot and killed in Washington Park in Pasadena, a place where we'd grown up playing ball. Unfortunately, Mickey struggled with a lifelong addiction, and now that he's gone, I can only believe he's in a better place. He'd thought the park was a safe spot for him, and he should have been right. But with the rise of gun violence in the US, it seems that there may be no true safe place for people these days (his killer used a semiautomatic). Thankfully, the murderer was found and booked on $4 million bail.

I miss Mickey every day. I also miss our mother, who died about seven years ago, and our grandmother. This is the hard part about getting older. You see some of the people you love most in the world pass away. Kobe Bryant's death was hard on me, just as it was the entire NBA. And just a few days ago, my friend Earl Cureton died suddenly. I'd actually just had him on my podcast, then two weeks later, he was gone at 66 years old. Life isn't fair. But the silver lining is that the reason those losses hurt so much is because I was able to have such great moments with those people when they were alive.

When you're rattled, you have to keep to your core principles. I've said it before, and I'll say it again. You have to stay determined and dedicated. You have to stay energized, breathing life into your desires, whatever they may be. You have to stay disciplined and keep your head on your shoulders. There are plenty of things that want to throw you off your game. But you have to remember that your internal courage and your fortitude are what keep you on the right path. It may sound corny, but these tenets and these lessons have kept me strong in the face of so much that could go wrong.

In 2014 I had a cancer scare. I was traveling one day and bit down on my tongue, which always hurts. But my tongue never quite healed. I was drinking water one day, and I felt a burning sensation. So I went to see a doctor. They immediately identified it as early-stage tongue cancer. They came back with a tray of knives to take a biopsy, and my head began to spin. Thankfully, I was able to have surgery at Winship Cancer Institute at Emory University in Atlanta. They had to remove a significant part of my tongue in order to keep the cancer from spreading. If it had gotten worse, the doctors said, I might have had a 50/50 chance of surviving it. The doctors also removed 57 lymph nodes from my neck. Thankfully, I've been cancer-free ever since. I also had hip surgery recently. I hurt my hip while walking, and I had to have a replacement. It's true—as author Chinua Achebe titled one of his books, *things fall apart*. It's important to remember that we're on this planet for a very short time. We only get a little while to enjoy the world and to treat each other well before we depart. What I do know is that it's important to tell each other that we care about one another.

That's why the Showtime Lakers' trip to Hawaii in 2022 was so special. Not long after that, our captain, Kareem Abdul-Jabbar, who has dealt with things including prostate cancer, recently suffered a bad fall and broke his hip at a concert. Our hearts want to believe that our friends will be around forever, but God only puts us here for a short while. It's the stuff that brings tears to your eyes. In Maui, my teammate Wes Matthews said he cried every day, remembering and celebrating our youth. Riley pulled out these videos, and we'd see our younger selves working hard on the court. It brought a tear to my own eyes, I must admit. Our teams practiced harder than we played, we wanted it so bad.

One of the most emotional moments in Maui was when Spencer Haywood spoke to us. We all gave speeches throughout the trip, but 'Wood had something emotional to say. He spoke from the heart, how he was at his lowest moment as a person in the 1980 playoffs. He talked about being dismissed from the team before we won the championship, but he also talked about how he'd fallen asleep at the wheel a few days before, which we didn't know at the time. If he hadn't been removed from the Lakers then, he said, he probably would have died. But that was his wake-up call, his rock bottom. That's what life is all about: redemption.

WHEN I THINK about our Showtime era, I believe the basketball gods put Magic and Larry together in the NBA intentionally. For those players to go to those two teams—there's no way it wasn't divine. If Magic had gone to Boston and Larry had gone to L.A., it wouldn't have been the same. The basketball gods made sure they went where they needed to go in order to revive the NBA and change the game. I always tell players that they have it great, from the fame to the money pros can make, but it's important to remember how that was built. It was Jerry West, Bill Russell, Wilt, and Walt Frazier. Then Magic and Bird. Then Jordan.

Regarding today's game, I could go on at length about it. But I'll keep my thoughts short. It's a good, entertaining product, but I wish the league didn't legislate out so much of the toughness and physicality. I know NBA commissioner Adam Silver recently talked about this with Kevin Garnett in an interview, saying that the skill of a player shouldn't be neutralized just because some goon could take him out, and I agree with that. But I believe there is more of a happy medium the NBA could find to bring some toughness and defense back to the sport. Some of the "flagrant fouls" the referees call these days makes me shake my head.

Of course I care about safety. But these are grown men! Along those same lines, I take issue with the load management players and teams seem to go for these days—from the regular season to the All-Star Game. When I played, if Magic took a game off, I'd be licking my chops. The starters didn't want to miss games, because they knew backups wanted to take their jobs. Now, I was never going to take Earvin's spot, but you get the idea. People want to see players play, and fans pay hundreds of dollars to do so. That money isn't a birthright. Players already have so many more advantages over my generation, starting with chartered planes. So . . . play!

As far as the future of the league, who knows where it will go. Maybe they'll raise the rims to 10 and a half feet as Kareem has proposed. Or maybe they'll bring in a four-point shot like the Big3. Or use more AI in telecasts. But I wish they'd bring back hand-checks, offensive post play, and short-shorts (ladies want to see some leg!). Today, there are few centers, if any, you'd throw the ball to in the post to start the offense. The NBA's version of him now is the 7'3" Victor Wembanyama, who wants to handle the basketball and shoot threes from the outside—now I've seen everything!

OKAY, NOW TO the sentimental stuff! For the past four years, I've had the great honor of being a Basketball Hall of Fame finalist. And in 2024 I made it! I've always said that I played the game for the love of it. When I started as a young man, I wanted to succeed and, with any hope, get an education through basketball. Thankfully, I was able to get a scholarship to the University of New Mexico, where I was seen by Jerry West and drafted by the Lakers. I never played basketball for the money. If you do things for the right reasons, money will follow. I tell kids today that if you treat the game the right way, it can take you around the world.

The basketball gods want you to give back to it. Today, I'm happy to say I'm very comfortable with myself and the life I've lived. Far from perfect, I've worked hard every day to grow. One achieves a status by doing little things day by day. Now I'm part of the Hall of Fame. When I got to Springfield, I didn't run through the door; I walked calmly (Showtime did enough running!). Knowing I'm an equal with the game's greats makes me so proud. I'm in there with MJ, Magic, Bird, Jerry West, and my idol, John Havlicek. I feel so honored to have been invited into those hallowed halls, knowing my peers and basketball legends feel I am deserving.

My other highest honor was the fact that Larry Bird said I was the toughest guy ever to guard him. Me, a skinny kid from Los Angeles who barely made the league. Someone who few thought had a chance. Heck, maybe the Lakers will put my jersey in the rafters one day too. Right there with Worthy, Magic, Kareem, West, and the others. But if not, I'll remain 100 percent satisfied with my career and truly blown away to have even had a shot at the Hall. In the past, I know others such as Larry Bird, Mychal Thompson, Isiah Thomas, and Robert Horry have advocated for me, and I can't thank them enough for their kindness.

As for the Hall of Fame, I wanted to have all of my kids there to induct me. To have the whole family in one place again, nothing could be better. After all, I gave them all my Lakers rings. On top of that nod, I've celebrated other great honors. The University of New Mexico recently humbled me with a big mural of me in their arena. Pasadena High School recently retired my jersey (I was the first player ever to receive that). I've also been selected to the California Sports Hall of Fame and the Lobo Hall of Fame at UNM. I've lived a blessed life. All because of that orange ball. And I don't know where I'd be without it or the support of my friends and family.

From slicing my knee to stealing cigarettes to getting cut from my high school team, from NBA championship trophies to the Defensive Player of the Year Award, from losing loved ones to enduring a pandemic, from addiction to recovery, from staying up until 3:00 AM watching tapes of Larry Bird to celebrating on the steps of the Fabulous Forum, from the mad Boston Garden fans to the intoxicating Hollywood celebrities, my life hasn't been like any other. And yet I've been able to experience just about every corner of the world. In the end, it's important to remember that life, like basketball, is a team game. Together everyone achieves more.

To get to that next level, I hope people can remember my philosophy—my Five D's brought me from uncertainty to five championship rings! As you've read in these pages, determination, desire, dedication, discipline, and decision-making can help anyone create a strong foundation and a lasting future in whatever career they put their mind to. And a Hall of Fame career too! These help build up the mind and character. They can get you through a difficult time in your life and sustain you when the world seems confusing. Remember those words. They'll come to your aid at times when you least expect it, whether you're a blue-collar worker or an NBA star.

But there is also more to life than any game. That's the final point I'd like to leave you with. Here, in these pages, this is my true self. I shared it in the hopes that you can take something from me. This is my way of giving back to the basketball gods and to you. With hope, there's a story that will make you change your life for the better—something I did to illustrate a stronger way forward. We're all struggling to get better. But I've learned along the way from people such as Bill Russell, Jackie Robinson, Muhammad Ali, and other great thinkers such as Malcolm X and Martin Luther King Jr. I'm not comparing myself to them; I just wanted to follow in their footsteps.

Chapter 21

The Year of Coop

EVEN THOUGH I HAD A HISTORIC PLAYING CAREER that dovetailed with a championship coaching one, I don't think I ever could have imagined what this past year has been for me. In the summer of 2024, I found out that I'd been elected to the Naismith Basketball Hall of Fame with my friend, mentor, and guardian angel Jerry West, who got in for his record-breaking third time, as a contributor. Jerry drafted me, coached me, taught me, and helped me through tough times, and to get in the same year with him, even though some outlets gave me a 0.9 percent chance of making the Hall, is a dream come true.

In the Lakers organization, there were a bunch of us known as Jerry's Kids: Byron Scott, A.C. Green, James Worthy, Mychal Thompson, me, and a few others—we were the ones Jerry had hand-selected to bring to Los Angeles. We all loved him, which is why I hated to see how HBO depicted him as a cussing maniac. When I worked for him, our offices were right next to each other. I knew the man well, and he was a special person. He saved my life when he saw that I was getting myself in trouble. He was my Lakers angel up until the day we last spoke, just a week before he passed.

After I'd been named a finalist for the 2024 class, I hoped my name would be called, but of course you never know. When I got the call from

HOF chairman Jerry Colangelo, it was 9:08 in the morning, and I was in bed. In the past when he's called, Jerry has said, "Coop, you're a Hall of Famer, but you didn't get in this time." Now, as he talked to me, I just felt numb. That's when he said, "Coop, you got in." I was waiting for the punch line. It was April 1, after all. But then Yvonne turned to me and said, "Babe, you got in!" I said, "What?" She said, "They said you got in!"

Instinctively, I let out a great big *yell* of joy. Then when I got my senses back, I asked if it was an April Fool's joke. "This is very, very cruel," I cautioned. But they assured me it was for real. After that, it was a whirlwind. I got another bunch of phone calls, and then Yvonne and I flew to Arizona for the Final Four in Phoenix. We got our rings and jacket sizes, and not long after, the entire class (sans Jerry West, who was dealing with health issues) took a big "team" photo, holding up our No. 24 jerseys. I'm just so grateful. I never thought I'd make it in.

They don't usually give such an honor to players who weren't multi-time All-Stars in the NBA. But with my induction, the Hall was recognizing defense and winning. Now I was immortalized with the best, from Walt Bellamy to Hondo to Connie Hawkins to my Lakers teammates. When I started to write my speech for the induction ceremony, I started to cry. I couldn't hold back the emotion. Some suggested I ask Larry Bird to be my presenter, but that would have been too weird! Since I retired, we've only crossed paths a few times in Indiana, but that's it.

But now, I'd like to thank the Los Angeles Lakers organization for everything they did for this skinny kid from Pasadena. I'd like to thank my coaches George Terzian, Joe Barnes, Norm Ellenberger and, of course, Pat Riley for their never-ending efforts to make me a better player. I'd like to thank Magic Johnson, Kareem Abdul-Jabbar, Byron Scott, James Worthy, Norm Nixon, A.C. Green (who recently won the Presidential Lifetime Achievement Award for serving the community), Kurt Rambis, Mitch Kupchak, Jim Chones, Mychal Thompson, Bob McAdoo, Gary Vitti, Spencer Haywood, Jamaal Wilkes, and so many others who wore the Purple and Gold.

During a Lakers playoff game, when the team took on the reigning champion Denver Nuggets in April 2024, Jeanie Buss and the whole organization honored me and my Showtime brethren during halftime. On hand were guys including Kareem, Magic, Byron, James, A.C., Kurt Rambis, and Jamaal Wilkes. We took photos at center court, and the entire place cheered me and my induction into the Hall of Fame. It was a special night to remember (even if the Purple and Gold couldn't beat Nikola Jokić and Denver).

I went through the trenches with all those guys on the way to earning five rings. Of course, I'd also like to thank the late Dr. Jerry Buss, the architect of Showtime and the greatest sports owner in history. I'd also like to extend great gratitude to Jeanie Buss, his daughter, who kept his legacy alive. My heart is in L.A., and I'd also like to send love to my Sparks family, from Lisa Leslie to Candace Parker to everyone else I coached. We won two rings in Los Angeles, and those women brought me strength and, later, tears to my eyes.

To make the Hall was incredible, and it's not something I could do alone. Truly, there are so many to thank. But at the top of the list has to be my kids, Michael II, Simone, Miles, and Nils—I couldn't have done it without you all; you are the apples of my eye. I love you. And to my beautiful and brilliant wife, Yvonne. Without you I'd be lost out in the California desert somewhere. To everyone else who has been part of my life, we did it! After all the beautiful things that have happened to my family and me, I never thought it could get any better. But now it has.

Even my son Nils has noticed all the attention. It had never been a thing for us to go out to dinner, but now people are coming up to me and congratulating me. That's opened my son's eyes. When he found out about the Hall of Fame, he called me from school and said, "Dad, you know what? You were pretty good!" I said, "Dude, I tried to tell you!" But it doesn't end there for the Year of Coop! I also found out that the Lakers would be retiring my No. 21 jersey and hanging it in the rafters, which they did on January 13, 2025. My grandmother used to tell me, "Keep living and you're going to experience some things." Man, she was right on with that. I never played or coached the game of basketball for accolades, but these days I'm getting all the ones I could ever have wanted.

It's interesting because I think my induction into the Hall is changing things for the world of basketball. People's minds are opening to the idea that a Hall of Famer doesn't only have to be someone like Michael Jordan or Kobe Bryant. Before my induction, there were defenders such as Dennis Rodman and Ben Wallace, but even they were All-Stars. There is the old cliched saying, "If I can do it, you can too." But today I actually believe in it. I understand that now. When I talk to kids, I can tell them that a skinny kid from L.A. who wasn't an offensive threat and who came off the bench is now in the Hall of Fame. And his jersey is up there in the rafters with the Lakers greats.

I truly believe in my heart—if I can do it, you can do it. If you put the hard work in, if you put the effort in and believe in yourself, believe in a higher power, make a commitment, anything can happen for you. Now anytime someone in my family, from my kids to my great-great-great-grandkids walks into the Lakers arena, they will see my number and their name hanging up there with guys such as Wilt, Kobe, Magic, West, Shaq, and Kareem. That means something. Believe in yourself, and you could be up there in the rafters too. Our legacy is there. It's making me believe I really belong.

The night it happened to me was beyond words. Magic read a few words as he inducted me as the 13th member of the Lakers to have my number retired. As I saw the black veil over my jersey in the rafters come down, exposing my No. 21, I couldn't hold back tears. The fans shouted, "Coooooooop!" All my old teammates were there, from Worthy to Jamaal to Rambis to A.C. to Byron to Coach Pat Riley. To have all this happen in my hometown of L.A. was beyond surreal. I told some of the stories in my speech that night that I've told in this book. And then there I was, up with the greats.

IT'S FUNNY, OR even ironic. The other day I was at an event and the great Boston Celtics champion Paul Pierce was there. When he approached me, I gave him the normal, "Boo! Get out of here, Celtic!" But then we started talking. Paul is from Los Angeles, and he started talking to me about how he used to watch our team growing up. And he said he wanted to be a Laker because of me. It made me think of when I was a kid growing up in Los Angeles and I watched the Celtics with Tom, my uncle. And how I'd watched John Havlicek, and how he made me want to play pro ball. What goes around comes around.

Speaking of which, I was back in Boston for the Big3 championship in the summer of 2024, not long after the Celtics had won their 18th NBA title, one more than the Lakers (but let's not talk about that). I'd taken my team 3s Company to the Finals, and we faced Gary Payton's Bivouac team—two former Defensive Player of the Year Award winners going head-to-head. The first team to 50 points would win the game, and while Bivouac got out to a big lead, we chipped away and chipped away. In the end, we lost 50–47. What could have felt like a 1985 victory instead felt too much like my 1984 summer in Beantown.

With eight basketball championships and now a Hall of Fame ring, I'm determined to get my 10th ring one day. I want to run out of fingers like Bill Russell! The Big3 has been a blast; I even got a chance to meet guys such as Snoop Dogg because of it. Snoop has invited me to his big home compound, this real special place where he lives that's almost like a small town unto itself. You can't just walk up there; you have to be invited. I went there with him and Ice Cube and got to see where people record, got to see Snoop's full-court basketball setup. And I'll just say this: the air in Snoop's compound smells, well, very good.

But those are the kinds of things that happen when you're a Laker. The cherry on the sundae, of course, is the Hall of Fame. I'm in with other all-time great defenders such as Dennis Johnson, Alvin Robertson, Hakeem Olajuwon, and Rodman. Following, I want to share with you the speech I gave during my induction ceremony. While I've said a lot in these pages, it sums up how I feel. Really, I'm just living the dream, and it's all thanks to how I was raised and the hard work I put in. My faith in God and my belief in my Five D's put me on the right path, and I wouldn't be the person I am today without them—I can't say that enough. Truly, the Year of Coop has been marvelous, and I hope it never ends.

Epilogue

My Hall of Fame Induction Speech
(October 13, 2024)

Ahmad Rashad's introduction:

Have you ever shopped for a Swiss Army Knife? They have a couple of tools built in with the blade: a tiny pair of scissors, a bottle opener, and a screwdriver. And you can just about do anything with one of those if you have one. Now, in the 1980s, the Los Angeles Lakers had their own version. He could fly to catch a Coop-a-Loop from Magic Johnson. He could fill a lane in transition and finish with authority. He could knock down three-pointers with the best of them. He was a human Swiss Army Knife. Even though he wasn't Swiss and he wasn't in the army. But he could lock down your best offensive player because he was one of the best perimeter defenders ever, making his team one of the most dominant of the decade. His name? Michael Cooper. Welcoming Michael to the Hall of Fame is the centerpiece of the back-to-back champion L.A. Sparks, Lisa Leslie, and his Showtime band of brothers, Magic Johnson and Pat Riley. Congratulations!

Michael Cooper:

Wow! Giving glory and honor to God, I want to thank all of you so much. I feel like I'm being welcomed into an amazing new family. One with some familiar faces. And for that I'm so grateful and honored. So grateful to the Hall and to all of you. As I stand here, I know that there are many people that I want to thank. That's how I want to spend my time with you today. There's something that I've accomplished that I believe makes me unique in this esteemed company. I've achieved something that not even Michael Jordan could! Everyone knows that he was cut from his high school basketball team. I was cut twice!

In fact, my early life was filled with setbacks. My father abandoned us soon after I was born, and my mother had to flee to Northern California to escape a violent and dangerous relationship. As a result, I was brought up by my incredible grandmother, Ardessie Butler. And right alongside her, my Aunt Honey, my Uncle John, and his brother Tom, my uncle. As you can imagine, we weren't allowed to call him Uncle Tom! They raised me to love sports, to be persistent, and to be fearless. Their support, wisdom, and faith made me the person I would become.

Then there was my high school coach, George Terzian. It may seem odd to thank the man who cut me twice, but he might have been more important to me than any other individual in my basketball life. Yes, he taught me how to play ferocious defense. But he also showed me that passion for sports could go hand in hand with devotion to God. Nothing before or since has mattered more. My life didn't follow a smooth path, though. No big schools recruited me, and I ended up at Pasadena City College. Now look, PCC was good enough for Jesse Owens and Jackie Robinson, so it was certainly going to be good enough for me. I was, and I am, beyond proud to have followed in their mighty footsteps. But it wasn't exactly a fast track to the NBA.

From there, I transferred to the University of New Mexico. And my time in Albuquerque was truly special. Coach Norm Ellenberger took my raw skills and made me a far, far better player. But I was still no NBA shoo-in. Finally, at the end of the third round [of the NBA Draft], with the 60th pick in the draft, someone took a gamble on me. You may have heard of him: Jerry West. The Logo, the icon of our game. He was a friend and a mentor, and I owe him more than he could ever understand, and I miss him more than I could ever express. Jerry West was always a voice of reason. And what a team Jerry and Bill Sharman put together. Before long, we were off and running, headed to title after title.

It was great to see so many of my teammates up here with me today—Spencer Haywood, Jamaal Wilkes, "Big Game" James Worthy—and unfortunately, the incomparable Kareem Abdul-Jabbar could not be here today. He showed me, as well as all of us, how to be leaders on and off the floor. Thank you, Cap. And get well soon! And of course there is Earvin "Magic" Johnson, the Magic Man. He made it all happen and showed us all how to win with joy, with consistency, and a whole lot of ass-kicking. Legends and inspirations, each of them. These men and our other incredible teammates who are here today—like Byron Scott, A.C. Green, Norm Nixon, Kurt Rambis, Bob McAdoo, and Mychal Thompson—and all of those who are not here too, will forever be my brothers, including Jim Chones. I love all of you from the bottom of my heart, and I'm so glad we went on this journey together playing in front of the greatest fans in the world, men and women whose decades-long support in every sense of the word means more than they will ever know. That's the Laker Nation fans!

I also want to thank the Boston Celtics and Larry Bird. As that old saying goes, "Iron sharpens iron," and the Celtics made us the sharpest tool in the box, and Larry kept me on my toes too. That's why the Lakers-Celtics rivalry was so special. And I know I speak for us all when I say none of it could have happened without Coach Pat Riley. He made me a better player on the court, and he made me a man off it. And while folks today talk about his incredible sense of style, no one should forget what an absolute genius he was as a basketball coach. Let's give it up for him! He too encouraged me to focus on my particular skill, and my defense enabled me to be part of five championship teams and got me Defensive Player of the Year in 1987, and that means that I'm now one of the few defensive-first players to join this amazing Hall, following greats like Dennis Rodman, Ben Wallace, Bobby Jones, and our friend, the wonderful Dikembe Mutombo, gone much, much too soon.

After I finished playing, I followed in Coach Riley's footsteps and became a coach, first back with the Lakers under Magic Johnson and the incomparable Del Harris. Then Dr. Buss gave me a chance to become head coach for the Los Angeles Sparks. When it came to the WNBA, Dr. Buss was, as usual, ahead of his time, recognizing what amazing athletes these women were and recognizing what a growth opportunity it was for the game. I'm indebted to him, to Jeanie, to Johnny Buss and Linda Rambis and their family for all their support over the years. With the Sparks, we won back-to-back titles with an amazing group of women. And I had the privilege of coaching the fearless Lisa Leslie Lockwood. She gets mad at me when I call her that, so I'm going to call her Smooth. Her name is Smooth. But I got a chance to experience her magnificence up close.

I've been so lucky to experience it all with my family, whom I adore. My children, with their significant others—Michael and Princess, Miles and Lisa, Simone my beautiful daughter and David. I love you guys so much, and although I wasn't there as much as you wanted me to be, I was there when you needed me to be. Thank you for that. I'm a proud dad and a lucky one. And my wife, Yvonne. Thank you for everything, sweetheart. You are my source of strength, my dearest friend, and my true companion. And I want you to buckle up, because we're going to ride this thing until the wheels fall off!

Before I sit down, I want to go back briefly to 1987, because along with the Defensive Player of the Year Award, I won something else that year, the J. Walter Kennedy Citizenship Award. It's an award given by the NBA to an individual who has shown service and dedication to the community. That honor means a lot to me.

I know I was blessed from above to be able to play this game I love so much. That's why as I stand here and join this amazing collection of legends, I know what I need to do next. I am determined to continue to make sure that I use this incredible platform to give back to a game and to a world that has given me so very much. Thank each and every one of you. Oh, and I'd be remiss if I didn't mention my youngest son, Nils, right there. The love of my life! He's going to follow in his dad's footsteps. I love you, son!